The Politics of the Universe

Robert Merideth * THE
POLITICS
OF
THE
UNIVERSE

Edward Beecher,
Abolition,
and
Orthodoxy

Vanderbilt University
Press
Nashville

Composed and printed
in the United States of America by
Heritage Printers, Inc.
Charlotte, North Carolina

Bound by Nicholstone Book Bindery
Nashville, Tennessee

The author and publisher make grateful acknowledgment to the editors
of the following periodicals for permission to reprint those parts of this
book that first appeared in their periodicals:
Journal of Presbyterian History, XLII, Nos. 1 and 2 (March and June 1964);
The Nation, CXCV, No. 9 (September 29, 1962); *Phylon: The Atlanta University
Review of Race and Culture*, XXIV (December 1963).

"Edward Beecher's *Narrative* and Conservative Abolitionism," copyright
©1965, by Robert Merideth, appeared as the Introduction to Edward
Beecher's *Narrative of Riots at Alton* (New York: E. P. Dutton & Co., 1965).

For my mother and father

Chronology

1803 Edward Beecher is born, August 27, third child and second son of Lyman (1775–1863) and Roxanna Beecher. The other children are: Catharine (1800–78), William (1802–89), Mary (1805–1900), George (1809–43), Harriet (1811–96), Henry Ward (1813–87), Charles (1815–1900), Isabella (1822–1907), Thomas (1824–1900), James (1828–86).

1810 The Beecher family moves from East Hampton, on Long Island, to Litchfield, in western Connecticut.

1817 Lyman Beecher delivers *The Bible a Code of Laws*, a sermon given at the ordination of Sereno E. Dwight as pastor of Park Street Church, Boston.

1818 The Standing Order in Connecticut falls; the Dedham case in Massachusetts begins; Edward Beecher matriculates at Yale College.

1819 William Ellery Channing's *Unitarian Christianity*; Lyman Beecher's *The Design, Rights, and Duties of Local Churches*, Salem, July.

1822 Catharine's fiancé drowns at sea; Edward Beecher's conversion experience, graduation from Yale as valedictorian, and position as Headmaster of the Hartford Grammar School.

1823 Lyman Beecher helps promote a revival at Park Street
      Church; Catharine begins a female seminary in Hartford.

1824 Edward Beecher at Andover Theological Seminary.

1825 Edward Beecher as tutor at Yale, May 1; Lyman Beecher
      accepts a pastorate in Boston.

1826 Edward Beecher preaches four times at Park Street
      Church in the summer and is ordained as its pastor in
      December.

1827 To Edward Beecher is revealed a suffering God and the
      pre-existence of souls; his *Address*, February 10, to the
      Auxiliary Education Society of the Young Men of Boston; Edward Beecher and Harriet begin a two-year correspondence about her religious difficulties.

1828 Edward Beecher, in inner turmoil, takes a vacation in
      Maine, where that winter he preaches twenty-eight revival sermons in twenty-six days; he takes another vacation in July to the scenes of his youth, and by October
      15, quiets his "inward man."

1829 The Yale Band signs its compact on February 21; Garrison speaks at Park Street Church on July 4; Edward
      Beecher marries Isabella Porter Jones on October 28.

1830 Edward Beecher resigns his Park Street pastorate on October 28 and on November 8 formally accepts the presidency of Illinois College in Jacksonville.

1831 Edward Beecher and Theron Baldwin, *An Appeal*.

1832 *Hints to Christians*; Lyman Beecher to Lane Seminary,
      Cincinnati.

1834 The Lane Seminary debates on slavery in February.

1835 The American Union for the Relief and Improvement
      of the Colored Race, formed in January; Edward Beech-

er's *Six Sermons* on Eminent Holiness, that summer; Lyman Beecher's family gathers for a reunion in September in Cincinnati; a large scale shift of clerical sentiment toward abolition, October–December; Edward Beecher's December 20 letter of approval to Lovejoy.

1837 Edward Beecher and Lovejoy attend the divided Presbyterian General Assembly in the summer; they help form the Illinois Antislavery Society; Lovejoy is murdered on November 7.

1838 *Narrative.*

1840 The Liberty Party and the American and Foreign Antislavery Society are formed; Edward Beecher publishes the first of a series of articles in the *Biblical Repository*, culminating in *Baptism, with Reference to its Import and Modes* (1849).

1843 Edward Beecher returns briefly to East Hampton; his reminiscence.

1844 Edward Beecher works to establish the Society for the Promotion of Collegiate and Theological Education at the West, then resigns from Illinois College and begins a pastorate at Salem Street Church, Boston; his article on Judge Ruffin appears in the Boston *Recorder* on May 2.

1845 The American Board controversy over slavery in the church leads to Edward Beecher's articles on "Organic Sin" in the Boston *Recorder*.

1849 Edward Beecher accepts a position as first editor of the *Congregationalist*; *Baptism* is published and *The Question at Issue* is delivered as a sermon, October 30.

1850 Millard Fillmore signs the Fugitive Slave Law on September 18.

1852 After having been run as a serial for over a year in the *National Era*, *Uncle Tom's Cabin* appears on March 20 as a two-volume book; the *Key* is begun the same year.

1853 *The Conflict of Ages*; Edward Beecher resigns as editor of the *Congregationalist*, December 9.

1854   Extensive reviews of *The Conflict*; clerical protest against the Kansas-Nebraska bill, March 1.

1855   Edward Beecher resigns as pastor of the Salem Street Church and returns to Illinois, this time to Galesburg, where Knox College is located; he publishes *The Papal Conspiracy Exposed*.

1856   Edward Beecher becomes a lecturer at Chicago Theological Seminary; Harriet publishes *Dred*.

1860   *The Concord of Ages*.

1863   Charles Beecher's heresy trial in Georgetown, Massachusetts; Edward Beecher acts as his advocate; *The Result Tested*.

1871   Edward Beecher returns east permanently; he serves for two years as assistant editor of the *Christian Union*.

1874   Edward Beecher supports Henry Ward Beecher in the series of church councils inquiring into the affairs of Plymouth Church.

1878   *History of Opinions on the Scriptural Doctrine of Retribution*.

1885   Between 1885 and 1890 Edward Beecher writes *Cornelia, A Tale of the Second Century Under the Reign of Marcus Aurelius*, an unpublished novel.

1895   Edward Beecher's death.

1896   Charles Beecher writes the "Life of Edward Beecher," an unpublished memoir.

Contents

Our students . . . come to us . . . through
two ranks of opposition—Old School and ultra
Abolitionists, though the conservatives among
the latter confide in and patronize us, and
most of our students are conservative Abolitionists.
—Lyman Beecher (1840)

It may not be clear at first to the ordinary
mind why slavery and theology should go hand in
hand, in national affairs. But if we reflect
that theology is but another name for the
politics of the universe, or the kingdom of God,
the problem becomes simple.
—Charles Beecher (1896)

The Politics of the Universe

Introduction

SOMETIME after ten o'clock Monday night, November 7, 1837, Elijah P. Lovejoy, abolitionist editor and Presbyterian minister, was shot five times and killed while defending the press of his newspaper, the Alton *Observer*, from an insensate Illinois mob. News of the murder—which Edward Beecher would later describe in the language of Christian tragedy—spread to the East during the next two weeks, and the country overflowed with passion. Those who lived through it testify that no other personal incident of the antislavery struggle, except the hanging of John Brown on the eve of the Civil War, so overwhelmed the North. Funeral sermons poured from the pulpits. Public memorials and resolutions flooded the papers. At a mass meeting to mourn Lovejoy in Boston, Wendell Phillips was moved to make his famous leap onto the stage of Faneuil Hall and into history as the most exciting agi-

tator of his time. William Lloyd Garrison deplored Lovejoy's resort to arms and his rejection of nonresistance, but
the American Antislavery Society nevertheless celebrated
Lovejoy's heroism, and the membership of local branches
swelled. Even southerners regretted the reign of King
Mob in southern Illinois. The exemplary New Englander,
John Quincy Adams, observed that Lovejoy's death had
jolted the Yankee conscience like the "shock" of an "earth-
quake," that it marked an "epocha in the annals of human
liberty," that it belonged in one sense to the yet unwritten
history of the struggle for liberty in Western civilization.[1]

Adams was prophetic. The Alton affair, as he said, has
come to represent one phase in the history of the struggle
for liberty in western civilization. Of that phase Americans have grown especially aware since the 1954 Supreme
Court desegregation decisions. Particularly because of one
book, however, the Alton affair also belongs to another
unwritten history, the history of culture (strictly defined)[2]
and consciousness in America.

Such a history, if ever fully and conscientiously written,
will not aim to provide a libertarian description of events.
Rather, its aim will be to locate, define, and chart patterns
of consciousness—to show the terms by which men at a

1. John Quincy Adams, "Introduction," Joseph C. and Owen Lovejoy,
*Memoir of the Rev. Elijah P. Lovejoy: Who Was Murdered in Defence of
the Liberty of the Press, at Alton, Illinois, Nov. 7, 1837* (New York: John S.
Taylor, 1838), p. 12.

2. See A. L. Kroeber and Clyde Kluckhohn, *Culture: A Critical Review
of Concepts and Definitions* (New York: Random House, n.d.); originally
published in *Papers of the Peabody Museum of American Archaeology and
Ethnology*, XLVII, No. 1 (Cambridge, 1952). For applications to American
Studies and the writing of history, see my *American Studies: Essays on
Theory and Method* (Columbus, Ohio: Charles E. Merrill, 1968), especially
the Introduction and the essays by others collected in Parts 2 and 3.

given time, often in response to events, apprehended, conceptualized, and confronted what they conceived to be their culture's meaningful questions. No historical writing, to be sure, and no such small contribution to the history of culture and consciousness as this book, should wish to ignore hard data: what happened? in what political, economic, sociological context? in what sequence? Lovejoy and Alton—as well as other major events of the middle nineteenth century, with some of which I also deal—are clarified in part as they are placed in their contexts; I have tried to place them appropriately. But events are clarified also by an analysis of the patterns of belief implicit in the vision of their contemporary interpreters, especially perceptive interpreters, who loom more imposingly in the unwritten history I have in mind than the events themselves. We can know Lovejoy and Alton, as Adams said, as chapters in the annals of human liberty. We can know them in appropriate hard contexts. We can also know them by knowing the minds (historically, that means the writings, the books) that, in a complicated metaphorical sense, *made* them. In that sense, Edward Beecher, whose *Narrative of Riots at Alton* I believe should be considered a major document in the unwritten history of American culture and consciousness, is a crucial figure in the understanding of Alton and America in 1837.

Like the *Memoir* (1838) of Lovejoy written by Lovejoy's brothers, Joseph and Owen; like Henry Tanner's *The Martyrdom of Lovejoy* (1881); even like William S. Lincoln's *Alton Trials* (1838), Beecher's *Narrative* poses as an eyewitness account. It has become a major source for such later studies of Alton as Frank H. Dugan's "An Illinois Martyrdom" (1938), historical novelist Philip Van Doren

Stern's *The Drums of Morning* (1943), John Gill's *Tide without Turning* (ca. 1960), Merton L. Dillon's *Elijah P. Lovejoy* (1961), and Paul Simon's *Lovejoy: Martyr to Freedom* (1964). Gill has described the *Narrative* as a "careful and scholarly work," "parts" of which are "beautifully written." Dillon thought it "probably the most eloquent defense of freedom of inquiry ever written in this country." Beyond data, beyond the defense of freedom of inquiry, beyond scholarship and language, however, the *Narrative* was also a complicated interpretation of the meaning of Alton.

For Beecher, Alton in 1837 was a dramatic epitome of the nation. The Alton affair was a dramatization of the central questions the nation confronted. Even its casting was representative: the protagonists were New Englanders; the antagonists were engaged in typically Southern histrionics; and the West furnished both stage and script. As a consequence, the *Narrative* took on the quality of national drama. And as a consequence of Beecher's theological genius, national drama became cosmic drama. Ultimately, the *Narrative* was a work of dramatic art—a re-creation controlled and shaped by Beecher's intense inner experience, by his special version of orthodox theology, by his vision of society, and particularly by his abolitionist theory. In it, Lovejoy acted as protagonist in an involved Christian-democratic morality play, a fate-drama serving as the nineteenth century's version of Greek tragedy.

Understanding the book in these terms, then, we may more fully understand the Alton affair. And in understanding Alton through the book, perhaps we will find ourselves in a position to understand something more about the complexity of the American consciousness in the years leading to the Civil War. For such understandings, we do well to turn to the author of the script from whose perspective we, for the most part, know the event—to Edward Beecher, who would find an explanation for the public struggle of his society in the inner conflict of its religious life.

Even with the help of so refractive a center for the exploration of culture and consciousness, however, such understandings are not easily achieved. They are not, unfortunately, to be achieved by working wholly within the conventions of traditional biography, and I have written at once something less and something more than Edward Beecher's biography. On the one hand, I have relegated major events in Beecher's life to relatively minor places in the book: for example, his lifelong concern with problems of baptism and revivalism, his extended response to *Essays and Reviews* in 1862, his anti-Catholic, nativist proclivities. I have not only relegated these; I have often refocused them, as when Beecher's anti-Catholicism becomes for me metaphoric illustration of his vision of the good and bad societies.

On the other hand, all my relegating and refocusing may be taken as an attempt to write a book with a thesis biographically argued and, I hope, established. I want to contend that through Beecher we may see the dilemmas of a generation as felt ideas, and that the special dilemmas of his generation were temporarily resolved by politicizing theology and—if I may use the word only once—theologizing politics. (I might well have made my subtitle something like "Politics as Theology and Theology as Politics in Ante-Bellum Orthodox New England.") Beecher's dilem-

mas, his struggle to resolve them, the actions his resolutions
both allowed and forced him to engage in, the ambiguities
and certainties he felt, the compulsions he was obliged to
heed: these provide to an unusual degree a paradigm of
the inner life of his generation. That his solutions to his
dilemmas were, from our point of view, sometimes absurd
(as in the argument for the pre-existence of souls), that his
actions were sometimes cowardly and sometimes heroic
from both his point of view and ours: these serve primarily
to illustrate the terms of absurdity, cowardice, and heroism
in his time. The special qualities of Beecher's solutions do
not make him peculiar. A generation is defined, not by
the varieties of its solutions to problems, but by the problems it confronts and the terms it finds available for the
confrontation. The value to the study of culture of what
logical positivists call meaningless questions (but which,
for a culture, are vitally meaningful questions) is great
and not to be denied by the peculiarity or absurdity of
answers to those questions.

An introduction is not, however, the place for anything
more than the indications I have already given of the
methodological rationale of the book. The book deals with
Alton, but only as Alton was the animating event, the
catalyst for Beecher's theological imagination. Alton
served him—as it will serve us—as the anchor, the base, the
ground in politics and in the world for meanings only God
and a meaningful universe (and his culture) could finally
provide. That in 1853 Beecher himself became the focus
of controversy—of a great theological and social debate—
serves our purposes all the more, in allowing us to test the
degree to which he represented the patterns of belief of
his generation.

In forming the center of this book, Beecher poses technical as well as methodological problems. I am extremely fortunate to have had available to me extensive manuscript sources, particularly Charles Beecher's "Life of Edward Beecher," fully as revealing and almost as lengthy a document as Lyman Beecher's famous *Autobiography*. More in short phrases than in blocks, and often, I have quoted from the "Life," as well as from Edward Beecher's letters and published works, in order simply to *expose* the state of mind it is my aim to characterize. I have supposed that Beecher's state of mind is to be apprehended more fully in his language than anywhere else. Sometimes (as, for example, in section 3) I find myself explaining a document in the manner of the New Criticism, or at least in the manner suggested by Bernard Bowron, Leo Marx, and Arnold Rose in their classic essay on American Studies method, "Literature and Covert Culture."[3] My practice, in short, requires some small adjustment of standard footnoting procedures, if the text is to be at once readable and accurately documented.

I have tried to solve my technical problems in the following manner. Whenever possible, consistent with the requirements of accuracy and clarity, I have cited the source or sources of sequences instead of single quotations; at times, one citation may refer to several paragraphs containing a number of short quoted passages. I have quoted all passages exactly as they appear in the source, even though, as Beecher wrote his sister Catharine in commenting on a manuscript she had sent him for criticism, he was hardly "distinguished" for his "accuracy" "respecting mistakes in spelling or in the position or omision [*sic*] of com-

3. *American Quarterly*, IX (Winter 1957), 377–386.

mas or periods."[4] Since I am so concerned with Beecher's language—and also since Beecher may be read nowhere but here—such an editorial principle seems to me preferable to silent changes. At the same time, I have tried whereever possible to avoid the intrusive [sic], hoping that, as a result of these remarks, readers will understand that all such passages have been double-checked and will be able and willing to insert silently the [sic] themselves, if they wish.

All of Edward Beecher's published works are cited in the notes by means of short titles; a full chronological bibliography appears at the end of the book. I have abbreviated often repeated names and repositories of documents as follows:

Names

CB	Charles Beecher
EB	Edward Beecher
LB	Lyman Beecher
HWB	Henry Ward Beecher
HBS	Harriet Beecher Stowe

Repositories

BPL	Boston Public Library
MHCL	Mount Holyoke College Library
SL	The Arthur and Elizabeth Schlesinger Library on the History of Women in America, Radcliffe College
Yale	Yale University Library

4. EB to Catharine Beecher, New Haven, March 29, 1822 (SL). In the interest of consistency, I have allowed myself two exceptions to the rule of exact reproduction. The variable spellings of "pre-existence" and "anti-slavery" have been regularized.

I hope your *inward man* will soon
be taught how to behave himself in
all circumstances & emergencies.
                    —Catharine Beecher (1828)

One:

The Inward Man

1

EDWARD BEECHER was reared in the "half Hebrew theocracy, half ultra-democratic republic" of New England villages whose "inner life" his sister Harriet reported in *Oldtown Folks*.[1] Of theocracy all the Beecher children grew fully aware. Their father, Lyman Beecher, at the peak of his vigor and fame in the twenties, would, more nearly than any other minister in mid-nineteenth-century Protestant America, approximate the power of the Roman Pope. But the children's awareness began earlier. From the beginning they were aware that Lyman Beecher was committed to the theocratic society. From the beginning they knew his theology—revivalistic, clinical, evangelical—as the means to a theocratic end. Though they all, like Charles, denied that the conversion experience and the dogmas of orthodox Protestant Christianity were "pre-

1. Boston: Fields, Osgood, and Company, 1869, pp. iv, 1.

sented" in a "gloomy or repulsive" manner, the children were still invariably "anxious" or "serious," had "obtained hope" or "met with a change," had been "awakened," "convinced of sin," "experienced religion," "converted," and "saved."[2] The evangelical rhetoric defined the major categories of their experience.

Life in Edward Beecher's first village was not, of course, completely describable in the language of religious dedication and piety. Beecher did and felt all the things a boy growing up in such an environment might do and feel, as his 1843 reminiscence, written upon returning at age forty to East Hampton on Long Island, makes clear. There he had "gawked" at the ocean from garret windows, picked blackberries on expeditions with his father, and, insofar as a seven-year-old boy could, helped put "sharks for manure" in the garden. Despite all its pastoral charm, however, the 1843 reminiscence ends with "Revivals, seriousness, anxiety and hopes. The Assembly's Catechism. The book of Revelation, read with awe in my little bed-room." Beecher in 1843 was primarily aware of East Hampton as the place where he "awoke into being in this world" and felt incipient, divine "emotions of beauty and sublimity."[3] He was aware that, like his brothers, he had been "consecrated to the ministry" from his "mother's womb."[4] For the first twenty-five years the story of his life had been that of a predictable, though ultimately futile and perhaps even tragic, attempt to assimilate and accept Lyman Beecher's

2. Charles Beecher (CB), "Life of Edward Beecher," pp. 1–3; hereafter "Life." For a list of abbreviated names and manuscript repositories, see the Introduction. CB's "Life" is discussed in the bibliographical essay on manuscripts.

3. Edward Beecher (EB), quoted in "Life," pp. 149–151.

4. CB, "Life," p. 3.

account of the universe. If the "ultra-democratic" thrust of the society in which he was nurtured had led him into abolition and reform and finally disturbed the theocratic certainties he strove to inherit, the disturbance had been, he was sure, neither early nor easily discernible.

Beecher's father borrowed the basic elements of his account of the universe from Jonathan Edwards. He advised his sons, "Next after the Bible, read and study Edwards" and qualified his advice only by insisting that Edwards must be "accommodated to use." Consequently, all the children felt toward Edwards "high obligations" and Edward Beecher, though he would "call no man master on earth," was influenced perhaps more than any of the others.[5] Edwards had dealt, definitively it seemed, with all the central issues: original sin, the freedom of the will, total depravity, virtue, grace, religious affections, the relation of God to man, of man to man, of man to state and church, the trinity, election, damnation, redemption, love, future punishment. To name any one of the issues is to imply a system which, as Oliver Wendell Holmes's satirical account of "The Wonderful One-Hoss Shay" (1858) would have it, was "so like in every part," so interlocked and interdependent, that the breakdown of any of its parts would seem to lead inevitably to total destruction.[6]

It was not, however, so much a breakdown as an eclipse that occurred between Jonathan Edwards's death in 1758

5. Lyman Beecher (LB) to George Beecher, November 5, 1830, in *Autobiography, Correspondence, Etc., of Lyman Beecher, D.D.*, edited by CB (New York: Harper and Brothers, 1864–1865), II, 238; hereafter *Autobiography*. EB to Colonel George A. Foote, New Haven, September 9, 1828 (Yale).

6. "The Deacon's Masterpiece: or, the Wonderful 'One-Hoss Shay' a Logical Story," *The Works of Oliver Wendell Holmes* (Standard Library Ed.; Cambridge, Mass.: Riverside Press, 1892), XII, 420.

and Beecher's birth in 1803. To the revolutionary generation in control in those years, God was no longer an oriental potentate with absolute, irrevocable powers; He had become a watchmaker, a distant First Cause, not an intimately felt Trinity. Men were not totally depraved; they were born shapes of white wax awaiting the impress of their culture. Sin was not original; it was social. Men were responsible for their choices. Society was the result of an act of will, of a compact between individual men in a state of nature; it no longer was meant to become the Holy Commonwealth. The clergy and magistrates were to retain only limited and distinct powers. Men were reasonable animals; their logic was naturally empirical, not theological. Religious affections, such as those which overwhelmed Edwards's society in the 1740 Great Awakening, were manifestations of excessive zeal to no purpose. Men were neither redeemed and elected nor damned and punished; they merely died and were rewarded according to their works on earth.

Beecher's father, born in 1775 during the eclipse of orthodoxy, felt (as he told his children) as if he had grown up in a shadow. He had been given a "good orthodox education"; he had been "serious-minded" and "conscientious"; and he had developed a "settled fear of God and terror of the day of judgment." At Yale College he suddenly discovered he was living in the time of the "infidelity of the Tom Paine school." Most of the students of his generation were "skeptical," the college church almost "extinct," the college in a "most ungodly state." He resisted his times, and his conversion experience, when it came, was "instantaneous," if painful. Reading Edwards on the affections, as he did, however, had been "a most overwhelming thing," "most entangling." It had induced in him a "state of permanent hypochondria—the horrors of a mind without guidance, motive, or ability to do any thing." The experience led him to counter his times, not altogether with Edwards, but with a new "clinical theology," a modified version of Edwards, in which "ability" and "certainty" were central dogmas. It was this "evangelical philosophy" by which, he said fifty years later in his autobiography, he had "relieved people without number" not only out of the darkness of the Enlightenment but "out of the sloughs of high [Edwardsean] Calvinism."[7] The philosophy served as an ideology in the father's forty-year war with the enemies of orthodoxy: with rum-sellers, slaveholders, foreigners, disestablishmentarians, Jeffersonian democrats, Roman Catholics, infidels, and Unitarians. And it was within the context of that "philosophy," in a world of battles and causes and enemies, that Edward Beecher grew up, "sure that his father was right,"[8] certain, in the father's phrase, of the "similarity" of their "minds, and views, and systems of action."[9]

In the spring of 1810, the Beecher family moved to Litchfield, Connecticut, another of those Hebraic-democratic villages about which Harriet Beecher Stowe wrote. Litchfield was special. Locked inland by the hills of western Connecticut, isolated, provincial, Federalist—"a kind of fountain-head of orthodoxy"—the village nevertheless thought it rivaled the large eastern cities of New England as a center of learning and culture. Miss Sarah Pierce's school for young ladies (which, we are told, "exceeded" in

7. *Autobiography*, I, 34, 43–47.
8. CB, "Life," p. 7.
9. LB to EB, September 5, 1826, *Autobiography*, II, 69.

"reputation" "that of any other in the country"), Judge
Tapping Reeve's "celebrated" law school (attended by
John C. Calhoun), the poet John Pierpont, Governor
Oliver Wolcott, military heroes of the revolution, and now
Lyman Beecher, who when he read the roll of his parish-
ioners read many of the most important names in the
state: all these made Litchfield one of the first villages in
New England.[10] Edward Beecher studied there and at
South Farms, a neighboring village, in preparation for
Yale College and for the ministerial career to which he
was fated.

Always, though, he learned most from his father. Beecher's faith, we learn from his brother Charles, was "so absolute, that there was never any wish to be skeptical, or to
raise cavils." But there was much he did not understand.
Orthodox Christianity was a complicated and sometimes,
it seemed, a contradictory matter. In such a situation, the
father's "skill in making things clear and rational" was a
"positive educational influence of great power."[11] The fact
of being Lyman Beecher's son, even when the father was
absent, made a difference. From his father's replacements
Beecher learned orthodoxy and the ministry from the
inside. In the letter he contributed to the biographical
sketch of Asahel Nettleton in Sprague's *Annals of the
American Pulpit* in 1856, for instance, he recalled that the

10. For a full sense of the Beecher family's image of Litchfield, see *Autobiography*, I, 204–229. Perhaps the best summary can be found in a passage
quoted by CB on p. 213: " 'A delightful village, on a fruitful hill, richly
endowed with schools both professional and scientific, with its venerable
governors and judges, with its learned lawyers, and senators, and repre-
sentatives both in the national and state departments, and with a population enlightened and respectable.' " See also Harriet Beecher Stowe (HBS),
Poganuc People: Their Loves and Lives (1878).
11. CB, "Life," p. 8.

famous revivalist substituted for his father for four or five months. They talked "freely" about the revival then going on in Litchfield; Beecher was Nettleton's roommate and sometimes the conversation continued through the night. Nettleton told Beecher his life story. He spoke "of his entrance into the ministry; of the manner in which he was led to engage in his labours as an Evangelist; of his theory of preaching, and of his principles and modes of labouring in revivals." For a young man whose "mind was habitually and solemnly" concerned with religion, all this, we hardly need be told, was "deeply interesting."[12]

During the time that Beecher in Litchfield was assimilating his father's orthodoxy, orthodoxy again was threatened by the Enlightenment, but now thinned and faded into the shadow of itself, and transformed into Unitarianism. The Unitarian shadow brought the cold, and the cold generated "fire" in Lyman Beecher's "bones." The father —observed, we may be sure, by the son—read "every thing that came out on the subject." He "watched the whole progress of the Unitarian controversy." His mind, he said, was "heating, heating, heating." As late as 1817, the year before his son started at Yale, however, we may suppose he had not become sufficiently incandescent to burn. His sermon "The Bible a Code of Laws," written to make all the orthodox "points" against Unitarianism, attacked the new version of the Enlightenment only obliquely, by the obvious implication that it was not the orthodoxy Lyman Beecher outlined.[13]

12. Short-title references to EB's published works—such as here to EB's letter in Sprague's *Annals*—are expanded in a full chronological bibliography at the end of the book.

13. *Autobiography*, I, 350–351. See also Sidney Earl Mead, *Nathaniel William Taylor, 1786–1858: A Connecticut Liberal* (Chicago: University of Chicago Press, 1942), p. 134n.

At last the famous Dedham case brought the father to white heat. The minister of the First (Congregational) Church of Dedham, Massachusetts, resigned in 1818. His church split on the choice of a successor; and the orthodox faction, losing out to the liberal parish, seceded to form a new church. After long and stubborn litigation, lasting over two years and followed closely by the orthodox community, especially by the *Spirit of the Pilgrims*, the Massachusetts Supreme Court in 1820 decided which faction owned disputed church property by ruling that "the members who remain, though a minority, constitute the Church . . . and retain the rights and property belonging thereto."[14] The ruling meant that the liberal (Unitarian) party of any local congregation, if it could maneuver the orthodox party into walking out, might take over valuable church property, lock, stock, and pulpit. The orthodox community charged that the judge, a Unitarian, had been biased; they bemoaned the plunder of the true church, but the decision became law. Civil law was not, however, God's law, and the Dedham case was only the beginning of controversy. Invited in the midst of the controversy to preach at the July 1819 installation of a former student in Salem, Massachusetts, Lyman Beecher outlined the "Design, Rights, and Duties of Local Churches." The church, he argued, is a *"society incorporated by the God of heaven with specific chartered privileges."* "To abolish the revealed terms of membership in the Church of God," as the court did, "and to form churches without reference to doctrinal opinion or experimental religion, and only by . . .

14. Quoted in Earl Morse Wilbur, *A History of Unitarianism in Transylvania, England, and America* (Cambridge, Mass.: Harvard University Press, 1952), p. 432.

certain civil qualifications," as the Unitarians were now trying to do, he thought was the "most pernicious infidelity . . . ever broached."[15]

This "most pernicious infidelity" had been a matter of semipublic record for some ten or fifteen years. But it was in May 1819, just before Lyman Beecher's Salem sermon, that William Ellery Channing had stated its case fully. Channing's "Unitarian Christianity" was destined, moreover, to control Edward Beecher's theological imagination for life. After reading that sermon, everyone (including Lyman Beecher's sixteen-year-old son) knew that the Unitarians insisted upon the application of reason, philosophy, and the principle of selection to the interpretation of Scripture; they emphasized the unity of God and denied the trinity; they denied the traditional orthodox doctrines of total depravity, election, and "God's irresistible agency." "Excess of feelings" was not, they said, proof of piety. With some equivocation they argued that Christ was "distinct from the one God," and thus not divine, and that his "mission" was not to give "infinite satisfaction" to God for our guilt, but rather to "educate" us through the influence and example of his perfect character. Finally, and above all (at least insofar as Edward Beecher judged it), they protested that God was *not* "above the principles of morality, above those eternal laws of equity and rectitude to which all other beings are subjected." "If," they concluded, "religion be the shipwreck of [the] understanding, we cannot keep too far from it."[16] It is to go to the heart of Lyman

15. Quoted in *Autobiography*, I, 415–418. See also Mead, *op. cit.*, pp. 134–139.

16. William Ellery Channing, "Unitarian Christianity," *The Works of William E. Channing, D.D.* (Boston: American Unitarian Association, 1903), pp. 367–384.

Beecher's—but not Edward Beecher's—view of the infidelity of Channing's Unitarianism to note that it became "pernicious" only in the context of the Dedham case. Were it not that Unitarianism between 1818 and 1820 threatened the church as a polity, as an institution, Lyman Beecher may have continued indefinitely, as in 1817, to attack the theology of reason only obliquely. The courts, and to a lesser extent Channing, made that response finally impossible.

So orthodoxy and Lyman Beecher refurbished their tactics. To counter the *North American Review* and the *Christian Examiner*, Unitarian periodicals through which the enemy, as he said, poured out their "floods of heresy upon the community," and to confront other enemies, the father at various times helped begin the *Christian Spectator, The Connecticut Observer,* and *The Spirit of the Pilgrims.* He wrote tracts and, with some success, urged others, like his friend (and Edward Beecher's teacher) Nathaniel Taylor, to write them. "The enemy," he observed, had once been "driven from the field by the immortal Edwards"; now the battle must "be fought over again."[17] But the "most pernicious infidelity that was ever broached" would not, as Beecher's father was aware, be staved off by sermons, journal articles, and tracts. "The Unitarians," he wrote to a friend, "can not be killed by the pen." By "action only" can they be "effectually met."[18]

"Action" meant a resurgence of the revivalism that had served orthodoxy so well at the turn of the century. Lyman Beecher felt certain that the "Unitarian people, with the

17. *Autobiography,* I, 438–439; for the tracts, see I, 335; for the periodicals, see I, 329, and II, 13, 122.
18. Quoted by Mead, *op. cit.,* p. 137.

exception of a few *veterans*, are no more Unitarians than
any uninformed people, who know nothing except that
they do not believe in Calvinism as caricatured *in ter-
rorem.*" They were, he thought, ready to be persuaded to
return to the church of their fathers. All they needed was
"the truth, divested of obnoxious terms" and "mildly, and
kindly, and luminously explained and earnestly applied."
Their souls were merely sick, not dead, and Lyman
Beecher, with the help of the clinical theology, could cure
them.[19] On such revivalistic inroads into the Unitarian
congregations he placed great faith. Was it not true—according to the much-used and -abused argument from tendency—that results speak more convincingly than books,
that if men were converted in great numbers by orthodox
doctrine, then that doctrine was true? The argument was
a little disingenuous; it could as well be applied to Unitarianism. But no-one could deny that orthodox doctrine
had lately been getting results. Since its nadir in the 1790s,
at the climax of the American Enlightenment, orthodoxy
had been riding the crest of revival after revival (one would
soon be able to count fifteen separate periods of revival
at Yale College alone in the first forty years of the nineteenth century),[20] many of them initiated and nurtured by
Lyman Beecher's evangelical genius. The second Great
Awakening, at the turn of the century, at the moment
Lyman Beecher began to preach at East Hampton, had
given him impetus. The renaissance of orthodoxy after the
fall of the Standing Order in Connecticut (1818) can be
attributed, in great part, to his efforts. When in 1823 he

19. *Autobiography,* I, 542.
20. Alice Felt Tyler, *Freedom's Ferment: Phases of American Social History to 1860* (Minneapolis: University of Minnesota Press, 1944), p. 30.

went to Park Street Church in Boston to help promote a revival in that infidel (Unitarian) city, he found, as he reported to his son Edward, "a great and auspicious change going on." The orthodox population was gaining in influence, "numerical, and political, and secular"; the "Unitarian population begin to be apprehensive about the soundness of their foundation." The enemy, he thought, was in retreat.[21] In 1826 he left his Litchfield, Connecticut, pastorate permanently, to become spiritual leader of Boston's Hanover Street Church and to continue the attack-by-revival on Unitarianism for five uninterrupted years. It was during those years that he became, for the many radical abolitionists who began and sometimes remained as orthodox clergymen or parishioners (often his), the symbol of everything wrong with the attitude of the northern church toward slavery and abolition. Lyman Beecher was, indeed, making his place in the "secret history of Boston," ironically not so much by the quantity of his converts to orthodoxy as by a "moral influence" that, he might later have reflected, went wrong.[22]

Edward Beecher went to Yale College in 1818 with the beginnings of his father's battle against Unitarianism ringing in his ears. A "great reader," possessed according to Charles Beecher of a "tenacious" and even encyclopedic memory, he had assimilated under his father's tutelage the controversial works of Channing and Worcester, Woods and Ware, Miller, Sparks, Stuart, Taylor, Norton, and the rest. He had read in Channing that the Unitarians looked "with horror and grief" on orthodox "views of the divine government." He had read the orthodox reply that Uni-

21. LB to EB, Boston, April 16, 1823, *Autobiography*, I, 517–518.
22. *Autobiography*, II, 63, 74.

tarianism was "irrational and unscriptural" and would "destroy for eternity every man who believes it." We may suppose he would have agreed with an 1820 pamphlet that "Unitarianism and the Orthodox worship different Gods."[23] Yale College would only intensify, not change, the attitudes nurtured by what Lyman Beecher led him to read. Beecher matriculated a year after the death of President Timothy Dwight, who in 1795 had undertaken to rebuild a "ruined college." Like Lyman Beecher (class of '97), Dwight had found Yale in what some described as "a most ungodly state," a hotbed of French infidelity, with "disorder, impiety, and wickedness" rampant.[24] By 1810, when Lyman Beecher in moving his family from East Hampton to Litchfield had pointed out to his sons their future alma mater, the college had been back in the orthodox groove for a decade. By 1818 Dwight had firmly imprinted his personality on the institution, and after his death his influence continued through the agency of Nathaniel Taylor, formerly Dwight's secretary and now pastor of the First Church in New Haven. Taylor, who in 1822 would become the first Dwight Professor of Didactic Theology at Yale, was Lyman Beecher's "most intimate friend, and that friendship Edward [Beecher] as it were inherited."[25]

Though "Taylorism" (Taylor's version of the "new school" or "new light" theology, of which Lyman Beecher's clinical philosophy was the practical counterpart) undoubtedly helped shape Beecher's mature theology, and though the father's position was never fully rejected, other

23. For CB's description of EB, see "Life," p. 84. For the quotations, whose location CB does not specify, see pp. 74–75.
24. Quoted by Charles E. Cuningham, *Timothy Dwight, 1752–1817: A Biography* (New York: Macmillan, 1942), pp. 177, 293.
25. CB, "Life," p. 10½.

members of the faculty besides Taylor also influenced Beecher. He studied mathematics with Alexander Metcalf Fisher, soon to become the catalyst, several times removed, of a major shift in his view of his father's universe. Benjamin Silliman, professor of Chemistry and Natural Science, sensed no conflict between science and religion, had no qualms about demonstrating the "great antiquity of the earth," and consequently helped Beecher respond intelligently to Darwinism and the English Broad Church movement in the early sixties. Chauncey A. Goodrich, professor of Rhetoric, had perhaps the most immediate influence on Beecher because, as Charles Beecher tells us, the influence was personal and religious; it was to Goodrich that Beecher went for help in "experimental matters." Beecher, however, "studied according to his own ideas," or at least liked to think he did (perhaps unconsciously resisting the many letters of advice his father wrote). He won the Berkleian prize in his sophomore year, became a member of the Phi Beta Kappa Society, and finally graduated as valedictorian of his class. But by his senior year he had not yet achieved the conversion experience he coveted beyond all worldly honors; there was "a certain baptism of the spirit, which he had not yet received."

For the first three years, Charles Beecher explains, he consented fully to the new-school theology; when his father and Asahel Nettleton came to New Haven for revivals he was "interested sympathetically." But he was not converted, perhaps because he "had not yet perceived the logical exigencies of the Conventional system." At last, in his senior year, a sermon moved him not only to realize but to sense that he was "in danger, and that if he did not become a Christian he would be lost." He renewed his efforts, "reading, striving, seeking, praying," a " 'blind sort of work.' " As all Christians of his time knew, the "struggle[s] of the imprisoned spirit for reunion to its primeval source are agonizing"; the "mysteries of the Soul are great." Beecher "testified" that "through all his childhood, as far back as memory could reach he never had a feeling of conscious alienation from God, or of hostility or revolt." Now he was in agony. "What he was striving for, was not mere intellectual knowledge of the system, but actual communion with God, 'face to face, as a man talked with his friend' "; he was seeking "objective reality."

Finally in his senior year he found it. All the "alternations of hope and fear; darkness and light, gloom and joy" were not, he felt, "greater than so august a change demanded." He had received the "baptism of the spirit" and was "converted." That was everything. But perhaps more interesting to us than the fact of his conversion is its immediate cause, which, he said, was the reading of certain passages in the Bible. Unlike his father, who read Jonathan Edwards, Beecher read scripture, and the language of the Bible "representing Christ as the bridegroom, and the church as the bride" made his heart, he said, "burn within." He came to think of marriage as a "type of the great and mysterious union of Christ and the Church."[26] It may or may not be relevant that during the same year, at the very moment he was writing his graduation oration on "Moral

26. CB's account here ("Life," pp. 10½–23) seems clearly a paraphrase of an original source; his own quotations from that source, uncited, I have indicated by double quotation marks. For a full supplementary account of EB's teachers and of Yale in EB's time, see Roland H. Bainton, *Yale and the Ministry: A History of Education for the Christian Ministry at Yale from the Founding in 1701* (New York: Harper and Brothers, 1957), especially pp. 79–112.

Influence," Beecher was infatuated with a New Haven girl. The available details are scanty and oblique. Evidently his family, or at least Catharine, thought she was not right for him. They spoke of "the necessity of a minister's having a pious wife." He came to a "decision to do" his "duty, & not to form any engagement at present."[27] Whatever subsequently happened, and aside from the "inexpressible" and clearly mystical sense of unity with the cosmos the experiences of his senior year gave him, he developed out of it all a theory of "correspondence by analogy." If it is crucial for Charles Beecher to note that it was in "these Scripture analogies" that "the Lord thus early revealed himself" to Beecher, "a revelation real, and direct, though not miraculous" (Charles does not mention the town girl), it is important for us to add that in his senior year he developed a way of looking at the world to be cultivated in his germinal 1827 *Address*, and at about the same time in the works of the Swedenborgians, the transcendentalists, Horace Bushnell, and some abolitionists.[28]

"It is not strange," as Charles Beecher remarks, that a young and loyal "mind, going through such profound and peculiar experiences, in such communion with God, breathing the atmosphere of revivals"—a mind, we should remember, still on the conscious level "sure that his father was right"—felt and spoke "strongly" about Unitarianism, as Edward Beecher did. But if he was "obliged to defend the divine character from the charges of that system," he felt he must in conscience conduct the defense "without

27. EB to Catharine Beecher, New Haven, August 30, 1822 (SL). In the postscript to his next letter, EB noted briefly that "As to my private affair, it is over & nothing more can be said than I have already said. It is as it should be." EB to Catharine Beecher, Litchfield, September 16, 1822 (SL).
28. CB, "Life," pp. 18–21.

violation of charity." His conscience forced him into a self-imposed "education of peculiar severity." He felt it necessary to "read every thing bearing on the subject, ancient and modern; to be resolutely honest in conceding to antagonists whatever elements of truth they possessed."[29]

In making such concessions out of conscience, Beecher was, whether consciously or not, rejecting his father's image of Unitarianism as the enemy. He was trying to defend the orthodox establishment, not by militant and unrelenting denial of Unitarian truth, but by assimilating its truth into the orthodox system. He was in effect, then, admitting that the new principles, in favor of which Unitarianism was, to use his own phrase, a "providential protest," were his principles too. Beecher saw that orthodoxy, if it was to come to terms both with the Enlightenment it had tried to reject out of hand and with the social realities of the nineteenth century, must do more than assimilate; it must itself undergo extensive "readjustment." The adjustment he began to contemplate, perhaps as early as his college years, was not evangelical in the manner of his father, though he not only acknowledged but insisted upon the importance of revivals. It was doctrinal. He wanted to perform theological plastic surgery upon the systems of orthodoxy and Unitarianism, to graft the truth of the latter upon the durable, but (for many) ugly, form of tradition. He sought, in short, a new system of theology and of the universe, more orthodox than Unitarian, which would resolve, and in resolving reveal, the inner conflict of his time.

That conflict, as Beecher finally analyzed it publicly in 1853 (though he thought he felt its effects much earlier), was epitomized by orthodoxy's own dialectic. The thesis

29. CB, "Life," pp. 80–81.

of the inner debate that went on in the minds of men was
that evil could be explained by the doctrine of either
original sin or total depravity, depending upon whether
one's immediate concern were first or second causes. Original sin, total depravity, God's unconditioned sovereignty,
man's culpability and dependence on grace: these were the
traditional first principles of Edwardsean orthodoxy. But
in the Enlightenment there arose an antithesis which af-
firmed the "principles of honor and of right" and which
required God to act according to human notions of justice.
So long as no one made an issue of the contradictions between them, an orthodoxy half Hebraic and half ultra-
democratic could hold both, if not in a new synthesis, in
at least a tentative and uneasy embrace. But when Unitarianism at the turn of the century made its protest in full
favor of the antithesis (and thus almost seemed to deny the
possibility of evil), when Unitarians took the antithesis
for themselves, the orthodox remnant were forced in self
defense to return, at least publicly, to their original thesis.[30]

The terms of Edward Beecher's problem were typical of
his generation's dilemma. He "sympathised" with his
father's clinical version of Edwardsean orthodoxy, yet he
was "impressed" by some of the "testimonies of the other
side." The essence of the "great controversy" of his "day,"
he at first merely felt but later fully understood, was not
the public debate between two wings of orthodoxy (really,
now, two sects) carried on in the law courts, the journals
of theology, and the pulpit. It was the constant and agonizing dialectic going on in men's minds that was important,
a dialectic in which two views of the world were "at war"
with each other and sought a new synthesis.[31] The inner

30. EB, *Conflict*, p. 124 ff.
31. CB, "Life," p. 73.

conflict really belonged mostly to the orthodox mind, for it was committed both to the traditional dogmas of Edwardsean Calvinism and, being a part of the new century, to the principles of honor and right, to social justice, as well. The Unitarians were not as complicated; they were the party of progress, bent upon denying tradition, wholly engaged in forging a reasoned new world. Like their spokesman William Ellery Channing, they were persuaded that Calvinism was beginning to give "place to better views. It has passed its meridian," they insisted, "and is sinking to rise no more. It has to contend with foes more formidable than theologians; with foes from whom it cannot shield itself in mystery and metaphysical subtilties,—we mean with the progress of the human mind, and with the progress of the spirit of the gospel. Society is going forward in intelligence and charity, and of course is leaving the theology of the sixteenth century behind it." The Unitarians felt they were riding the wave of the future, and in such a situation they did not feel compelled to reconcile their "better views" with the traditions of "sixteenth-century" theology.[32] It remained, then, for the orthodox community to accommodate the new principles of honor and right—to transfer, for instance, the Hopkinsian doctrine of disinterested benevolence to the social and political realities of the nineteenth century, one of the most pressing of which would be slavery.

But during Beecher's college years (1818–22) and, indeed, as late as 1827, most, if not all, of the conflict went unrecognized. Outwardly, at least, Beecher remained his father's son. "Naturally ambitious," "aspiring," "conscientious," and "cautious" as a student, he looked forward to

32. William Ellery Channing, "The Moral Argument against Calvinism" (1809), *Works*, p. 468.

graduation as the time for "the commencement of action."
After experiencing a "state of indecision" for a few weeks,
he acted. He accepted, as reward for being valedictorian of
his class and a Beecher, a position as Headmaster of the
Hartford Academy at $500 per year. The two years he
subsequently spent in the capital of Connecticut were years
of high hope, but, as Charles Beecher insisted (perhaps too
much), "at the utmost remove from an impractical, dreamy
idealism." His typical day was completely filled: at least
seven hours at his school (he taught twenty-six students in
sixteen different classes), an hour of exercise cutting wood,
one and one-half hours for prayer and the Bible, forty-five
minutes for three meals, and an indeterminate amount
of time reading student papers, preparing for classes, attending meetings, honoring invitations from students'
families to "take tea" (he visited, he wrote, in "the best
society in Hartford"), tutoring his brother George, preparing his weeekly lecture on "moral and practical subjects," studying music and mathematics for fun, writing
letters and critiques on theological subjects and writing
privately in his commonplace book, and doing the "thousand little thing[s]" such as washing and drying ("about
20 minutes every day") that a bachelor must do. All this
was valuable preparation for his more important job in
the next decade, in Illinois. But evidently the contradictions and "cares of schoolkeeping" weighed heavily upon
him. Teaching at first made him feel "dejected and full of
fear," perhaps because of his sense of "deep responsibility
for the care of so many immortal souls." He found it "un-
pleasant" to "go back to the dry uninteresting rudiments
of cases, tenses, concords, & governments," especially when
he had to "beat knowledge into thick sculls," but he conscientiously tried to improve his Latin and Greek. And he

tried to convert his students, intensely aware of the contribution he might make to the "happiness of the Universe." He tried to follow "the example of Jesus," to imitate his "meekness, patience, and long-suffering."[33]

If teaching kept him out of the "humour of correspondence,"[34] it perhaps also led to his decision in 1824 to attend Andover Theological Seminary, a decision perhaps best understood, however, less as an attempt to escape schoolkeeping than as the beginning of the fulfillment of his destiny as a minister and theologian. There at the leading orthodox seminary, born out of the uncertain marriage of the Old Calvinist and Hopkinsian wings of the orthodox church, Beecher took Hebrew, theology, and other seminary courses as a member of the junior class. He studied under Moses Stuart, the master of Biblical criticism, and once a week attended a theological discussion held by Leonard Woods, noted for his attempt to reconcile the two wings of orthodoxy that had built the school. He became acquainted with the men behind two journals originating there—the *Biblical Repository* and the *Bibliotheca Sacra*—

33. For the information and quotations in this paragraph, see especially "Life," pp. 18, 23–24, 28, and EB to Catharine Beecher, Hartford, February 14, 1822 (SL); the contents and context of the letter make it virtually certain that its date ought to be 1823. For minor points, see also three other letters from EB to Catharine: September 16, October 27, and December 11, 1822 (SL). For the Latin and Greek, see the four pages of inquiries on matters of pronunciation, declension, and rules to EB's teacher, Professor James L. Kingsley, Hartford, March 24, 1823 (Yale, Kingsley Collection). These, as well as EB to Willard Fisher, Hartford, October 12, 1824 (Yale), help clarify a small problem in chronology:

Charles H. Rammelkamp in his DAB sketch says that EB taught at Hartford Academy for one year; CB says two years. CB was right. EB took the position in October 1822 (see EB to Caleb Fisher, Litchfield, October 27, 1822 [Yale]), and, as the letter to Willard Fisher indicates, he was just beginning in October 1824 to decide what he would do next. The point is important in assessing his relationship to Catharine and Harriet.

34. EB to Willard Fisher, October 12, 1824 (Yale).

journals in which he would eventually publish scholarly theological articles.[35] There, on the whole, he found his circumstances "very pleasant," his health, always a problem, "good," the advantages "great."[36] There he flowered into a minister who could give "help" and "comfort" to his father, as, for example, when he contributed his "piety and talents" to the revival in Litchfield that year.[37] But Beecher remained at Andover less than one academic year, perhaps because (as his brother William wrote in a letter) he did not want to waste three years studying Hebrew, perhaps because (as later events would make especially probable) he found Andover's "emphasis on dogma and polemics" and its brand of conservatism distasteful.[38]

In any case, at just the right moment he was offered a job as tutor at Yale. His sister Catharine urged him to accept. New Haven, she wrote in March 1825, is "the best place for you." She had never, she said, really feared that Beecher would be "much altered" by Andover; it was not as if he were "pliant & likely to copy the models" he had there. But no doubt she was relieved when on May 1 of that year he went to New Haven.[39] In fact, as she could not have known, the change partly determined Beecher's future. When he arrived in 1825, religion at Yale again was, in the perennial orthodox phrase, "at a low stage," even though the college had been dominated by orthodox teachers and had recently gone through a series of revivals. The

35. See "Life," p. 28, and Henry K. Rowe, *History of Andover Theological Seminary* (Newton, Mass., 1933), pp. 50–61.

36. EB to Willard Fisher, Andover, January 31, 1825 (Yale).

37. LB to William Beecher, October 26, 1825, *Autobiography*, II, 28.

38. William Beecher to EB (in Boston), July 8, 1827 (MHCL); Rowe, *op. cit.*, p. 50.

39. Catharine Beecher to EB (at Andover), Hartford, March 26, 1825 (MHCL).

students had become "lawless." Beecher, we are told, engaged in a one-man effort, organizing Bible classes, appointing "committees for gospel effort," lecturing in the theological class room, "virtually undertaking a revival." At first he was unsuccessful; insults were "heaped on him." But eventually his lecture room was filled. Finally the "reaction came. Order was restored. Religion revived. Yale College was changed." We may wish to discount the enthusiasm with which Charles Beecher implies that his brother changed Yale. More likely, the year at Yale changed Beecher, or at least his career. He impressed a handful of divinity students who would in 1829 become known as the "Yale Band" and subsequently invite him to Illinois to become president of a new college. The episode does suggest, however, that Charles was right in describing his brother as "a resolute earnest practical man, who was determined to do his duty, and did it as perfectly as possible" (given, that is, certain inherited limitations) "to humanity."[40]

Yale was temporary for Beecher. In the summer of 1826, he was seriously considering an offer of a professorship at Dartmouth. His father advised him not only to reject the position but to refuse to "consent to be invited."[41] At about the same time, he preached four Sunday lectures at Park Street Church, the scene of his father's 1817 lecture, for the Beechers the "Gibraltar of orthodoxy,"[42] for others the

40. CB, "Life," pp. 30–31, 33.
41. LB to EB, Boston, August 3, 1826 (MHCL); also in *Autobiography*, II, 67. In a letter from New Haven, August 1, 1826 (MHCL), EB had put twenty questions to his father, the answers to which were to help him decide whether to become a professor at Dartmouth or to take a parish at Andover. The context suggests that it was a second letter of inquiry. The result was that EB did neither.
42. CB, "Life," p. 36.

"brimstone corner" of Boston. To become pastor of Park
Street Church would be a distinguished beginning for a
young man. And, as his father wrote him, there was an
"earnest desire" among the congregation to have him, a
"manifest providential indication" he should accept. Lyman Beecher also wanted him to "do it without fail." Edward would be a "great consolation" to him "just at this
time"; there were "the little clouds" of a revival, which
with "four weeks of exertion such as you, with myself and
others, may make" might produce "an overpowering
shower."[43] As a result (and, as we shall see, with some
doubts) Beecher "settled over" Park Street Church in December 1826. Finally, it seemed, Lyman Beecher's model
son had begun to realize his destiny. He whose faith had
been "so absolute, that there was never any wish to be skeptical, or to raise cavils" was now a minister, working side by
side with his father to bring orthodox truth to a heterodox
(Unitarian) city. He had, it seemed, demonstrated in action
his inner certainty that his father was right.

2

Appearances were in this case deceiving. The predictable surface of Beecher's life disguised its inner turbulence.

43. LB to EB, Boston, April 19, 1826 (MHCL); also in *Autobiography*, II,
61–62. On the general subject of EB's career, LB wrote at least thirteen
long letters to EB during 1826, dated January 8, April 19, June 11, July 20,
August 2*, August 3, August 4*, September 4**, September 5, September
12*, October 16*, November 21, December 7. The unstarred letters, now at
MHCL, are reprinted with unacknowledged and extensive deletions, additions, and distortions in the *Autobiography*, II, 46–86. The single-starred
letters are available only in manuscript (MHCL). The double-starred
letter (September 4) appears only in the *Autobiography*. One becomes aware
in comparing versions of these letters that LB's relation to his children,
particularly EB, was closer, warmer, more open and involved than the
Autobiography alone has indicated to scholars.

As the first of the Beecher children to experience conversion, as a young and brilliant scholar, headmaster, tutor, and now minister, he was, to be sure, the "envy and the example" of his brothers and sisters.[44] They sought his advice; he in turn prayed that their "inner man" would be strengthened, as his had been, by the spirit of God, that they would have faith, that they would "be able with all saints to comprehend" Deity.[45] But all the Beecher children had "difficulties"[46] accepting their father's system; and, ironically, the difficulties (which so consistently led them toward heresy that in the forties and fifties their collective eccentricity was called "Beecherism") may be traced partly to the father. The example of Lyman Beecher, in league with Nathaniel Taylor and others, leading one wing of the church to revise orthodox doctrine into a "new divinity" suggested to the children that orthodoxy was not immutable, that it had a morphological history. And the father's insistence that the children "Receive no opinions upon trust" pervaded the atmosphere of their youth, from the remarkable dinner-table debates he encouraged to his pronouncements in print: "Dare to think for yourself. Let no creed bind you because it is reputed orthodox, until you perceive its agreement with the Scriptures; but then, though every where spoken against, adopt it."[47]

44. CB, "Life," p. 17.
45. EB in 1825, as quoted by CB, "Life," pp. 29–30.
46. Chapter 7 of the "Life" (p. 38) was entitled "Difficulties Attending the Evangelical System."
47. LB, "The Bible a Code of Laws," A Sermon Given at the Ordination of Sereno E. Dwight as Pastor of Park Street Church, Boston, September 3, 1817, *Autobiography*, I, 352–353; quoted in part in Mae Elizabeth Harveson, *Catharine Esther Beecher, Pioneer Educator* (Philadelphia: privately printed, 1932), pp. 28–29. For more of the flavor of the dialogue that pervaded the life of the family, see also *Autobiography*, I, 149; Forrest Wilson, *Crusader in Crinoline: the Life of Harriet Beecher Stowe* (Philadelphia,

Antedating Emerson's plea for self-reliance by more than twenty years, the father's charge was intended to promote neither the permanent suspension of belief nor the elevation of transcendental intuition to final truth. It came from a man who *knew* he was right and who could not doubt that debate would affirm orthodoxy. The liberty he offered his children was calculated to bring them to the orthodox God, and if his calculations did not always add up as he hoped, it was not finally—he perhaps was never aware—his fault. He kept trying. "What shall it profit you," he wrote his son, engrossed at Yale in his studies, "though you should gain all knowledge and lose your own soul?" "Oh, my dear son," he pleaded in another letter, "*agonize* to enter in. You *must* go to heaven; you *must not* go to hell!"[48] On the one hand, then, Beecher was charged to dare to think for himself; on the other hand, his heritage was to agonize his way into heaven. What would happen when the Hebraic heritage conflicted with democratic daring, or when the agony would lead him to dare too much?

Beecher first sampled the conflict vicariously, through the experience of his older sister Catharine, whose fiancé, the precocious Professor Alexander Metcalf Fisher, died by drowning in April 1822 when the packet ship *Albion* went under off the coast of Ireland. Fisher had never joined the church; his charm and goodness were only "natural," not the result of a conversion experience, as Catharine later discovered in searching through his private papers; therefore, unless he had experienced grace in his last moments,

London, New York: J. B. Lippincott, 1941), p. 30; and Charles Edward Stowe and Lyman Beecher Stowe, *Harriet Beecher Stowe: the Story of Her Life* (Boston and New York: Houghton Mifflin; Cambridge: Riverside Press, 1911), p. 9.
48. LB to EB, June 22, 1820, and April 7, 1821, *Autobiography*, I, 429, 460.

he was, according to Lyman Beecher's version of orthodoxy, damned to eternal torment. His status in the afterlife was at best uncertain, at worst and probably, permanent damnation. From her father and brother Catharine sought solace for what seemed unjust. Her father's explanations, later published as "one of the best presentations of New England theology which had then appeared," were not consoling. Many did "indulge the hope" that Fisher was "pious," the father granted, but for that we have no evidence, we cannot "remove the veil," we have "no absolute resting-place but submission" to God in the knowledge of his "perfect administration" of justice. Lyman Beecher admitted privately to his son that "at times" he felt at his "wit's end to know what to do," but clearly nothing was "safe" but to "assert ability, and obligation, and guilt upon divine authority"—that is, the doctrine which contended that if Fisher had not been saved, it was his fault, not God's—"throwing in, at the same time, as much collateral light from reason as the case admits of." He felt it his duty to destroy the "indefensible positions" Catharine tried to "set up" through "depravity, and fear, and selfishness, and reason." He had, in short, to "answer objections and defend the ways of God."[49]

Edward Beecher agreed. Between May and December 1822, he exchanged at least two letters a month with Catharine, often more, sympathizing with her over Fisher's death and, at the same time, urging her, in every way he knew how, not to let the "warning" pass "unimproved." Like his father, he tried to use Fisher's death as a means to Catharine's salvation. Like his father, he failed. His warn-

---

49. LB to Catharine Beecher, New Haven, May 30, 1822, *Autobiography*, I, 478–479; LB to EB, August 2, 1822, *Autobiography*, I, 384–385.

ing that she was "in danger of being lost forever" did not move her because, as she had written to Beecher even before Fisher's death, she could not "feel."[50] She had had, she said, a "secret" hope Beecher could do something to "remove" her "difficulties," but early in their correspondence that hope was "gone." The "difficulty," she wrote, "originates in my views of the doctrine of original sin. . . . I feel that I am guilty, but not guilty as if I had received [at birth] a nature pure and uncontaminated. . . . Is there any satisfactory mode of explaining this doctrine, so that we can perceive its consistency while the heart is unrenewed?"[51]

According to one account, only partially true and begun, evidently, by Lyman Beecher Stowe, chronicler of the Beecher family, Edward Beecher never stopped trying to answer Catharine's question. Her question became his. It provides one clue to the turbulence of his inner life. And it explains his theological masterpiece thirty years later, *The Conflict of Ages* (1853).[52] In the beginning in 1822, though, Beecher was without satisfactory answers, and his

50. EB to Catharine Beecher, New Haven, May 30, June 14, and March 29, 1822 (SL); EB quotes Catharine on her inability to feel in the March 29 letter.

51. Catharine Beecher to EB, Litchfield, July 1822, *Autobiography*, I, 481–483.

52. The account appears in print for the first time to my knowledge in the 1911 biography of HBS by her son and grandson, *op. cit.*, p. 49. Unfortunately, not only does it oversimplify the source and significance of EB's achievement in *The Conflict*, but it has been accepted whole by nearly all subsequent students of the Beecher family; see, for example, Wilson, *op. cit.*, p. 58. Lyman Beecher Stowe (probably the man responsible for the simplification) makes his case by quoting out of context a letter from EB to Catharine, New Haven, June 7, 1822 (SL); see *Saints Sinners and Beechers* (Indianapolis: Bobbs-Merrill, 1934), p. 89, which is a generally useful but often inaccurate chronicle of all members of the family.

responses to Fisher's death were wholly conventional. He helped settle Fisher's estate.[53] He warmed over his father's cold logic with sympathy. He advised Catharine to rebuild her life around a service ideal and to spend her talents in doing good. He helped her form the Hartford Female Seminary and wrote the definitions for her theologically unusual course in Mental and Moral Philosophy (which, since they involved "much that might result in theological controversy," were not published),[54] and in general provided a model of orthodox action for her to imitate in adversity.

Catharine passed what she learned on to her younger sister Harriet, who, in the autumn of 1824 when she was thirteen and when Beecher was preparing to leave Hartford for graduate study at Andover, went to Catharine's seminary.[55] Through Harriet, Beecher would again vicariously experience the characteristic agony of orthodoxy. Between February 1827 (the time of Beecher's ordination as pastor of Park Street Church) and February 1829, he

53. EB was the official executor of Fisher's effects and debts at Yale (which became the subject of several long letters to Fisher's family), not only because of Catharine, but also because he was a close friend of Fisher's brother Willard. He also sought out the sole survivor of the *Albion* and reported Fisher's last moments, which might have been crucial to the state of his soul, to Catharine. He consulted as well with Catharine about Fisher's epitaph and other such matters. Most of the relevant letters are dated 1822 and in SL.

54. Catharine Beecher, *Common Sense Applied to Religion; or, the Bible and the People* (New York: Harper and Brothers; Montreal: Benjamin Dawson, 1857), p. ix. See also Harveson, *op. cit.*, p. 151; "Life," p. 88; and Catharine Beecher to EB, Hartford, August 23 [28?], 1828 (MHCL). The text for the course, *Elements of Mental and Moral Philosophy* (1831), was printed only for private use. A quarter of a century later, it was assimilated into *Common Sense.*

55. Catharine Beecher, *Educational Reminiscences and Suggestions* (New York: J. B. Ford and Company, 1874), p. 31.

exchanged letters and talked with Harriet about her struggle toward a genuine conversion experience. By this time
he had begun to find answers to Catharine's question, and
his letters to Harriet were very different from his earlier,
very orthodox letters to Catharine. He was ready to dare
more.

Harriet's dilemma followed a pattern approximating
her elder sister's, one which became increasingly widespread as the century moved toward the Civil War. Bound
by the God of her father, intellectually accepting His
"power and justice," Harriet nevertheless *felt* that He was
not "such a God as I need." She needed a God "merciful
and compassionate," "a being who sympathizes with his
guilty, afflicted creatures." One way out of the dilemma
was to join the Unitarians (or, for that matter, any of the
other liberal sects) in rejecting what seemed to be an orthodox God at once dispassionate and consumed with revenge.
But to do that would be to deny all the emotional truths of
childhood. It would require that Harriet wrench her entire
being out of a context that seemed natural and inevitable.
Not many could escape their inheritance so directly, as the
relatively small number of Unitarians and their relatively
slow rate of growth attested. Besides, there was a less violent
way. If one could find a homemade solution, one within
the limits of permissible variation in orthodox doctrine,
he might both remain orthodox and resolve the conflict
raging within. Catharine, for instance, discovered her private solution in a theory of "common sense and the moral
nature of man." Though it sounded suspiciously Unitarian, it gave her the emotional solace that her father's orthodoxy refused, without forcing her into obvious heresy.
Beecher offered Harriet comfort in a view of God he ini-

tially revealed to her one afternoon they spent together. He removed "Many" of her "objections" to God and made her "not as unhappy" as she had been. Harriet longed, she wrote Beecher, to adopt his system, but she was afraid for several reasons. First, it seemed to take from God's "majesty and dignity" to suppose "that his happiness can be at all affected by the conduct of his sinful, erring creatures." Second, such a view of God would lessen that "reverence and fear" which are major motives to action. Third, the God of the Book of Job did not seem to be Beecher's God of "mercy and pity," the God who "sympathizes with his guilty, afflicted creatures." But despite these objections— which help confirm that Beecher was not only thinking, but discreetly talking, heresy in the late 1820s—Harriet was close to being convinced: "Somehow or another," she wrote, "you have such a reasonable sort of way of saying things that when I come to reflect I almost always go over to your side. . . . Oh, Edward, you can feel as I do; you can speak of Him! There are few, very few, who can."[56]

The image of Deity that Beecher offered Harriet and Catharine, in both conversation and letters, was one of a sympathetic, suffering God, modeled on Jesus Christ. He was "God 'long-suffering,' God 'grieved,' when his work of 'sealing' was resisted." As he was to write publicly and argumentatively in 1860, Beecher privately in the 1820s

---

56. For the HBS letters, see Charles Edward Stowe, *Life of Harriet Beecher Stowe: Compiled from Her Letters and Journals* (Boston and New York: Houghton, Mifflin and Company; Cambridge: Riverside Press, 1890), pp. 36–48. Catharine made public her private solution in *Common Sense*, where she also criticized the arguments of *The Conflict*. Some aspects of my account of HBS I borrow from Charles H. Foster, *The Rungless Ladder: Harriet Beecher Stowe and New England Puritanism* (Durham, N. C.: Duke University Press, 1954), p. 94 ff.

drew for his sisters "the line between the true character of God, as revealed in Christ, and the Absolutist character as conceived of by even the best of men under corrupt or partially reformed systems. To deny the possibility of suffering in God," he argued, "is to deny that Jesus 'the man of Sorrows' is the express image of his person. In his pity, in his sympathy, in his agony in the garden, yea in his suffering on the cross, he expressed to us all that could be expressed of the pity, sympathy and grief of a father's heart."[57] Clearly, as the sisters were aware, this was not the God of Job that Beecher was imagining. Nor was it altogether the God of their father and the orthodox church. Was it not, rather, if not entirely a homemade God, then a recently made one, constructed like Catharine's "common sense and the moral nature of man" to satisfy the dual demands of an orthodox heritage and a psychological situation that orthodoxy, having precipitated, was no longer capable of resolving? Had their brother, then, the theological conservative of the family, found himself in the same disconcerting and anomalous inner dilemma his sisters had experienced?

Though Harriet was not sufficiently aware of Beecher's inner life to ask such questions, they should be asked. And the answers are to be found in her brother's diaries for the crucial year 1827. During that year, his first as a minister, Beecher tried to exorcise the doubt that had slowly been enveloping him, by writing to himself. Since his senior-year conversion at Yale—the period also of Catharine's debate with her father's God—the central orthodox doctrine of total depravity had plagued him. It seemed, he

57. CB, "Life," pp. 59, 302–303, describing and paraphrasing from *The Concord* (1860).

recalled in 1827, "to imply depravity antecedent to the exercise of reason," "a state of mind existing antecedent to developement." If "there be a cause in every one leading to such a state of mind how is he to be blamed?" Beecher was, of course, asking a question that had disturbed the orthodox community from the beginning. The Unitarians posed the same question. But for all its history and time-liness, the ordeal of asking was no less excruciating, and Beecher probed his spirit, sometimes incoherently, for an answer. He reasoned in his "commonplace-book" for 1827:

Pain, sickness and death come on the human race antecedent to the developement of reason. Such a constitution resembles punishment applied in anticipation of a crime. . . . there seems to be something in the nature of every human being morally odious as the certain cause of Sin. This one would think is a calamity and not a crime, a ground of pity and not of condemnation. . . . [To call total depravity] voluntary seems like removing a difficulty by language only. In short, original, native, entire depravity is a hard doctrine to be explained. . . . Why all men should tend so constantly to wickedness, against the light of Nature, and against the Christian revelation, is mysterious except on the ground that such a cause exists. And to come into being with a certainty of becoming miserable, and voluntarily so, is a great calamity.
. . . the question is, is not the present system a malevolent one? . . . if it reduces all things to a system of mere machinery, and of pain attached to conduct which seems voluntary, and pleasure to conduct which seems good. . . . we land in [a universe] of skepticism, yet, if such is the natural consequence of reasoning, we cannot help it. . . . Evil exists. If it does prove malevolence in God we are lost, or else must love a partial being. We cannot analyze the thing. . . . Why has God so made

men that a conviction of depravity, the most essential thing to a sense of mercy, is so hard to be obtained?[58]

Undoubtedly Beecher's deep concern about the "spiritual death" of his two sisters—he used the phrase in an 1825 letter to Willard Fisher to describe a certain "deadness of the soul to all spiritual things," especially an inability to feel orthodox doctrine as truth—contributed to his own conflict and doubt.[59] But simple chronology forces us to seek other explanations for his inner turmoil and for his participation in a pattern of religious experience which, I mean to suggest, characterizes his generation. Five years had elapsed between Fisher's death and 1827. The exchange of letters with Harriet was only accidentally contemporary with Beecher's experience, not its source, as the letters show. The fact is, rather, that Beecher was one of those persons for whom events larger than himself and abstract argument had personal meaning. Unitarian protests like Channing's, as Charles Beecher says, "touched" him: "The system his father defended, did it not impugn the honor, and rectitude of God? Did it not stain the beauty of that being?"[60] In short, the logic of the unfolding nineteenth century, embodied as Beecher saw it in Unitarianism, may be considered the ultimate, if not the immediate, cause of his "spiritual death." The "principles of honor and right"—manifested in the bewildering array of reforms throughout the first half of the century: in the temperance

58. EB (May–October 1827), as quoted in "Life," pp. 38–41.

59. "This state of mind I have felt," EB wrote Fisher from Andover on April 7 (Yale). Sometimes he called the state "moral death," which he described in *Six Sermons* (p. 198) as "the point of utter self-renunciation, self-loathing, and self-abhorrence."

60. CB, "Life," p. 37.

reform; in the reforms in education, in penal codes and prisons, in institutions for the deaf, blind, and insane; in the peace reform and the women's rights movement; and most significantly, in the antislavery movement, as well as in the numerous cults and utopian communities the principles generated—the principles of honor and right for which Unitarianism was a "providential protest" attracted Beecher just as they attracted his contemporaries, orthodox and heretical alike. But how could he logically and emotionally consent both to the reforms that embodied these principles and to the orthodoxy of his father (with which, since his ordination as a minister, he had become not only familially but formally connected)? Was there not an "irrepressible conflict between the facts of human depravity and the principles of honor and right"?[61] Must Beecher, like Orestes Brownson, drift literally from denomination to denomination seeking answers, only to end up as a Roman Catholic? Must he abandon one principle to the other? And even if he must, which principle could he abandon, committed as he was to both in the deepest recesses of his being?

Like his sisters and large numbers of his orthodox contemporaries, Beecher had to resolve the two forces that pulled him so excruciatingly in opposite directions, if, that is, he was to keep his sanity. The "transition" in his "own case," as he described it years later, was sudden, dramatic, illuminating, and perhaps best characterized, in Charles Beecher's phrase, as a "virtual revelation": it was as if he "had been groping in some vast cathedral, in the gloom of midnight, vainly striving to comprehend its parts and relations, [and] suddenly before the vast arched window

61. CB, "Life," p. 76.

of the nave a glorious sun had suddenly burst forth, filling
the whole structure with its radiance, and showing in perfect harmony the proportions and beauties of its parts."[62]
To Beecher was revealed the doctrine of the pre-existence
of souls. Souls, he perceived in that instant, are born into
this world, not newly created and corrupt, but as spirits
who fell from innocence in a free and previous existence.
Like Wordsworth in the famous "Intimations" ode,
Beecher thought that

> Our birth is but a sleep and a forgetting;
> The Soul that rises with us, our life's Star,
>   Hath had elsewhere its setting,
>   And cometh from afar:
>   Not in entire forgetfulness,
>   And not in utter nakedness

But unlike Wordsworth (whom he read), Beecher could
not assent to the next line; he was sure we do not come
into the world "trailing clouds of glory . . ./ From God."
We come rather out of the dark cloud of our fall from
Grace into a world best described as a "moral hospital" to
expiate our pre-existent crime. God suffers and grieves at
our fall, but having given our spirits freedom, He is restrained by His own law and justice from absolving us.

In one flash of insight, Beecher had found a way to counter Unitarianism's objection to the orthodox perception of
human depravity. No longer could God be charged with
being unjust and arbitrary, for the souls that became men
had fallen of their own volition. Orthodoxy was thus vindicated (if in revised form): men *are* depraved but God is

---

62. EB, *Conflict*, p. 191; for CB's characterization of the experience, see
"Life," pp. 43–44.

clearly free from blame. Life's purpose is, moreover, to atone for one's own original sin (forgotten though it may be by us all) through the reform of this world. The "irreconcilable conflict" of his generation had, for Beecher, been resolved. Armed with his two doctrines of a suffering God and the pre-existence of souls—both of which, as Charles Beecher observes, colored his "whole career, to an extent a superficial observer cannot well realise"—Beecher could live with both orthodoxy and his times, involving himself deeply in both without contradiction. He had found a "mode of adjustment."

But "thenceforward there was something akin in his experience to that of the apostle when he was caught up to the third heaven and heard things which it was not lawful to mutter." Like "Moses descending from the mount—his face transfigured—must he needs draw a veil over his countenance." The father "had no place in his system for this new revelation—The great champions of evangelical faith, Taylor, Goodrich, Stuart and others heed not—he must be silent, as became his youth. He must be 'dead and his life hid with Christ in God.' " Beecher felt compelled for the sake of church unity and because of his youth to "yield to his father's request to postpone utterance of his new views." And even if his father had not objected, there were few who, like his fourteen-year-old brother Charles, would "instantly as by a kind of intuition" accept the doctrine of the pre-existence of souls and sixty years later be able to say they had "never doubted it since." Beecher became isolated—"Shut up to God," in his own phrase. The revelation that he was sure would be a balm for the inner agonies of the orthodox of his generation could not be spoken. Indeed, he could not "converse much" even with "his father, or with Dr. Taylor, or anoy other leading minds, on the new revelations made to him," for it only "excited in them alarm, and solicitude." To compound the problem, this "young man of twenty-three, fresh from academic life . . . side by side with his father, the leader of his denomination, in the zenith of influence . . . already much honored by older men, leaders of the host; stationed conspicuously in the focus of New England thought, intense but narrow and provincial"—this young man had a "dogmatic system to defend distinctly based upon a doctrine" with which he could no longer agree, *"the fall of the race in Adam."* Not until 1853 would Beecher feel sure enough of himself to reveal to the orthodox world his revision of the doctrine of Adam's fall, and his solution to the inner conflict of his age. In the interim, he had to find a way to tell his truth without telling it all—a way to operate within his new assumptions about the nature of God and God's universe without giving away his heresy. *He* knew that he was only restating and "adjusting" orthodoxy; *he* knew that his sympathies were still orthodox. But who else would agree with that interpretation of his new vision?[63]

3

On February 10, 1827, a few months after he had taken the Park Street pastorate, and at the request of the Auxiliary Education Society of the Young Men of Boston, Beecher delivered, then published in revised and extended form, a lecture ostensibly about "the importance of the christian ministry, and the duty of men to extend its in-

63. CB, "Life," Preface, pp. 36, 44–46, 52; EB's phrase appears on p. 52.

fluence and to increase its numbers."[64] Charles Beecher, commenting on the *Address* seventy years later, thought its significance reposed in two different kinds of passages. First, Beecher had written that the "material system" is intended, "as the Bible plainly indicates, to assist in reforming the depravity of the mind"; that the system was by "forethought and design" adapted to furnish analogies and illustrations of spirit, to "illustrate the principles of the mind" and of God's "moral government"; that things were "faint and feeble" emblems of spirit. Such passages, Charles Beecher said, clearly indicate that Beecher was anticipating the transcendental doctrine of correspondence as it later appeared in America—in translations of Swedenborg, in Carlyle, in Emerson and Bushnell.

In other passages in the *Address*, Beecher had described the world as a "battlefield—the waterloo of the Universe."[65] For Beecher "the power of contending elements in the natural world," of which men were aware, provided an analogue for moral conflict, of which men were not aware. Do you not, he put it to his audience, see that there is a "great moral conflict" going on between God and the Devil? Do you not see the signs of moral conflict all around us, especially in the sinful mind hopelessly struggling with God? Do you not see, therefore, that the "victory of the kingdom of God on earth, will not be miraculous, or the result of physical power; [that] it will be a moral victory?" In short, as Charles Beecher saw, the imagery of moral conflict ("contending elements," "controversy with God," "victory") controlled Beecher's theological imagination.

64. Unless otherwise indicated, all quotations in this section are from EB's *Address*.
65. CB, "Life," p. 50.

The imagery, one should add to Charles Beecher's account, dominates the later work also, and provides the language in which Beecher would describe the Armageddon in the West between the Papal Conspiracy (the antichrist) and God's host; the conflict in men's minds between the ortho- dox doctrine of the fall and the Unitarian principles of honor and right; and the dilemma of conservative aboli- tionism—how to conserve orthodox institutions while en- gaged in an assault on social corruption.

But the significance of the *Address* is to be found neither in its anticipation, if it was that, of transcendentalism, nor in its images of cosmic conflict. Rather, its meaning and drama lie in what is retrospectively clear: that in this, his first major public performance, Beecher was trying to strike a difficult but tenable compromise between his father's re- quest to keep silent and his duty to his new truths. Mea- sured by number of words, the *Address* was not even primarily about its ostensible subject, the importance of the Christian ministry. It was prefaced by an "exhibition," which took most of the space and which covered the provi- dential history of the universe not only since Adam and Eve but since their pre-existent fall. Beecher, we may sup- pose, was attempting to put all his assertions into a context containing his revelations of a suffering God and pre- existence, but this without becoming explicit about his revelations. His assertions, in the sense he meant them, would be true. But his full meaning would have to be hid- den between the lines.

Such a task seems impossible, but Beecher's success was, from the point of view of his intention, remarkable. His personal vision of God as suffering and limited, for ex- ample, is there; but it lies hidden, necessarily, in a conventional rhetoric never unequivocally advocating such a God. God is not, Beecher wrote, a "great quiescent being, incapable of any deep feelings," as many "by a strange delusion" have been led to suppose. The "cold chill" which in many seems to "check every current of warm and tender emotion" at the mention of Him is unjustified. The widespread "secret dissatisfaction with God and his law" is to be attributed to the mistaken image of "a sovereign God who cannot sympathize with us in our tender feelings." Rhetoric such as this would seem to imply a sympathetic and suffering God. But Beecher never discusses Him directly; he only hints and implies. Moreover, God as he appears in the *Address* is both omnipotent and benevolent; but evil is nevertheless paradoxically "inevitable as an incidental result at some period of the progress" of the divine system, a paradox which may be resolved for Beecher only by the assumption (never stated in the *Address*) that God's omnipotence is limited to the natural world. The God Beecher projected, then, is at the same time "just" and capable of "deep feelings," omnipotent but constrained by the inevitability of evil. Passages and paradoxes like these, offering the barest hints of a new synthesis of the orthodox universe, are buried within extended sections of stock orthodox rhetoric. We may suppose that Beecher could not do without them.

Similarly, what are we who know of Beecher's secret doctrine of the pre-existence of souls to think of the almost-too-casual suggestion in the *Address* that the audience "consider first the application of the law [of God] to a pure spirit, as the most simple case"? Introduced as a hypothesis, a convenience for the purposes of theoretical discourse, it was in fact a part of Beecher's private distinction between the moral and material universe (between soul and "world," spirit and matter) and God's very different relation to each. God was, he privately thought, omnipotent only in the world of matter; in the world of morals, of spirit, He was limited. Only by such a distinction could he explain to himself how the fall of man (in the form of pre-existent "pure spirit[s]") could be "free," that is, not attributable to God, and at the same time preserve something of the orthodox concept of God's sovereignty. Beecher's "hypothesis," we must again suppose, was a way for him to suggest his truth, and to apply it, without standing for it.

The "exhibition" of the "nature and design of the kingdom of God" touches on every fine point of orthodox theology, and in most respects sounds eminently—remarkably —correct from an orthodox point of view. Throughout, however, there seems to be double-entry bookkeeping going on, in which Beecher's private resistance to orthodoxy, carefully noted in his diary, is replaced in the *Address* by affirmations of his father's faith. Publicly, he found himself, for instance, able to affirm that "to assert that sin is not criminal, where existing motives are not powerful enough actually to prevent it, would excuse all sin; for when does sin take place in any other circumstances?" But privately, he had thought that "there seems to be something in the nature of every human being morally odious as the certain cause of Sin. This one would think is a calamity and not a crime, a ground of pity and not of condemnation."[66] Or again, the "entrance of moral evil" into the universe, he

66. In this and the next paragraph, I quote not only from the *Address* but, as indicated in the text, from EB's diary (May–October 1827), reproduced in "Life," pp. 38–41. See Section 2 for the full diary passage.

said confidently in his lecture, "does not imply any want of benevolence in God." Privately, however, he admitted to himself: "Evil exists. If it does prove malevolence in God we are lost, or else must love a partial being. We cannot analyze the thing." In his lecture he predicted and prayed for the "victory of the kingdom of God on earth." But "the question is," he conceded in his diary, "is not the present system a malevolent one?" "Pain, sickness and death come on the human race antecedent to the developement of reason. Such a constitution resembles punishment applied in anticipation of a crime," he reasoned in his diary. But in his lecture, he "omitted to mention bodily suffering. I do not wish to settle the question as it regards this," he said. "Corporeal pain may exist, but it must be as a drop in the ocean."

It may be that what seems dishonest bookkeeping is in fact dishonesty—that Beecher feared the obloquy that would follow the exposure of his theological aberrations, that he lacked the courage his convictions required. It may also be, however, that in part we face a problem in chronology. Perhaps, as I suppose, the affirmations of the *Address* were carefully qualified answers to the questions and doubts in the diary. Perhaps Beecher thought that compromising his truth was the best way finally to get a hearing for it. He did, after all, believe everything he said in the *Address*, though with certain unstated qualifications.[67] He

67. I assume a chronology something like this: (a) In January and early February 1827, EB prepares the initial version of the *Address*; (b) he delivers it on February 10. Members of the society like it and ask him to publish it. He agrees but (c) feels obliged to revise extensively because he is personally and privately in the midst of theological uncertainty; he is unsure of himself—he wants to be careful. Read closely, the note he added to the published version of the *Address* suggests his caution: "Justice to my-

did, for example, believe that sin was criminal; it was only, in the words of his diary, a "calamity and not a crime" *if* there were no pre-existent state and no pre-existent fall. But he knew, even though he did not say so publicly, there *was* such a state and such a fall. Given the premise of his moral syllogism, his private reservations and public affirmations squared with each other. But he did not give his premise. In the same way, Beecher did believe that "the entrance of moral evil" into the universe implied no "want of benevolence in God"—but only if one knew as he did that God was limited, omnipotent only in the material world, not in the moral sphere. Were he to have outlined clearly and unmistakably his image of a limited and suffering God in the *Address*, one would not wish to audit his books. But that was precisely his problem: whether to remain, as his father wished, "silent" concerning the private assumptions from which he derived, and by which he justified, his conclusions (themselves orthodox enough), or to tell all and alienate himself from the orthodox community. The compromise he worked out in the *Address* was at least better than standing mute.

---

self and the community requires the following statement of facts. The Address was originally prepared and delivered in such circumstances that I was not able to discuss the subject as its importance seemed to demand. I deemed it therefore my duty, in preparing it for publication, merely to retain the original subject, and to make any alterations or additions which the nature of the case seemed to require." (d) Extensive revision turns out to require a whole new essay; writing it becomes a very difficult task, given EB's inner turmoil. He scribbles his doubts and uncertainties in his diary for May–October as he works, and (e) when the *Address* is finished he has "solved" his problems. Duplicity of a kind is involved in the solution: assertions are not put into the context that makes them possible, and EB still feels doubts. Nevertheless, with unstated reservations, he does believe everything he says.

Moreover, the imagery of the *Address* offers considerable evidence that Beecher's compromise of his cosmic revelation in favor of orthodox unity was, though conscious, in a sense inevitable. The idea of Christian "unity" is primarily a social idea; Beecher's imagery paradoxically joins social conservatism and radicalism—it suggests a man whose social consciousness is unarticulated and inherited, a man who does not yet perceive his contradictions.

On the one hand, Beecher spoke of the "stability" of God's government, of the "good of his enlarging empire"; God is a king; opposition to Him is like an "antisocial conspiracy" of "outcasts from human society" against "human governments." The Bible is the "constitution of the universe," and its literal and limited interpretation "should at once become a matter of intense national interest." It is like "the noon-day sun" in contrast to the "delusive meteors of pretended science, and of philosophy falsely so called." For instance, read properly, it shows that God, in "administering the principles of law and justice, elects and saves as many as the public good will permit," but no more. If there is, as I think, a relation between Beecher's yet-unexamined social attitude and his theological imagery, and given only this imagery, he should be described as a royalist, in favor of a constitutional monarchy of earth and universe, in favor of "stability," and opposed to all "antisocial conspiracy."

On the other hand, as different images demonstrate, he was a man with a radical vision of what society ought to be. The changes he

would produce in the social relations of life, in systems of education, in the principles of business, and in government, are great and important. . . . Restore the human heart to God, and selfishness will no more desolate the earth, war and slavery will cease. . . . Restore business, and the mechanical and agricultural concerns of life to God, and the fever of selfish competition will cease, and the whirlpools of speculation will not ingulf thousands in ruin; nor will the seeming necessity of adopting dishonest maxims, and calling them principles of trade, longer sear the conscience as with a hot iron. . . . No remnants [he cried] of the feudal system shackle us. . . . How glorious the spectacle, if the whole system of our political, literary, scientific and social institutions should be organized in accordance with the principles of the kingdom of God. . . . Does any one reply, "This is all a vision?" If so it is the glorious vision of the man of God of old.

Beecher's conscious manipulation of theological doctrine in the *Address*, then, his compromise, may have been the inevitable result of unexamined, inherited social attitudes. When in subsequent decades, especially in the 1830s, he began to think about society and to examine his political stance, his thinking would, in turn, be influenced by his theological revelations. Now, though, in his 1827 *Address*, he had passed his first test; he had made "little or no impression" on the public, "preoccupied" as it was with the "controversies of older and more noted men."[68] He had, it would seem, found a *modus operandi*, a way to use his revelations without revealing them and disturbing orthodox unity. He therefore decided, as he wrote looking back in 1853, not to "set forth in haste" his revelations. He would "review and reconsider," "mature" his thoughts, avoid a "crude and ill-digested presentation of so great a theme," and defer publication in "respect to the judgment of honored friends."[69] This is not to say that he would not bring

68. CB, "Life," pp. 51–52.
69. EB, *Conflict*, p. 6.

his revelations in, as he did in the *Address*, by the back door. Nor did the 1827 *Address* mark the end of his uncertainty about the rightness of his decision to compromise. But there were "topics enough for awakening sinners, and edifying saints" without stirring up new debate. He would try to devote himself to them.[70]

4

One of those topics was revivalism, to which Beecher had given his full assent years before he wrote *Hints Designed to Aid Christians in Their Efforts to Convert Men to God* (1832). As a boy he had learned evangelical tactics from Asahel Nettleton and others, as well as from his father; as a college student he had admired Jonathan Edwards's *Treatise Concerning Religious Affections*; when he went to Boston's Park Street Church, he went to help his father promote a revival; and from 1827 on, as a minister, he was himself a revivalist. At Park Street Church, where he remained for four years, he engaged in "constant calls, visits, and conversations with inquirers." This, added to the other tasks of a minister and to the emotional climax the diary records and the *Address* reveals, forced Beecher from "prolonged nervous strain" to take a long vacation in the winter of 1828.

His month in Maine was strenuous and satisfying. He preached twenty-eight revival sermons in twenty-six days. He was instrumental in the conversion of his future wife, Isabella Porter Jones, a distant cousin whom he would marry in October 1829. Most important to him, he renewed in Maine the "constant, full, and most delightful

70. CB, "Life," p. 46.

communion with his Lord" that was so necessary to him.[71]
His *sense* of God was intensified. He was able to

> realise that God does long to bestow upon me infinite love, and
> that I ought to give him infinite love in return. . . . I realised
> that I could be perfectly absorbed in him, and drawn into him,
> so as to be mingled with him and made a part of his Essence, so
> as to be in the most absolute sense one with him; yet I felt that
> the exciting cause of such love, must be the knowledge of his
> love to me and of his infinite desire to communicate his Essence
> to me in full and overflowing communication of love such as
> should affect my whole frame until I could feel that the love of
> God is strong as death, that the coals thereof are coals of fire
> that hath a most vehement flame; yea so intensely did I desire
> the love of God that I felt willing that it should burn one up if
> it were but love, and I could rejoice to die by such a death; or
> I was willing to be even filled full of pain by it, if I might yet
> feel that the pain was caused merely by intensity of love;—Or,
> I was willing to be dissolved, and mingle once more with God
> as a part of his being and thus to lose existence by returning
> into the being of my God, knowing that I should thus be in him
> still, and be a part of him and not be lost altho' I should be un-
> conscious of it when I had ceased to have any existence sepa-
> rated from his.[72]

Reminiscent of the piety of earlier New England Puritanism—of Edwards's *Personal Narrative*, of Edward Taylor's Meditations, of Hopkins's willingness to be damned
for the glory of God—Beecher's "willing to be dissolved"
hints at a second religious experience and perhaps explains
why he began to doubt his compromise of his revelations
in the *Address*. The Maine revival was, as Charles Beecher

---

71. CB, "Life," pp. 35, 53–54, 61.
72. EB, as quoted in "Life," pp. 62–63; the ellipsis in this quotation is
either EB's or CB's, not mine.

said, "highly beneficial"[73] because it temporarily provided
an answer in action to his "earnest prayer" that he might
not need to compromise, that he might "dare to pour out
and express ardent and infinite love, even before those
who might hate me for it, or be disgusted with it, as enthusiastic and unreasonable."[74] But the congregations of
the Maine provinces were not those of theologically sophis-
ticated Boston, where the debate between orthodoxy and
Unitarianism had reached a climax.

The major issue in the Unitarian controversy to which
Beecher returned was, according to Charles Beecher, "the
character of God." The "essential question" was not the
"arithmetical puzzle," the "mechanical" and "numerical"
quibble of unity *versus* trinity, of how $1=3$. The real question was whether Christ's "meekness, mercy, sympathy,
sorrow, tears, [were] true expressions of what is infinite in
the heart of God." Theoretically, the orthodox, like the
Unitarians, denied God's sorrow; sorrow would limit His
perfection. Yet "popularly the effect was as if they had not
denied it." The language of popular orthodoxy implied
that God "did humble himself, and sympathise, and suffer."
Beecher's problem was that he wished to go further; he
wanted to define a suffering, limited God speculatively and
theoretically. He wanted to meet the age's demand for a
just universe with a revision of orthodoxy. But drawn as
he was between his father, his ministerial tasks, and his
work writing for the orthodox *Spirit of the Pilgrims*, on
the one hand, and the "sincere esteem" he felt for Channing and certain of Unitarianism's central principles, on
the other, he again fell ill.[75] Only six months after his first

73. CB, "Life," p. 61.
74. EB, as quoted in "Life," p. 63.
75. CB, "Life," pp. 66–67, 84.

vacation he took a second one, this time revisiting East Hampton, New Haven, Hartford, and other places which had shaped him, as if in résumé of his youth.

In Hartford he talked with his sisters, upon whom he had first tried out his revelations. He and Catharine discussed his problem for three hours. She wrote him in August 1828, after he had returned to Boston:

> Your "explaining & expounding" was quite satisfactory, & I hope your *inward man* will soon be taught how to behave himself in all circumstances & emergencies. I wish I could catch my *inward woman*, & give her such an inspection & exposition, but she is such a restless thing that I cannot hold her still long enough to see her true form & outline. . . . I am however a little afraid that in the millennium your peculiar notion *not to be mentioned* about a *pre-existent state*, will not be found in the elementary works of mental philosophy or theology.[76]

Perhaps it was Catharine's lukewarm reception of his "peculiar notion" that led Beecher to begin rethinking assumptions: "How do we know that things are as they seem to be? How be certain that if God seems to be good, he really is so? . . . Can the human imagination create ideas of glorious displays of God forever, which seem real, when there is no such reality?" He was, as Charles Beecher observed, "continually meditating on the great themes on which Christians were in controversy, and on which he had received from the Spirit new revelations."[77]

Charles Beecher devotes a disproportionate number of pages to rationalizing his brother's state of mind during the Park Street years. He writes that Beecher was "strongly

76. Catharine Beecher to EB, Hartford, August 23 [28 ?], 1828 (MHCL).
77. CB, "Life," pp. 69–70 (probably paraphrasing very closely EB's diary), 84½.

impelled" to make his "precious" revelations public, but many considerations restrained him: his idea that the church was Christ's bride, their relationship "typified" by that of marriage, might be misunderstood as "mystical, visionary, and degrading to the majesty and dignity of God"; other of his ideas, ill proportioned, ill digested, crude, still in the formative stage, might prematurely censure existing customs and institutions and "tend to unhinge and distract society"; the "wicked and impure might scoff, and the holy feel hurt"; New England's "spiritual aristocracy" would, with its "immense force," ostracize him. Finally, simply to resist the satanic motives of pride and ambition, he ought to be quiet.

In short, it would seem that either during or shortly after the summer of 1828, Beecher talked himself into silence for a second time. After his second vacation, he returned to Park Street Church and a year of constant and "unintermitted" revivals. He preached six or eight sermons a week, at times he had a hundred "inquirers" at once, he wrote for orthodox journals, and he pushed "investigations in history, philosophy, and theology."[78] By October 15, his inner struggle had ceased, and he was able to inform his father that he now found himself "uncommonly tranquil." He had, he realized in looking back over the past year, "lost the balance" of his mind and become "unconsciously the slave of that visionary certainty which is caused by nervous excitement." He admitted he had been "proud, & ardent, & always in danger of extremes." Not even now did he "dare to speak with certainty." But his "increasing persuasion" was that his conduct (that is, his prudent compromise) was "in the main judicious."[79]

78. CB, "Life," pp. 85, 88, 93–94.
79. EB to LB, Andover, Wednesday, October 15, 1828 (MHCL).

Beecher felt sure enough of himself to marry a year later, on October 28, 1829. His first son, Edward Lyman, was born on May 5, 1831, an angelic but congenital idiot whose existence led Beecher for the next forty years to question all his motives, as if the child were a visitation of God's wrath. Of ten other children to follow, only two would survive their parents. But in 1829 they were in the distant future. The immediate future lay westward. In September 1830, Beecher began studying Flint's maps of Illinois, reading travel books, and mulling over Asa Turner's invitation to become the first president of Illinois College in Jacksonville, Illinois. After consulting his father (who had already been invited to accept the presidency of Cincinnati's Lane Seminary) and others, he resigned his Park Street pastorate. The church's inflexible orthodoxy and its strict stand on the baptismal issue had not been congenial to Beecher, and his expressions of sorrow at leaving were largely ritual. His experiences at Park Street, however, had at least served as the indirect occasion for two books.

Beecher wrote *Hints to Christians* with the help of his father's friend and colleague Thomas H. Skinner,[80] whose congregation (the Fifth Presbyterian Church of Philadelphia) had decided on January 31, 1832, to make "vigorous" and "persevering" efforts toward the "immediate conversion of sinners." Beecher was in Philadelphia soliciting money for Illinois College, as if, Skinner wrote Lyman Beecher, providence had sent him at just the right time. During Skinner's revival he preached "like an apostle."[81]

80. The style, diction, and emphasis of the book all indicate that EB was responsible for most of it, though officially he was only the junior co-author. Unless otherwise indicated, quotations in this and the next three paragraphs are from the *Hints* and are to be attributed to EB.

81. Thomas H. Skinner to LB, Philadelphia, February 16, 1832, *Autobiography*, II, 253–255.

And to "assist" the lay congregation in its work, he wrote like one. The *Hints* was only a tiny (2½" x 4") handbook but it read like a manual for the evangelization of the world. It showered its readers with moral imperatives and dogmatic directives:

Show that sin is rebellion against God; that ceasing to sin is ceasing to rebel. . . . [The chief end of] divine truth [and of] . . . the means of grace [is] . . . to produce immediate repentance. . . . [The] object of sinful attachment is different in different individuals. . . . In one, the claims of God are directly resisted by covetousness; in another, by pride; in another, by the love of pleasure; and commonly the resistance proceeds from some particular modification of these generic sins. . . . [Never be] unsupplied with a judicious selection of religious tracts. . . . [Understand] the laws of the mind as well as those of the body. . . . Tell them that they are already in a state of condemnation for their sins; that they are utterly guilty, vile and polluted in the sight of God, and can be saved only on the ground of unmerited mercy. . . . Let them know that to become religious is an intelligent, voluntary, indivisible act of the mind, in which it ceases to rebel against God, submits to his authority, and accepts of his mercy. . . . [If] through injudicious affection, or natural sympathy for distress, you forbear to urge the claims of God, and fully to take his part against the sinner, and enforce immediate obedience, you do, in effect, take part against him, and neutralize the influence of his claims on the soul. The love of God must be stronger than parental or any other affection, and we must be faithful to him and his kingdom, however painful to us, or to our friends. . . . Not only is it important that the truths represented be adapted to convert the soul, but also, that every thing be avoided in the manner of presenting them, which has any tendency to prevent the desired result. . . . How often has the whole power of truth been destroyed by something unhappy in the manner of presentation. . . . [Avoid, therefore,] a hasty, heartless manner [as well as] . . . a gloomy and forbidding

manner. . . . This produces on the minds of the impenitent conviction, that so far as love to God is concerned, you are perfectly happy, and that your sorrow is caused by a sincere and
deep interest in them. . . . [Avoid, too,] a harsh, imperious spirit.
. . . Be self-possessed. . . . Meekness is invincible; but the moment
you permit your passions to be excited, you are stripped of all
your power. . . . [Actions] speak louder than words. The real
state of a man's mind will develope itself by his habitual mode
of living. . . . Study diligently the character of those with whom
you converse, and adapt your remarks accordingly.

The *Hints* explicitly advised the amateur congregation
to "Avoid every thing polemic" and to "Represent divine
truth as a matter [for] practice, not for speculation." But
Beecher did not follow his own directions. The happy
intimacy between the popular version of orthodoxy and
Beecher's revelations allowed him to make use of his peculiar solutions to orthodox dilemmas.

His emphasis on Christ's suffering, for instance, could
very well have been orthodox rhetoric, the stock response
to Biblical fable: (be with Him, he wrote, "in his deep
poverty, his amazing privations, his cruel persecutions, . . .
his mountain retreats, his midnight prayers, his conflict
and agony in the garden, his shame and reproach . . . on
the cross"); so those who read the manual probably understood it. But Beecher was asking Skinner's congregation
to concentrate on the suffering of Deity as a "means" to
convert sinners. He did not, on the other hand, mention
the doctrine of Adam's fall, which repelled him; the doctrine was a standard one in this context, and its very omis-
sion may be taken as evidence that Beecher was imposing
his own revealed version of orthodoxy on the manual and
Skinner's congregation.

Or, again, the disjunction between the material and
moral halves of the universe that Beecher had "hypothe-

sized" in his 1827 *Address* finds a place in the *Hints* in the form of a conventional comment on "motives." God influences men, not by capricious force, but by surrounding him with motives to repent. It is then clearly a "criminal aversion to duty" if men ignore them (even though, Beecher admitted, they "always and obstinately" do). It is the sinner's fault, not God's, a "crime," not a "calamity": again we note those crucial terms of the 1827 diary and *Address,* as if Beecher could not get rid of them; and again Beecher avoided stating the assumptions upon which the distinction depended for its validity.

Measured against Beecher's mature writing, the *Hints* is didactic and slight, to be understood as a test of his ability to exploit his heresy without announcing it. It reveals in full that Beecher was a moralist and evangelist—qualities that constantly controlled his behavior—and that he was a tactician for whom muscular Christianity was a way of life, who charted his success according to the number of sinners he was instrumental in converting, and whose books were ultimately (if not always immediately) intended as contributions to a revival of religious experience. But he was also a scholar and historian of the first caliber, and though not published until 1849, a second and very different kind of book grew out of his years at Park Street Church. *Baptism, with Reference to its Import and Modes* shows Beecher in the best possible light as controversialist, linguist, philologist, scholar, and historian. It shows his concern for "a careful induction from facts," his awareness that in time "new ideas produce new words and new senses of old words," and his understanding that men write "in accordance with the views" of their "day."[82]

As early as November 1826, Beecher had begun to ex-

82. EB, *Baptism,* pp. 10, 19, 35.

amine "the baptismal question," and, as the time for his ordination drew near, the question increasingly troubled him. He wrote his father in December that he had been called to the ministry before he had fully investigated and finally resolved it. Unable to ponder the problem for years, he had to "administer this ordinance" immediately, even though he was not sure he could "conscientiously adhere to the present mode." He confided to his father that he should not have "answered the call so soon," that his conscience was unsatisfied.[83] Lyman Beecher said that he himself felt "no doubt"; that he was sure Edward, when he had time to study the issue, would agree with him; that really the Bible revealed enough on the subject "without ecclesiastical history and combats with windmills in the fog of distant ages." "Your present state of mind," the father wrote, comes from a "tender conscience," one "preternaturally sensitive and fearful." This, he pointed out, had worried many a man till he "became a Baptist through excess of conscience." Beecher had better come home, put off being ordained, and work out his problems, "especially" if he should be "veering" toward the Baptists. The father would take care of "the business of the delay of time." Beecher should not mention the occasion of delay; it was unnecessary and publicity could do no good and might do harm.[84]

83. EB to LB, New Haven, December 4, 1826 (MHCL), printed in part in *Autobiography*, II, 86. It was in this letter also that EB wrote to his father that, as there was "no one" whom he "love[d] better," so there was no one whom he could "more desire" to have preach for him on "so interesting an occasion" as his ordination. But as I have observed in my bibliographical comments on manuscripts, LB did not do the preaching.

84. LB to EB, November 21 and December 7, 1826, *Autobiography*, II, 85–87.

Since the ordination went off on schedule, we may assume that Lyman Beecher was able to assuage his son's tender conscience. But it is not clear why the conscience was so sensitive in the first place. It may have been merely a matter of doctrine that bothered Beecher, but in the same series of letters, as Lyman Beecher indicates, he mentions also his problems with the doctrines of "an authorized ministry," the damnation of infants, "etc." May his uncertainty in these matters be taken as symbolic action, in which a growing resistance to his father and to the central dogmas of the old orthodoxy—hidden as it was in the conflicts and revelations of his inner life—could be transferred to more peripheral, more formal, and less painful issues? One may suspect that such was indeed the case, but it is a hard, perhaps impossible, matter to demonstrate. Beecher thought the baptismal question a real issue in his life, as it in fact became. His reluctance to "administer" the ordinance contributed to his difficulties at Park Street Church, and perhaps finally to his resignation. In the 1830s he spent much of his free time working to resolve what had become so real an issue; and in the forties he published a series of articles on baptism in the *Biblical Repository,* engaged in an undesired and protracted, but respectable, controversy with British Baptist leader Alexander Carson, and published (in 1849) his 342-page book. The primary formal question in the book was whether *to baptise* meant to immerse, as the Baptists insisted, or, as Beecher argued, to purify (immersion being only one of the several possible "modes" of purification). Beecher tried to prove that a generic interpretation of *baptism* was the only possible reading one could give the word. But his purpose was not, essentially, formal and philological. He saw a "large and influential denomination," substantially agreeing with Presbyterians and Congregationalists on matters of dogma, yet sustaining separate educational, missionary, and ecclesiastical organizations, all "on account of a different interpretation" of the word *baptise*.[85] This, it seemed to him, was a tragic waste. Was there not "something wrong and offensive to God in the present divided state of the Church"?[86]

The Baptists may have agreed about the division but, as we might suppose, they rejected his interpretation of *to baptise* "with scorn." Beecher failed in this, as he failed in his later and more important efforts to play the role of mediator and to bring about a major reconciliation within the divided orthodox church. But in failing he learned much about the ways of men and institutions. "In practice, words are things," he observed. "Systems grow out of words." The "life of a whole denomination" may depend upon them. Once institutionalized, fundamental errors do not "easily die." If they have no "logical life," they have "an organic life of tremendous power." Institutions show a "uniform tendency" to "sink from the spirit to the form"; they are unable to admit truths which conflict with "the fundamental principles on which they are organized."[87] The tremendous power of words and institutions would also impress Beecher in 1838 (*Narrative*) and 1853 (*The Conflict of Ages*), when, as a social architect attempting to revise institutionalized abolitionist and theological dogmas, he would again find the going difficult.

85. CB, "Life," p. 138.
86. EB, *Baptism*, p. 2.
87. EB, *Baptism*, pp. 50, 121, 169, 179.

You are to train the architects of
human society, the guides of human
life. The destinies of generations
are often involved in the training
of one lofty mind.

Two

—Edward Beecher (1869)

No more can an architect of society
work without the appropriate means.
It is not self-denial, but self-
sacrifice, to live in anguish from
a view of what ought to be done and
could be done, with a consciousness
of the power to do it with appropriate
means, and yet without the ability
to secure these means.

—Edward Beecher (1850)

An Architect of Society

5

ON May 31, 1851, some twenty years after he went west
and seven years after he had returned east, Beecher
might have heard Henry Thoreau define the West for the
people of Worcester, Massachusetts, as "but another name
for the Wild" and then argue that "in Wildness is the pres-
ervation of the World." He could have accepted neither the
definition nor the thesis. And if on July 12, 1893, two years
before he died, he had heard Frederick Jackson Turner's
thesis, announced at the meeting of the American Historical Association in Chicago, the major city of the very
state in which Beecher's experience denied the telling, he
surely would have protested. Reversing Turner, he would
have said that the wilderness does not master the colonist;
it does not find him "a European in dress, industries, tools,
modes of travel, and"—above all—"thought"; it does not
then force him to return to a primitive state of existence
before he may become an American. Beecher would have

thought that Turner was, like Thoreau, making "an extreme statement" so that he might make "an emphatic one." He may have found the remark of a later historian—that a "settler could hardly encamp on the prairie, but a college would spring up beside his wagon"—an extreme statement too, but one that described more precisely than the others the West he had experienced.[1]

For Beecher the West meant the Mississippi Valley, where wildness was only incidental. The West was the locus of an ultimate providential crisis, the battlefield of a "final war of mind" in which Satan's power would be shattered, the human race emancipated, and, as Beecher's father wrote in 1835, the "religious and political destiny" of America decided.[2] The satanic principle of absolutism, embodied in part in a proslavery society and in part in the Roman Catholicism which intended a total attack on American institutions—religious, political, educational, and social—was to be defeated in the West, once and for all, by the Protestant principle of freedom.

Victory would mean reconstruction, and as a social architect Beecher had in mind a master plan for the recon-

1. Henry D. Thoreau, "Walking," in *The Works of Thoreau*, edited by Henry Seidel Canby (Boston: Houghton Mifflin; Cambridge: Riverside Press, 1937), pp. 660, 672; see also Canby's introductory commentary on the lecture as delivered at Worcester. Frederick Jackson Turner, "The Significance of the Frontier in American History," *The Frontier in American History* (New York: Henry Holt and Company, 1935), p. 4. Earnest Elmo Calkins, quoting a "sardonic observer" in *They Broke the Prairie: Being Some Account of the Settlement of the Upper Mississippi Valley by Religious and Educational Pioneers, Told in Terms of One City, Galesburg, and of One College, Knox* (New York: Charles Scribner's Sons, 1937), p. 84; see also Louis B. Wright, *Culture on the Moving Frontier* (New York: Harper and Brothers, 1961), p. 178.

2. EB, *The Question at Issue* (1850), p. 12. LB, *A Plea for the West* (Cincinnati: Truman and Smith; New York: Leavitt, Lord and Company, 1835), p. 11.

structed millennial society. His model was the New England-Congregational past. The West, and after it all of American society, would be a purified and perfected New England. Part of the "work" involved would be that of "preserving uncorrupt" and "perpetuating" "true" systems of theology and "right social organizations"; it would be to a large extent a work of *re*-creation.[3] For that work western colleges were the appropriate means. And for Beecher to forsake temporarily the ministry to become a college president was less a personally motivated act than an act of great religious and social dedication.

The seven Yale theological students who on February 21, 1829, had signed a compact affirming the interrelation of evangelical religion and education in the West felt the same way. They were ready to go to Illinois, they said, to establish there a seminary of learning. A little less than a year later, in January 1830, instruction began at Illinois College in Jacksonville; that summer the Illinois Association (as the "Yale Band" formally called itself) elected Edward Beecher president.[4] In September and October, Beecher with his "habitual cautious deliberation" thought it over, consulted others, including his father, and accepted. He spent the first week in November packing books for the college library (books like Keil's *Opuscula Academica*, Muruscher's *History of Dogmatics*, works in ancient and modern history, and standard editions of Stewart, Reid, Brown, and other philosophers—hardly volumes a man committed to the wild would buy), and on November 5 he left

3. EB, *The Question at Issue*, p. 3.
4. Record of [the] Illinois Association (a manuscript located at the Illinois College Library), p. 32. Charles Henry Rammelkamp, *Illinois College: A Centennial History, 1829–1929* (New Haven: Published for Illinois College by Yale University Press, 1928), pp. 23–24.

the East. On the trip he wrote his formal letter of acceptance:

I deeply feel the importance of the enterprize in which you are engaged. . . . I trust that you are actuated by the same spirit, which animated our ancestors, when in a time of great weakness and peril, once yet strong in God, they laid the foundation of those institutions which have made New England the glory of all lands—and that it is your purpose to carry into full execution all the designs of those holy men whom I am persuaded God raised up that in them and in their seed all the nations of the earth might be blessed—and in executing this design to extend their institutions and their spirit to every part of this nation.[5]

In early December 1830 Beecher arrived in Illinois, in that decade to be the scene not only of the "final war of mind" but also of Lovejoy's martyrdom.

Beecher was elected President of Illinois College partly because of the high regard in which he was held by the members of the Illinois Association. During his year as a tutor at Yale in 1825–26, four of the seven had been juniors, one a senior; six were later students of Nathaniel Taylor, Lyman Beecher's best friend and Edward Beecher's former teacher, at Yale Divinity School.[6] As always, though, the Beecher name and influence helped him. Julian M. Sturtevant, for example, born in 1805 in Warren, Connecticut,

5. CB, "Life," pp. 96–97; EB to "the members of the Illinois Association," New Haven, November 8, 1830, from the copy by M. Grosvenor, Secretary, in the Record of [the] Illinois Association, pp. 33–34.
6. There are relatively full and accurate biographical sketches of both original and later members of the association in George F. Magoun, *Asa Turner, a Home Missionary Patriarch and his Times* (Boston and Chicago: Congregational Sunday-school and Publishing Society, 1889), especially pp. 52–53, 60–63. The occasional discrepancies between Magoun's account and Rammelkamp, *op. cit.*, pp. 17–25 ff., affect not at all the general point that Illinois College was a Yale venture and that it was in part EB's performance

eight miles east of Litchfield, had been held "almost spell-
bound" as a boy by Lyman Beecher's "eloquent" preaching, by "the power of his fervent enthusiasm and the glow
of his magnificent imagination." Asa Turner, with whom
Edward had corresponded about going west, studied with
Lyman Beecher in Boston in the spring of 1830 at the
invitation of Edward's brother George. Jonathan Baldwin
Turner, Asa's younger brother, professor of Rhetoric and
Belles Lettres at the college, described himself as George's
"old and well-tried friend"; he stopped in Cincinnati to
see the family as he came from Yale to Illinois to join the
faculty in 1833. Truman Marcellus Post, professor of Languages, praised Lyman Beecher's "wise treatment" of his
"religious difficulties" as "of great service" to him. William Collins, a former deacon of Lyman Beecher's church
in Litchfield, made the "largest single subscription" to the
school when it was still an idea and served as a trustee.
Nathaniel Coffin, eventually the treasurer of the college,
was related to the Beecher family through marriage.[7]

The name also helped Beecher perform the primary
duty of every western college president. Illinois College

---

at Yale that led to the presidency of the college. The Yale faculty, one may
add, was not so enthusiastic as the students, though Taylor, Professor Gibbs,
and President Jeremiah Day gave the group their "entire and cordial approbation."

7. For Sturtevant, see *Julian M. Sturtevant, An Autobiography*, edited by
J. M. Sturtevant, Jr. (New York: Fleming H. Revell, 1896), pp. 29–30; for
Asa Turner, see Magoun, *op. cit.*, p. 64; for J. B. Turner, see Mary Turner
Carriel, *The Life of Jonathan Baldwin Turner* (privately printed, 1911; reprinted, Urbana: University of Illinois Press, 1961), p. 14; for Post, see
T. A. Post, *Truman Marcellus Post, D.D.: A Biography, Personal and Literary* (Boston and Chicago: Congregational and Sunday-school Publishing
Society, 1891), p. 45; for Collins, see CB, "Life," p. 100, and Rammelkamp,
op. cit., pp. 15, 17, 293 (and note the minor discrepancies in the two accounts); for Coffin, see "Life," p. 54, and scattered comments in Rammelkamp.

could become a "permanent blessing," it could "exert a benign influence on the cause of literature, science and religion" in the Mississippi Valley ("destined so materially to affect the destinies of this nation and of the world"), only if well endowed, he wrote in his formal letter of acceptance. In 1831, 1835, 1837, 1840, and 1842, Beecher spent long periods of time away from Jacksonville, often in the East seeking money. Between 1842 and 1844 he spoke in all the New England provinces and in nearly every church in Boston on the "religious philosophy of Western society" and on "how to save the West"—in a special and final appeal made in conjunction with his father and other presidents of western colleges, in order to set up a system by which gifts could be made "more regular, constant, and adequate."[8]

The argument which Beecher, with the help of Theron Baldwin (eventually to become secretary of the Society for the Promotion of Collegiate and Theological Education at the West), presented on those trips, appears in its initial version in the *Appeal* of 1831—which at the same time describes the Illinois of Beecher's experience. Beecher and Baldwin pointed out that the valley as a whole was three or four times as large as the East, with a population of almost 4,000,000, to be doubled (they thought) every eleven years, an increase "without any parallel in the history of the world." At that rate, a united political front in the West would, in thirty years, "sway the councils and destiny" of the country. Illinois itself, geographically central to the valley, was the fourth largest state in the Union, almost equal to all of New England; its population in five years

8. EB to Leonard Bacon, Cambridgeport, December 12, 1842 (Yale). CB, "Life," pp. 146–147.

had doubled to 161,000. But, like the rest of the states, its schools were few and inadequate, and the "prevalence of popular ignorance" was "truly alarming." Only a quarter of the children were attending school, with a large proportion of the remainder illiterate. No member of over half the families in one county surveyed could read. If in a democracy, Beecher and Baldwin argued, the majority of men are "ignorant and corrupt, we are undone." Communities like men have their infancy; when, if not in its earliest stages, is the "most favorable time to lay deep the foundations of society"? Not a moment can be lost. The population and "obstacles increase," and before the present generation passes away, the "fate of our free institutions" will be decided. Illinois College's contribution would be to educate teachers and ministers who would, in turn, teach and minister to the people of the state. With their help the geographical and moral "wilderness will vanish." Out of "chaotic confusion" a "moral edifice will arise, complete and harmonious in all its parts, and resplendent with beauty and glory."[9]

Bringing noble order out of such chaos would require great effort. Eventually Beecher was "worn out, year after year, in journeys and solicitations for money," to the "suspension" of his more "appropriate duties" and the "corrosion" of his mind and health. The role of academic beggar became oppressive, exhausted him, and, as his successor wrote, took him from teaching and from "those literary and theological pursuits to which he was intensely devoted."[10] Once the Society for the Promotion of Col-

9. EB and Theron Baldwin, *An Appeal*, pp. 3–15.

10. EB, *The Question at Issue*, p. 26; Sturtevant, *op. cit.*, p. 238. For an account of EB's solicitations, see Rammelkamp, *op. cit.*, pp. 85–87. The phrase "academic beggar" appears in Wright, *op. cit.*, p. 179.

legiate and Theological Education at the West was established in 1843—even though, as he said in his letter of resignation the next year, his "views of the importance of the western field" were unchanged—he would be finished. He was, as Charles Beecher insisted, "no recluse, no sedentary philosopher," but there was a limit to the "self-abnegation" of a man of his "predominant tastes."[11]

If begging for money and promoting his view of the West did not take absolutely all Beecher's energy and push him completely to his limits, the hardships of frontier life helped make up the difference. The trip west—which he made often—took twenty-four days: seven by stage from New York to Pittsburgh, five by steamboat to Cincinnati, nine to St. Louis, and three to Jacksonville. His first winter there was the winter of the deep snow famous in Illinois tradition. He was caught returning from Vandalia, where he had been attempting to obtain a charter for the college from a "suspicious and unwilling" legislature. The blizzard lasted for two months, Beecher was snowbound for twenty days, and only in some "incredible way" did he make it back to Jacksonville.[12] Jacksonville itself was a crude, booming town. Between 1830 and 1833 its population increased five or seven times (from 446 to between 1800 and 3000). In 1832 William Cullen Bryant described

11. The letter of resignation is quoted by Rammelkamp, *op. cit.*, pp. 92–93; CB, "Life," pp. 146–147. CB contends that EB was largely responsible for the formation of the society. At the May 10, 1843, organizational meeting held at the New York Tract House, EB "pointed out so clearly the need of a new organisation, that it was resolved on the spot to form one." I find no other support for such a judgment.

12. Rammelkamp, *op. cit.*, p. 45. See also Eleanor Atkinson, "The Winter of the Deep Snow," *Transactions of the Illinois State Historical Society*, X (1909), 49–50.

it as "a horridly ugly village, composed of little shops and dwellings stuck close together around a dingy square, in the middle of which stands the ugliest of possible brick courthouses, with a spire and weather-cock on its top."[13] Still, together with Alton and Springfield, Jacksonville was one of the three centers of population and culture in the state, and Beecher's circumstances were nearly the best the state could offer. When not traveling, he taught Mental, Moral, and Social Philosophy. His salary by 1837 was a modest but reasonable $1100. And his living quarters were free, though he had to share them. Julian M. Sturtevant, professor of Mathematics and Natural Philosophy and Beecher's second in command, lived with his family in the south wing of the new college building, and most of the students and faculty lived in the rest of the inadequate structure.

On balance, then, compared to what Beecher might expect in the East, life in Illinois was hard but livable. It was not wild. And the point of enduring was to bring intellect and order to the frontier. In that respect, until he was marked as something of an extremist late in 1837, Beecher was the community leader—in trivial as well as important matters. He brought the first piano to Jacksonville; he and his wife helped organize several benevolent organizations; he received through the Jacksonville post office more (and better) pieces of periodical mail than almost anyone else; he was president of the Illinois State Lyceum and a vice president of the Western Literary Institute and College of

13. Quoted by Frank J. Heinl, "The Bryants at Jacksonville," *Journal of the Illinois State Historical Society*, Jacksonville Centennial Number, XVIII, No. 1 (April 1925), 218. For the population statistics, see Heinl's "Jacksonville and Morgan County, An Historical Review," *ibid.*, p. 5.

Professional Teachers.[14] In 1841, Marietta College in eastern Ohio conferred on him the D.D. degree. And he and the members of his family who visited were the brightest luminaries in what Sturtevant called a "brilliant" social circle. Jonathan Turner, in one of a series of delightful letters to his fiancé, contended that she could not find a village east of the Hudson "possessing so many men of literary eminence and moral worth, nor a community of greater refinement in taste and manners."[15] Turner perhaps had in mind Stephen A. Douglas, Elihu Wolcott (of the family that provided three Connecticut governors and leading citizens of Litchfield), Samuel D. Lockwood (jurist), Joseph Duncan (congressman and governor), and John J. Hardin (lawyer), among others. Perhaps he also had in mind some of Beecher's students (of 62 graduated during Beecher's tenure, 34 became clergymen): William H. Herndon (who often spoke of "the abiding impress of the scholarship and political principles of Beecher, Sturtevant, Turner, Post and Adams," impressions, we are told, that "abided in his mind and were passed on to and helped mold the character of Lincoln"), Newton Bateman, State Super-

14. Georgia L. Osborne, "Pioneer Women of Morgan County," *ibid.*, pp. 249, 253. Randolph C. Randall, *James Hall: Spokesman of the New West* (Columbus: Ohio State University Press, 1964), p. 159. Harveson, *op. cit.*, p. 91. Frank J. Heinl, "Newspapers and Periodicals in the Lincoln-Douglas Country, 1831–32," *Journal of the Illinois State Historical Society*, XXIII, No. 3 (October 1930), 423; according to Heinl, EB received the following periodical items: *Sunday School Journal, Boston Recorder, Theology, Home Missionary and American Pastor's Journal, Spirit of the Pilgrims, Southern Advocate, Home Messenger, Christian Monthly Spectator, Annals of Education, Minutes of the General Assembly.*

15. Sturtevant, *op. cit.*, p. 253. Jonathan Baldwin Turner to Miss Rhodolphia Kibbe, Illinois College, May 14, 1833, quoted by Carriel, *op. cit.*, p. 15. Rammelkamp, *op. cit.*, p. 93, names Catharine, Harriet, Henry Ward, and Charles as visitors; Thomas was a student at Illinois College.

intendent of Public Instruction and President of Knox College, and Richard Yates, Illinois' war governor.[16] Near the head of all such lists of Jacksonville's eminent men, nearly every commentator names Beecher.

His colleagues gave him affection and respect. Truman Post "loved, admired, and revered" him and described him as "a great-brained and great hearted man—of earnest devotion and with the guilelessness of a child." He told Charles Beecher he had been disgusted in 1853 at the "shallow, flippant, and unfair spirit" with which *The Conflict of Ages* was received. Beecher, he said, "inspired that idealisation of the Christian life" which comes to us only in our youth, and in this case "in the morning of a new world" where everyone was "constantly confronted with the gravest and most primordial problems in Social, Educational, and political architecture." Jonathan Turner told his fiancé he had become "strongly attached" to Beecher, "surely a most lovable man." Even before Beecher came west, Sturtevant had "great confidence" in his abilities; he rejoiced that he was "so competent, so strong and so devoted."[17]

Such support from the faculty stood Beecher in good stead in 1837 during the abolitionist crisis at Alton. He had gone there in the first place as the faculty's informal representative to "render what aid he could by counte-

16. For the names and the description of Herndon's comments about the college faculty, see Heinl, "Jacksonville and Morgan County, An Historical Review," *op. cit.*, p. 34 ff. See also David Donald, *Lincoln's Herndon* (New York: Alfred A. Knopf, 1948), p. 10 ff. For the statistics about EB's students, see EB's account in "Life," p. 116.

17. Truman Post to CB, undated, quoted in "Life," pp. 113–114; see also T. A. Post, *op. cit.*, p. 51 ff. Jonathan Baldwin Turner to Miss Rhodolphia Kibbe, Illinois College, May 14, 1833, quoted by Carriel, *op. cit.*, p. 15. Sturtevant, *op. cit.*, p. 177.

nance, address, or counsel." When he returned after Lovejoy's murder, Truman Post published in the *Emancipator*
a long and open letter "To the Citizens of Alton." And
Sturtevant, Beecher's successor, though he had earlier (at
the fall 1837 meeting of the Illinois Synod) counseled the
"more moderate and cautious view of the situation" in
Alton and opposed the re-establishment of Lovejoy's newspaper *The Observer*, now supported Beecher and Lovejoy,
who had been Sturtevant's house guest several times. "It
was our duty," Sturtevant wrote years later. Despite the
"intense hatred" of many men of "wealth and social standing and even of religious reputation," in this the faculty
was "unanimous."[18] But such unanimity on the questions
of slavery and abolition was hard won and did not develop
overnight. For most of the Illinois College faculty, as well
as for those of their type throughout the country, there was
a long period of uncertainty. It was not so much slavery
itself as it was the issues the radical abolitionists raised in
regard to it that nearly destroyed the hopes the faculty and
Beecher had for the good society; but it was just those
hopes that, in the end, made them abolitionists of a sort.

6

Perhaps without realizing it at the time, Beecher had
already been confronted personally with the social issue
that, more than any other, would impede his attempt to

18. The faculty's formal resolution to send EB as their representative is
quoted by T. A. Post, *op. cit.*, p. 95. As originally published, Post's letter
was anonymous; it is reprinted in Joseph C. and Owen Lovejoy, *Memoir of
the Rev. Elijah P. Lovejoy: Who Was Murdered in Defence of the Liberty
of the Press, at Alton, Illinois, Nov. 7, 1837* (New York: John S. Taylor,
1838), pp. 338–362; hereafter *Memoir*. Sturtevant, *op. cit.*, pp. 222–225.

reconstruct the New England past in the western present. On July 4, 1829, over a year before Beecher went west, William Lloyd Garrison had delivered an address on slavery at Park Street Church, by invitation of the Congregational societies of Boston. As minister of the church, Beecher sat on the platform. He heard the man with whom his social imagination would be greatly involved for more than a decade point out the "signs of the times." He heard him offer as "distinct and defensible" the proposition that the free states were "constitutionally involved in the guilt of slavery," that slavery was a "national sin" (a proposition with which Beecher would agree in proposing his 1845 theory of "organic sin"). Beecher heard Garrison, then still irreproachably orthodox and a member of Lyman Beecher's Boston congregation, attack the paradox of missionary and benevolent societies scattering "their contributions like raindrops over a parched heath" but bringing "no sustenance to the perishing slave." It took special courage to argue in this way since the Congregationalists generally, and Park Street Church especially, were primary perpetrators of the paradox.[19] But for the most part Garrison told his audience the things they wanted to hear because he agreed with them. He agreed with the Congregationalists' support of the Colonization Society; he agreed that "the emancipation of all the slaves of this generation is most assuredly out of the question"; he granted that "we have not the right" to use "coercive measures"; he appealed to the orthodox definition of human nature as corrupt in support of his prophecy that a struggle was ahead; and he

---

19. Park Street took pride in being "truly a missionary church." See *The Semi-Centennial Celebration of the Park Street Church and Society* . . . (Boston, 1861), p. 117.

agreed that "Moral influence," vigorously applied, was "irresistible" and that the outcome therefore was not in doubt. He also acknowledged that "immediate and complete emancipation" was "not desirable"; no "rational man," he said, "cherishes so wild a vision."

Two months later Garrison changed his mind. A little more than a year later, on the front pages of the first issue of the *Liberator*, he admitted he had "unreflectingly assented" in the Park Street lecture "to the popular but pernicious doctrine of *gradual* abolition. I seize this opportunity to make a full and unequivocal recantation, and thus publicly to ask pardon of my God, of my country, and of my brethren the poor slaves, for having uttered a sentiment so full of timidity, injustice, and absurdity." Conscience thus "satisfied," Garrison announced in the next paragraph his famous formula for verbal violence: "I *will be* as harsh as truth," he said, "and as uncompromising as justice. On this subject, I do not wish to think, or speak, or write, with moderation. . . . I am in earnest—I will not equivocate—I will not excuse—I will not retreat a single inch—AND I WILL BE HEARD."[20]

If he had earlier agreed vaguely with Garrison's passionate gradualism, and even perhaps with his attack on the Congregationalists' missionary efforts, we may be sure that Beecher at this point was antagonized by Garrison's

20. Much of Garrison's speech is reprinted in Wendell Phillips Garrison and Francis Jackson Garrison, *William Lloyd Garrison, 1805–1879: The Story of His Life Told by His Children* (Boston and New York: Houghton, Mifflin and Company, 1894), I, 127–140; hereafter *Garrison*. For the formula, see I, 225. An interpretation of the speech different from mine appears in John L. Thomas, *The Liberator: William Lloyd Garrison, A Biography* (Boston and Toronto: Little, Brown and Company, 1963), pp. 91–113. See also CB's account of the episode, which I expand, in "Life," pp. 90–92, 119–123.

new position and tone. "These two men like the pith balls on an electrical machine seemed for a time to fly apart," observed Charles Beecher. But for both "the electricity was the same, positive."[21] When, then, Beecher left Park Street Church for the West in November 1830, he was "decidedly hostile to the doctrines of immediate emancipation." Not until late in 1835 did he finally discover, like Garrison, that "the doctrine of gradual emancipation was fallacious, and that of immediate emancipation was philosophical and safe." In the interval, he had not "participated at all in the public discussion which was so deeply exciting the nation, but had been merely an attentive and thoughtful spectator." He had been, he said in the shorthand code that to his readers meant he disapproved of Garrison, "dissatisfied with the spirit of much which had been written on the subject; and with the disposition so common, of pushing true principles to an extreme."

According to the *Narrative*, Beecher changed his mind in 1835 only after "a careful examination of the history of experiments" in abolition.[22] Among many public conflicts between abolitionists and the American community since 1830, he may have had in mind such "experiments" as the beginnings of abolition in the British West Indies in 1833, the surge of respectable mobs against abolitionists from 1833 on, or the gag rule in Congress. No doubt he was also thinking of the Lane Seminary debates, if only because the Beecher family was deeply involved in them.

The story of the debates, often told, is primarily the story of Theodore Dwight Weld and the New York abolitionists, led by Arthur Tappan. In February 1834, over

21. CB, "Life," p. 120.
22. EB, *Narrative*, pp. 21–22.

the objection of most of the seminary faculty, Weld staged an eighteen-day student debate on slavery. An overwhelming number of the students were converted to the doctrine of immediate abolition and began to befriend Cincinnati's Negro population. As would be the case in Alton more than three years later, the predominantly southern (or, at least, anti-abolitionist) townspeople protested. The executive committee of the seminary's Board of Trustees then decided that summer to prohibit further discussion of slavery in the school. Weld and most of the student body quit the seminary in protest and eventually moved to Oberlin College to finish their education. Their debates and their action, widely publicized, have provided an event on which some twentieth-century historians rest, in part, Weld's considerable reputation as an abolitionist leader.[23]

For those same historians, the villain of the affair was Lyman Beecher, who, like his son, had become a western college president in the early thirties. The charge against him is that, as president of the seminary, he permitted the trustees to do the "distasteful job" of repressing Weld, a deed he wanted done but had promised his benefactor Arthur Tappan he would not do; then he attempted to "dodge the responsibility for it."[24] The charge may be true, but it is not self-evident that his actions and motives were completely dishonorable and devious. Beecher's father was a church politician, not an abolitionist of the Garri-

23. For the best recent account, see Benjamin P. Thomas, *Theodore Weld: Crusader for Freedom* (New Brunswick, N. J.: Rutgers University Press, 1950).

24. Gilbert Hobbs Barnes, *The Antislavery Impulse, 1830–1844* (Gloucester, Mass.: Peter Smith, 1957; originally published by the American Historical Association, 1933), p. 230 (note 17).

sonian sort: he thought the abolitionists' "means" not only ineffective but ruinous. If he did contribute to repressing Weld, it was out of concern for the reputation of the semi-nary—a pardonable concern—and not because he was un-interested in the slavery issue. Lane, he pointed out, had been the first seminary to admit a Negro student. And as he wrote to Tappan on April 23, 1833, before the debates, he saw no inconsistency in favoring at the same time, as he did, both abolition and colonization. He would, he said,

make use of the current of human fears, and passions, and in-terests, when they may be made to set in our favor, instead of attempting to row up stream against them.

I would press the consciences, so far as they have any, of the Southerners, and shake their fears, and press their interests, as the Abolitionists are doing; but then, that the pressure might avail, I would not hermetically seal their hearts by cutting off the facilities of emancipation, and tempt them to delay it till insurrection might do the work, but offer them an easy, prac-ticable way of doing their duty, as the Colonizationists are doing; and I can perceive no need that the two classes of philan-thropists should fall out by the way.[25]

Lyman Beecher's supposition that the "two classes of philanthropists" need not fall out took institutional form on Christmas Day 1834, just after the seminary had lost nearly all its students. Partly at his urging, Boston's Con-gregational ministers attempted to launch a new benevo-lent society, The American Union for the Relief and Improvement of the Colored Race. According to its pros-pectus, written by Leonard Bacon (a prominent coloni-zationist as well as clergyman), the new organization

25. *Autobiography*, II, 323.

was conceived in order to oppose neither the Colonization Society nor the immediatists; its purpose was to provide organization for those who, while opposed to slavery, felt comfortable with neither.[26] Garrison thought that the Union merely repeated in watered-down and ineffective language the aims of the immediatists and that its main purpose was "TO PUT DOWN GARRISON AND HIS FRIENDS." Whatever its underground intentions, the new society was a failure almost from its first convention in January 1835. Its existence, however, serves to lay bare the Congregationalists' dissent from the man they had six years earlier asked to speak to them on the Fourth of July. To borrow a phrase from the Garrison children, it was the symbolic and formal beginning of the anti-Garrison movement within "the pietistic, theological and sectarian elements of society."[27]

The American Union Lyman Beecher supported defines Edward Beecher's attitude toward slavery and abolition before 1835. "At that time most of the Dr's children including Edward, agreed with him."[28] At the September 1835 gathering of the family in Cincinnati, father and children no doubt talked over the American Union and Weld's exodus. Perhaps, as he had written in a letter of July 15, 1835, the father once again warned not only the eldest son, William, but some of the other children—Henry Ward, Harriet, Charles, Catharine, Edward, all important figures later in the movement—to avoid commitment. "I am still of the opinion," he wrote,

26. Theodore Davenport Bacon, *Leonard Bacon, A Statesman in the Church* (New Haven: Yale University Press; London: Oxford University Press, 1931), pp. 235–236.

27. *Garrison*, I, 474–475.

28. CB, "Life," p. 120.

that you ought not, and need not, and will not commit yourself
as a partisan on either side. The cause is moving on in Providence, and by the American Union, and by colonization, and
by Lundy in Texas . . . and I hope and believe that the Abolitionists as a body will become more calm and less denunciatory,
with the exception of the few he-goat men, who think they do
God service by butting every thing in the line of their march
which does not fall in or get out of the way. They are the offspring of the Oneida denunciatory revivals, and are made up of
vinegar, aqua fortis, and oil of vitriol, with brimstone, salt-
petre, and charcoal, to explode and scatter the corrosive matter.[29]

But the father was unsuccessful in persuading William, as
finally he was unsuccessful in persuading most of his children. In the late thirties the Beechers became, if not Garrisonian immediatists, partisans—Edward Beecher first and
most dramatically.

7

Commencement at Illinois College, where Lovejoy and
Beecher met in September 1834, provided a time and place
for the orthodox clergy to gather. We may suppose that
most of them, like Lovejoy, felt "real difficulty in ascertain-
ing" their duty on the slavery issue. Most of them probably
agreed that "Slavery is a curse, politically and morally,"
that they might become abolitionists "at some future day,"
that the "necessity" of "forsaking the Colonization enterprise" might eventually confront them. Some there may
already have favored "gradual emancipation immediately
begun," but not many, and those few not passionately. In

29. LB to William Beecher, July 15, 1835, *Autobiography*, II, 345.

the fall of 1834, most American clergymen, including the Jacksonville ministers, rejected outright Garrison's call for immediate abolition. The situation was much the same at the 1835 commencement. "We only propose," Lovejoy had written editorially that year, "that measures shall now be taken for the ABOLITION OF SLAVERY, at such distant period of time as may be thought expedient, and eventually for ridding the country altogether of a coloured population." "Gradual emancipation is the remedy we propose."[30]

But during the summer just before the September 1835 commencement, Beecher's highly praised and widely distributed *Six Sermons* appeared. Subtitled "The Nature, Importance, and Means of Eminent Holiness throughout the Church," the sermons revealed a state of mind congenial to immediate abolition, though they never explicitly mentioned the issue. As one historian has observed of evangelical orthodoxy in general at this time, Beecher was cultivating "a kind of plain man's transcendentalism." He was gearing an ancient creed "to the drive shaft of social reform."[31] There are, Beecher wrote, "certain great crises, or turning points" in history, and American society is now at such a point. The Protestant church is "aroused, excited, and agitated." The "conversion of the world to God is no longer regarded as merely the glorious but distant vision of inspired prophets"; it is a "vivid reality." If we are to "abolish all corruptions in religion, and all abuses in the social system"; if we are to expose "all institutions, usages, and principles, civil or religious," to a "rigid and fiery

---

30. *Memoir*, pp. 118–121; 126, 128 (from editorials of June 1834; April 16, 30, 1835).

31. Timothy L. Smith, *Revivalism and Social Reform in Mid–Nineteenth-Century America* (New York and Nashville: Abingdon Press, 1957), p. 8.

scrutiny"; if we are to "reorganize human society"; if we are to "take it down and erect it anew," we must act now. We must—and this was the point, so he wrote it in capital letters—engage in "THE IMMEDIATE PRODUCTION OF AN ELEVATED STANDARD OF PERSONAL HOLINESS THROUGHOUT THE UNIVERSAL CHURCH." No other benevolent enterprise could "deserve to become the all-absorbing object of the soul."

The cultivation of eminent holiness, of "perfect purity," of "entire perfection" would seem, in practice if not in theory, to exclude antislavery action in favor of an immediate and "mighty revolution in the church." Beecher counseled immediacy, but only in religious matters—or at least there first. There is a *"state of mind,"* he admonished his fellow reformers, *"which if first produced will secure all else."* Christians should avoid, therefore, the "unchristian feeling exhibited in some of the great movements and discussions of the day," which is "alike humiliating and surprising."[32] No doubt Beecher had Garrison in mind as he wrote that last passage. As the thrust of the *Six Sermons* might lead one to predict, however, Beecher soon changed his mind about the application of his doctrine.

At about the same time, in fact, many ministers were to change their minds. In October, November, and December 1835 there occurred a pervasive change of sentiment among the orthodox clergy, a large scale clerical rejection of colonization and gradualism, in favor, if not of Garrison, then of the basic principles Garrison stood for. During that fall, riots, mass meetings, and suppression of the discussion of slavery had irritated the open sores of the country. What Garrison described as "The Reign of Terror"—the beginnings of the gag rule in Congress, the suppression of aboli-

32. EB, *Six Sermons*, especially pp. 193–203.

tionist documents in the mails, major riots in Washington, Philadelphia, Baltimore—had culminated in the famous mob of "respectables" who on October 21 dragged Garrison through the streets of Boston.[33] With good cause, many Americans were beginning to link the antislavery issue to the freedoms: the freedom of speech, assembly, the press. These, more than slavery itself, provided a rallying point for Beecher's clerical colleagues, and it was in such a context that Lovejoy, on October 1, published the statement of principles of the American Antislavery Society and editorially announced his agreement with most of them.

One week later, a group of eminent citizens (among them the men who had put up the capital to establish the *Observer*) asked Lovejoy in an open letter to "pass over in silence every thing connected with the subject of Slavery." They admitted that the right of free speech was guaranteed by the Constitution, but that did not "imply a moral right, on the part of the Abolitionists, to freely discuss the question of Slavery, either orally or through the medium of the press." That would be to allow "the agitation of a question too nearly allied to the vital interests of the slave-holding states," to allow, "ultimately, a disseverment of our prosperous Union." Lovejoy did not respond immediately, but when he did he was decisive. "I cannot," he said on November 5, "surrender my principles, though the whole world besides should vote them down—I can make no compromise between truth and error, even though my life be the alternative."

By early November 1835 then, the issue was joined, sides taken, principles clarified. Lovejoy was not thinking of Beecher when he wrote, "the heaviest blows have been

33. *Garrison*, I, 488; II, 1–72.

those which I have received from the hands of some of my brethren," but for a while he may have wondered where Beecher stood.[34] He wrote Beecher, probably toward the end of November, presumably inquiring what he ought to do when the owners of the *Observer*, as a consequence of his November 5 editorial, requested him to resign. Beecher's reply was held up by the press of work until December 20, but it was encouraging: "I approve," he wrote, "the principles which you have adopted & consider them capable of an unanswerable defense. I approve also of the manner in which you have spoken as truly in accordance with the meekness & yet courage demanded in a soldier of the cross, in fighting the battles of the Lord." Only a short time ago, Beecher reminded Lovejoy, he had "felt unable to judge decidedly" whether the editor had done "well to speak" when he did. But now he had decided; he supported Lovejoy totally in his "recent conflicts." When he saw

the demands of the friends of the systems of slavery, & their determination to muzzle not only abolitionists, but all who are determined gradually & wisely to remove the system, whatever be their ground, I think the time for silence has gone by. . . . even the religious party at the South are more erroneous than I had supposed. The paper laid in before the Synod of Virginia is as bad as the St. Louis Resolutions. Though it was indeed ably opposed—yet the fact that so many respectable men advocated it is alarming. If religious men do not understand this subject any better than that, it is time that some one teach them. . . . I say go on. you will find as you have already that the stand you have taken will increase the number of your friends.

34. *Memoir*, pp. 137–139, 142, 150. See also Merton L. Dillon, *Elijah P. Lovejoy, Abolitionist Editor* (Urbana: University of Illinois Press, 1961), pp. 62–63.

One of the friends, of course, would be Beecher, who, though he found himself temporarily "so confined to the college" that he could "do little" except through "opinions and influence," offered them both; "whatever I can do by these," he wrote, "is yours."[35]

Beecher was Lovejoy's "closest associate" in 1836 and 1837. They consulted each other on strategy and principle often, and if Lovejoy was the protagonist of the Alton drama, Beecher became not only his interpreter but his chief supporting player. As Beecher became an abolitionist, Lovejoy's theological position became more radical.[36] Both attended the 1837 meeting of the Presbyterian General Assembly in Philadelphia, where the lines between theology and politics became blurred and where the church split. It was at the 1837 meeting that the old-school wing, in the majority, "exscinded" four Northern, intensely abolitionist synods, ostensibly for their new-school theological tendencies, but in fact also upon political grounds. "It may not be clear at first to the ordinary mind," wrote Charles Beecher,

why slavery and theology should go hand in hand, in national affairs. But if we reflect that theology is but another name for the politics of the universe, or the kingdom of God, the problem becomes simple. Two systems or schools of theology were contending, called at that time Old school and New School.

35. EB to Lovejoy, Illinois College, December 20, 1835 (Wickett-Wiswall Collection of Lovejoy Papers, in the Southwest Collection of Texas Technological College, Lubbock).

36. John Gill, *Tide Without Turning: Elijah P. Lovejoy and Freedom of the Press* (Boston: Starr King Press, n.d. [about 1960], distributed by Beacon Press), pp. 93–94. Gill appropriately supposes that EB and Lovejoy "must have talked about religion, the 'old school' and 'new school' theologies, and the way conservatives in the church used the issue of orthodoxy to prevent discussion of slavery."

The former enthrones absolutism, the latter constitutionalism. According to the one things are right because God wills them, according to others God wills them because they are right. Old School theology enthrones a great slave holder over the universe; New School [theology] enthrones a great Emancipator.[37]

Lovejoy and Edward Beecher realized what was happening in Philadelphia, if only because they had gone through a series of related crises in southern Illinois. Another was imminent. Returning from the Philadelphia convention in July 1837, Lovejoy had five months to live; the scene of his martyrdom would be Alton. For those months we have a weekly—at times day-by-day and hour-by-hour—account of his and Beecher's response to events. Much of the account appears in Beecher's *Narrative*.

To prepare for Beecher's peculiar interpretation of the Alton affair, however, we need only observe that in July, partly because of "the impression produced on many by the violent proceedings of the General Assembly" and the belief that "unjust measures had been introduced into the church to defend slavery," Lovejoy's friends urged him to issue a call for a convention to form a state antislavery society.[38] Lovejoy wrote to Beecher, as he must have written to others, asking for support. Beecher, knowing that he would be understood as speaking for Illinois College, knowing that its continued existence depended on southern toleration, if not enthusiasm (as Truman Post put it, there was in Jacksonville "a collision between two antagonistic civilizations, one born directly or indirectly of slavery and

37. CB, "Life," pp. 121–122.
38. The account that follows draws primarily from the *Narrative*, pp. 20–28, 36–40, 100–106, and in supplementary fashion from Dillon and Gill, *op. cit.*

the other of freedom; between different views of humanity as well as Christianity—views as to the rights and relations of men in states, societies, churches, and in the kingdom of God")[39]: knowing this, Beecher at first replied that he "decidedly preferred to stand" on his "own ground—to join no society—and to speak as an individual," if he spoke at all. He could, he added—and the addition made all the difference later—join a society only if it "would assume such grounds" as he could "approve."

The destruction of the second *Observer* press by a mob in August (the first had been dumped in the river when Lovejoy first moved from St. Louis to Alton in 1836) changed the complexion of things for Beecher. The "friends of religion and good order" and the churches in Alton seemed to be "paralyzed." Many of the "wise and good"— that great uncommitted group of respectable citizens who, in Beecher's analysis of the social structure of Alton, controlled the city and must therefore be guided toward, if not abolition, at least support of the constitutional right of free discussion—evidently felt that "though the prostration of the law was a great evil, the publication of the Observer was one still greater." As in 1835, the issue became again a matter of basic principle, of civil rights; and for Beecher it remained primarily that. But Beecher, as he admits in the *Narrative*, was an incredibly naïve abolitionist. At the September 1837 commencement exercises at Jacksonville, he proposed to change "the character of the convention" so that not only abolitionists but "friends of free discussion" could also in conscience attend. He had in mind the "wise and good," but he was innocent enough to

39. Quoted by T. A. Post, *op. cit.*, p. 91.

suppose that "no violence need be apprehended"—that the same men who would destroy the *Observer* press would not "dare to claim a seat." He had, he said, "no doubt the leading citizens of Alton would countenance the meeting by their presence," and he left for the convention with "cheering expectations."

From this point the story is familiar. Beecher was soon disenchanted. The local colonization society, led by Usher Linder and the Reverend Joel Parker, attacked the convention before it assembled; when it did assemble, they packed it with anti-abolitionists; the delegates finally had to regroup at private homes.

Beecher's "preference still" was to speak as an individual, to "be held responsible for no sentiments, or measures" but his own. On the other hand, he felt obliged to join the "unpopular and despised minority" because "a great moral question" was involved—and because, given the attitude of the colonizationists, he had no choice but to surrender his father's and his own "fondly cherished hopes of Christian union." He would join the reassembled convention, then, but only if: first, they for the present "stand on entirely independent ground" (that is, they remain unaffiliated with the national society, controlled, he thought, by Garrison, and merely "entertain the most fraternal feelings" toward it); and second, they as a society accept his views on slavery. Since the group could hardly overrule the most prominent and, as it turned out, most influential man there, they solved the tactical problem Beecher's attitude forced upon them very simply. They allowed him to draw up the Declaration of Sentiments, made him one of a committee of three to prepare an address to the citizens of the state, and voted him a committee of one to propose topics for discussion at

the next annual meeting.[40] The convention's public tone
and most of the printed material emanating from it were
consequently Beecher's.

His reticent radicalism, the paradoxically conservative
temper of his mind, comes out in his *Narrative* summary
of the discussion of his draft of the Declaration of Sentiments. It was, he said, "the object of the brethren not to
admit of any exception" to the doctrine that slavery is in
all cases sinful; they would allow nothing "which should
weaken the power of truth on the conscience." Beecher's
object was "so to guard our language as not to bring a false
accusation against any man, and not to blame any one for
not doing impossibilities." The upshot of the disagreement
was that everyone finally consented to make an exception
when a slaveholder had done all in his power to free his
slaves, but could not. In that case, the community was guilty. (Eight years later Beecher would develop the same compromise into a theory of "organic sin.")

After the convention adjourned, Beecher remained
with Lovejoy. There was still unfinished business: the *Observer* press, destroyed for the third time just before the
convention, had to be replaced; the neutral respectables of
the community had yet to be won over. But in both instances Beecher was unsuccessful. The neutrals listened to
him but really neither understood nor accepted his arguments. When the fourth and final *Observer* press arrived
the next Monday, in the dead of night, everything nevertheless seemed safe; "all felt that the crisis was over." The
next morning, just before he left for Jacksonville—as he

40. *Proceedings of the Ill. Anti-Slavery Convention, Held at Upper Alton
on the Twenty-sixth, Twenty-seventh, and Twenty-eighth October, 1837*
(Alton, 1838), pp. 12–13. Printed as an Alton *Observer* extra.

describes it in what is rhetorically perhaps the most magnificent passage in the *Narrative*—Beecher felt assured that a "bloodless battle had been gained for God and for the truth; and that Alton was redeemed from eternal shame." He was exultant. But that night the "infuriate mob" murdered Lovejoy; the "bloody tragedy" Beecher had alternately feared and gainsaid "was consummated."

8

In Jacksonville the consequences of Lovejoy's death and Beecher's involvement were ugly. And the weight of obloquy fell most heavily on Beecher, despite faculty support. He was, he said in the *Narrative*, "publicly, severely, and pointedly attacked; accused of jesuitism, fanatical zeal, dereliction of official duty, and treasonable designs." Perhaps no one, he felt, had "been more severely censured by enemies, or regarded in greater error by some sincere and valued friends." Many suggested he resign. One Wisconsin newspaper reported with *"unalloyed pleasure"* that the trustees had dismissed him. He did not resign; he was not dismissed; and, despite the decline of the college (which never became, as many thought it might, the major school in the state) and the antagonism of the Jacksonville community, his antislavery activity did not end with the Lovejoy incident—it really only began there, as if Beecher, like the rest of the country, could be awakened only by violence. Respected even by Garrison, who thought of him as the staunch friend of Lovejoy, Beecher became something of a national figure in the abolition movement. In 1838, although he declined with regret an invitation to attend the annual meeting of the American Antislavery Society, he promised nevertheless to do all in his "power to promote its interest, and to promote the holy cause in which it is engaged." As if to make good on his promise, he accepted election as one of the managers of the society in Illinois in May of that year.[41] Even before that, he had written to the executive committee of the society informing them of his "design to publish an account of the events at Alton" and suggesting that the commemorative service they planned for Lovejoy "be fixed late enough to allow the account to be sent through the land."[42]

The *Narrative* was drafted at white heat, shipped to New York perhaps as early as January 1838, and stolen from the mail. (The "Advertisement" to the book merely says it "must either have been lost or otherwise disposed of.") Beecher copied it again and this time sent it to Alton to be printed. Meanwhile, according to Charles Beecher, so much time had elapsed and events were "rushing so fast" that, when finally published, the book "excited little atten-

41. For the quotations from the *Narrative*, see pp. 7, 17. For the repercussions and their effect on Illinois College, see Rammelkamp, *op. cit.*, pp. 103, 111–112, and Sturtevant, *op. cit.*, p. 225. For the report of dismissal, see the *National Enquirer*, III, No. 18 (January 11, 1838), 71. For Garrison's judgment, see *Garrison*, III, 14. For EB's promise and election to the American Antislavery Society, see EB to the society, Illinois College, March 11, 1838, in *The Pennsylvania Freeman*, IV, No. 11 (May 24, 1838).

42. As reported by EB to Owen Lovejoy, Illinois College, December 25, 1837 (University of Michigan). At the same time EB was writing the *Narrative*, Owen Lovejoy was trying to decide whether to write the *Memoir*. He evidently asked EB's opinion of the project. EB replied in this letter that a memoir "ought to be prepared—but not exactly in the ordinary way." Lovejoy, he said, "will always be known by the events of his life whilst editor of the Observer & especially by its close." The "main body of the work," therefore, ought to provide a narrative of those events, and to that can be added a biographical sketch and extracts from his writings. EB would be glad to assist, he said, but he could not write it. The plan of the *Memoir* seems very similar to EB's projection.

tion."[43] The information in most of Part I of the *Narrative* (the first 108 pages) had become common knowledge. Part II (the last 51 pages) and the introductory chapters, however, were peculiarly Beecher's, less a narrative than an interpretation, a theological analysis of a political tragedy. As the publisher said in his "Advertisement," no doubt thinking of the second part, the "general views taken of the antislavery discussion, and its general bearings on the moral interests of the world, are striking, and in many respects original." The book would last "independently of the interest growing out of merely transient or local excitements."[44]

But the full meaning of Beecher's theological explanation of the Alton affair was not clear in 1838, perhaps not

43. For help tracing the writing of the *Narrative*, the best one may do is look to the letter to Owen Lovejoy, in which EB observes that his book is "not yet completed" and therefore he cannot comply with Owen Lovejoy's request to send part of it to Cincinnati. "I have been delayed in part by pressure of business, in part by the failure to obtain needful documents from Alton, & in part I have chosen to wait until I heard the response of public opinion on existing statements." He concludes that he is "going on as fast" as he can. CB, "Life," p. 131, says that after the original draft was stolen, a "duplicate copy was forwarded and printed," but he offers neither dates nor details. According to the publisher's "Advertisement," three months had elapsed between the time EB sent the original to New York (surely no earlier than January) and the time the copy was printed and published at Alton.

44. The publisher was probably paraphrasing EB's own hopes for the book. In his letter to Owen Lovejoy, EB described his "design" as "to argue not merely the question of right, but of the prudence & wisdom of the steps taken, & to endeavour to put your brother's reputation on that ground also in a true light, & to show the nation & the civilized world where the responsibility truly lies. It is not a mere narration, but also an analysis of principle, & an argument on facts." He had waited so long to write, he continued, in part so that he could offer a "mature judgment on all the facts of the case in an hour of cool reflection." He wanted to make such "inferences" as would "render the work most permanently useful."

even to Beecher himself. Its "striking" and "original" features, its concern for what Charles Beecher called the "politics of the universe," were more implicit than explicit. Beecher did not explain what he really meant in the early chapters and in Part II of the *Narrative* until 1845, when he developed and named his theory of "organic sin."

His diaries between 1838 and 1845 are "very copious, and instructive" on the subject of slavery.[45] He began asking himself, somewhat like Garrison, whether the Constitution was "pleasing in the sight of God." It was, he knew, at "the foundation of National Life and feeling." Yet he also knew that constitutions and "agreements made in contravention of the law of God" are "criminal," for "God's law is the fundamental law of the Universe." "All laws adverse to" God's law are, "on the Scale of the Universe," unacceptable, he thought. Is not the nation then bound to "repeal" its evil agreement with the South—indeed, to repeal the Constitution itself? He felt himself implicated in a kind of sin: "to treat slaveholding as no crime, and to give the same honor to those who are guilty of it as to others, is to sustain it." Beecher was aware that the "work" of disengagement from national sin would involve "as great a struggle as can in the nature of things exist, and terrible malignity and reaction, for which those who occasion it are not to be blamed, but the sinners." But the "nature of God, and duty to him render it unavoidable." "Associate," then, "to diffuse knowledge" and for "mutual strength," he wrote to himself as if it spilled out. "Discuss. . . . Act—Act—Act."[46]

The imperatives of the diaries were almost at once translated into action. When the Illinois Antislavery Society

45. CB, "Life," p. 136.
46. EB, diaries as quoted in "Life," pp. 133–136.

was being formed, for instance, Beecher had intransigently required that it "stand on entirely independent ground," that it remain, as it did, unaffiliated with the American Antislavery Society. Then, in 1838, Beecher became one of the national society's agents in Illinois. The explanation of what appears to be a contradictory act lies in a letter to James Birney, secretary of the national society, written about the time of the Alton affair. Beecher wrote, he said, to "prevent all misunderstanding" and to state his reasons for not "becoming auxiliary to them." He told Birney that he could not abide the national society's *Declaration of Sentiments*, written, as everyone knew, by Garrison. Birney replied that the *Declaration* was "to be regarded as containing the sentiments of those who organized the American Antislavery Society, *and of them only.*" Only the society's constitution need be "assented to by auxiliaries and members," he continued, trusting that Beecher would "find in this nothing" he would "consider unsound." Anyone who favored the abolition of slavery "by peaceful means" was welcome. As a result of Birney's assurances, Beecher felt he could in conscience allow the Illinois society to become "auxiliary" to the national organization, and even become himself an agent of the national society. In Birney he had found, he thought, the "true spirit of liberality and enlightened toleration."[47]

He did not find the same quality in Garrison. Though in retrospect it is obvious that Garrison's existence as a foil and conscience was crucial to Beecher's development as an abolitionist, Beecher did not think him an "enlightened" man. Moreover, Garrison was wrong. His central assertion

47. Unless otherwise indicated, quotations in the remainder of Section 8 and in Section 9 are from EB's essays on "organic sin" in the Boston *Recorder* (1845). EB's description of his letters to Birney appeared on Nov. 27, 1845.

in the national society's *Declaration* that God had defined
slaveholders as "manstealers" in the New Testament was,
Beecher observed, historically false. On the contrary,
Beecher said (and this became vital to the theory he was
developing), slaveholders were in fact members of early
Christian congregations. Clearly the "time for an open assault on the system had not come" in the early centuries
after Christ. That was a time of "deep moral ignorance."
Slaveholders had not developed "such a knowledge and
sense of its [slavery's] guilt that they did violence to their
own consciences." God then—though no longer—"winked"
at slavery and "endured it." Our generation, Beecher continued, lives in the pre-millennial period, the time to which
God has assigned the revolutionary reorganization of society. The universal principles of "honor and right" that
have grown up in our time commit us to the abolition of
slavery as part of God's plan for the kingdom of heaven
on earth. But we should not therefore distort history. It
was "plain" to Beecher that all Christians who accepted
Garrison's position were "defeated . . . the moment the
historical fact is proved against them . . . and are logically
compelled either to renounce the antislavery cause, or to
take the ground of infidelity in its defense," as Garrison
had. No man, Beecher said, "can reason against the truth
with impunity."

Beecher took issue with Garrison on a second and, for
him, even more crucial point. All slaveholding is indeed,
Beecher agreed, sinful. But the guilt, the sin, is not to be
placed squarely and entirely on the back of the individual
slaveholder, where Garrison placed it. There are "grades of
guilt." And as Beecher described *his* Declaration of Sentiments, drafted in 1837 for the Illinois society and pub-

lished in the *Emancipator*, he had been very aware of these distinctions then:

In it I first unfolded the true laws of social organization, then analyzed the false and sinful relation between master and slave created by slave law, then declared the duty of the body politic to abolish the sinful system without delay—then unfolded the duty of the individual master, if the system was not abolished, to take his slaves out from under it by dissolving the legal relation between him and them if he could,—for it is by this legal relation that the slaves are kept under the system of slave law and exposed to all the wrongs which it authorizes. But if the community will not dissolve the legal relation, the fault is theirs, not his.

As Charles Beecher wrote and then crossed out in his manuscript, as if he feared misunderstanding, Edward Beecher was "as radical as Garrison";[48] but his radicalism had different sources and took different (conservative) forms. Garrison was magnificently intense, hortatory, eloquent, uncommitted to any existing institution, but he had to seek his justification for action in moral absolutes; ultimately he took what Beecher called the radical "ground of infidelity." Beecher, calm, urgent, and primarily analytical, was committed to the central traditions of Christianity; his justification for action was his orthodox sense (recently revised by his revelations) of God's relation to man and state. He became a theoretician of "conservative abolitionism"—a term that has never since been precisely defined.

9

The definition of conservative abolitionism contains both political and socio-religious differentiae.

48. CB, "Life," p. 136.

Politically, it may symbolically but very briefly focus upon two new organizations of 1840—the Liberty Party and the American and Foreign Antislavery Society—in both of which conservative abolitionists participated, at all levels. There is no evidence, for example, that Beecher participated formally in the formation of the Liberty Party, which held its first convention in April; but there can hardly be any doubt that he worked and voted for its presidential candidate Birney, whom he admired. He felt the man behind the convention, Gerritt Smith, his "highly respected friend," and when he returned to Boston permanently in the early 1840s, he talked over antislavery matters with Smith a number of times. Beecher did, however, formally participate when, in May 1840, only a month after the Liberty Party convention, he joined Birney and Smith—as well as other prominent abolitionists: the Tappans, Whittier, Jay, Leavitt—in breaking away from the American Antislavery Society in reaction against Garrison. He became a member of the executive committee of the new American and Foreign Antislavery Society and, like other conservative abolitionists, gave the new organization his active support.

Socio-religiously, the definition, again symbolically, but now in more detail, may focus upon the American Board of Commissioners for Foreign Missions, particularly its 1845 meeting. As early as the mid-thirties Garrison had attacked the American Board, which, he said, accepted money from southern slaveholders and whose agents to the Indian missions not only allowed the Indians to own slaves but also owned slaves themselves. He and the other radical abolitionists took the board as a symbol of everything they protested in the attitude of the American churches toward slavery. Parker Pillsbury, for instance, thought it more significant in this respect than "any other ecclesiastical association in this or any country." Oliver Johnson observed that the board in the late thirties and early forties was rising to great "prominence and power, and drawing to itself the sympathy and almost idolatrous reverence of the churches, especially in New England." And it was, he thought, "deadly hostile to the antislavery movement from the start."[49]

At its September 10, 1844, meeting in Worcester, Massachusetts, the board finally began to take official account of its critics. Its corporate members (some of them the most eminent ministers in the country) and some of its approximately 6,000 honorary members (of whom Beecher was one) listened that year to three "memorials" asking that the board take a stand on slavery. It was reluctant. It put off the matter till the next year so that, as its members said, information might be gathered. When, then, the board convened in 1845 in Brooklyn, everyone came prepared. Official reports of the meeting tell us little more than that a "deeply interesting discussion ensued" when the committee on the antislavery memorials offered the information it had gathered. Outside accounts of the debates, fortunately, are fuller. The discussion, according to

49. *Garrison*, II, 141, and III, 30. Parker Pillsbury, *The Church as it Is; or, The Forlorn Hope of Slavery* (2nd ed., rev. [a reprint of the "Second edition—revised and improved," Boston: B. Marsh, 1847]; Concord, N. H.: Republican Press Association, 1885), p. 28; Oliver Johnson, *William Lloyd Garrison and His Times: or, Sketches of the Anti-Slavery Movement in America, and of the Man Who Was its Founder and Moral Leader* (Boston: B. B. Russell and Company; San Francisco: A. L. Bancroft and Company; Portland: John Russell; Philadelphia: Quaker City Publishing House; New York: Charles Drew; Chicago: Andrews and Dorman; Indianapolis: Fred L. Horton and Company, 1879), p. 74.

Leonard Bacon, occupied the greater part of the entire session, at least two days. It was *"free;* there was no restraint put upon the utterance of any opinion, however extreme." There were more than six hundred members present. Amos A. Phelps, the American Antislavery Society's secretary, argued the radicals' case; on the other side, Beecher and his brother-in-law Calvin Stowe gave speeches "characterized by eminent learning and great force of argument."[50] The question formally before the board was a very specific one: should the board require the excommunication of church members under its jurisdiction (particularly in the Cherokee and Choctaw missions) for being slaveholders? But during the debate, more fundamental issues were raised, especially the issue Beecher had focused on in rejecting Garrison: Is slaveholding absolutely, at all times and without exception a sin, in the same category as, say, murder? Is the divine law to be applied to all slaveholders in the same absolute fashion as it is to be applied to "man-stealers," "whoremongers," and "liars"? After several amendments had been proposed and voted down, the board unanimously accepted the report of the committee. The report said, in effect, "no" to both questions. It is a fascinating document, revealing not only the rough consensus of a major segment of the American clergy in 1845 but also the rationale behind their position.

According to the report, there was no need in the first

---

50. *Report of the American Board of Commissioners for Foreign Missions. Presented at the Thirty-Sixth Annual Meeting, Held in Brooklyn, New York, Sept. 9–12, 1845* (Boston: Printed for the Board by T. R. Marvin, 1845), p. 62. Leonard Bacon, "The Collision Between the Anti-Slavery Society and the American Board," reprinted from the *New York Evangelist* (1846) in Bacon, *Slavery Discussed in Occasional Essays, from 1833 to 1846* (New York: Baker and Scribner, 1846), pp. 135–136.

place to discuss slavery generally. On its "wickedness" as a system and on its "disastrous moral and social influences" there was "little difference of opinion." Everyone, the report continued, agreed that the "unnatural state of society" in which slavery and other evils "originate" is a consequence of "human depravity—of that all-absorbing selfishness—that predominance of the lust of the flesh, the lust of the eye, and the pride of life, which are developed in our fallen nature." The American church may respond to slavery in its foreign missions only by trying to secure "holiness in the hearts of individuals." The situation may be "rectified," the report said, as if echoing Beecher's 1835 *Six Sermons* on Eminent Holiness, only by "diminishing the power of that terrible principle in which this, as well as all other wickedness and moral disorders originate." Is, then, the board, while engaged in its primary task of regenerating the human heart, "to be held responsible" directly for "reorganizations of the social system"? Is it, in "proceeding on these principles," any more "connected with slavery" than with "every other evidence and result of imperfect moral renovation" in its converts and members?[51]

For the leaders of the church, the questions were rhetorical. But the radical abolitionists still refused to see things their way. Beecher found, as he had in Alton, that his speeches on organic sin at the board meeting "excited far more attention" than he "supposed possible." While they were spoken of in "flattering terms" by men he respected, they also made him "the subject of extended cen-

51. *Report of the American Board . . . 1845*, pp. 54–57. The committee's report was also printed separately; see *Report of the Committee on Anti-Slavery Memorials, September, 1845. With a Historical Statement of Previous Proceedings* (Boston: T. R. Marvin, 1845), pp. 4–8.

sure, and violent assault." One "gentleman," as Beecher reports it, wrote a "poetical letter to the Devil, recommending to him to force an alliance" with all doctors of divinity, and "representing the distinction with regard to organic sins" as beyond even Satan's "subtlety." Elihu Burritt thought the theory deserved "to be called the Astral System of Moral Philosophy." The convention of the American Antislavery Society, meeting just after the debate at the American Board convention, gave its "unmitigated censure" of the theory in two long resolutions; the speakers, Beecher said, attempted "to render ridiculous the distinction between organic and individual sins."

Beecher felt he could not allow such distortions of his position to go unanswered. He thought he had been "solicitous to leave no entrenchment behind which slavery could defend itself." But evidently the radical abolitionists thought differently. A. A. Phelps, in the debates at the board meeting, at the convention of the American Antislavery Society immediately after, and later in the Boston *Recorder*, described the theory as "the last entrenchment of slavery in the free states." It was to such criticism that Beecher replied in a series of twelve essays on organic sin in the same paper.

The theory, Beecher patiently explained, was the same as that implicit in the Declaration of Sentiments he had written in 1837, the same as that implicit in the *Narrative*, the same as what he believed when Birney assured him in 1838 he might in conscience join the national society. He had now merely given it a name. "This ground I take," he said, "not for want of zeal in the antislavery cause, but because I am so zealous in it that I am unwilling to see it exposed to logical and moral disgrace, by a defence false in its grounds, and tending to produce a fierce, fanatical and uncandid spirit." As his readers were aware, Beecher was again attacking Garrisonism. The "defence" of abolition he was offering was meant to replace Garrison's argument that *all* slaveholders were, individually, sinners. This, Beecher thought, provided no antislavery rationale for the action (or lack of it) the American Board must inevitably take. The theory of organic sin did. It defined slavery as a sin that individuals in their individual capacity cannot commit and one, therefore, in which the "body politic" is the sinner, the "great, the omnipresent slaveholder." Lyman Beecher, in writing his approval of his son's speech and action, told Edward to "come out in one sentence & say that Organic Sin means *National Sin*—make it stand out—& stop all this flummery that Phelps will make about the word."[52] But Beecher meant something more precise than his father's phrase, a catch phrase since the 1830s, could indicate. "If the organization of THE BODY POLITIC creates false and sinful *Permanent relations* between the individuals who compose the body politic, that, and that only, as I use the term, is an organic sin."

When, then, Beecher contended that the antislavery society's position savored of "false metaphysics and false philology," he was not being devious; he was not, as his opponents charged, propounding a "theological fiction" to explain the relation between individuals and their society. It was not true, as the radicals charged, that the "antislavery sentiments expressed by such men as Messrs. Bacon, Hawes, Beecher, Stowe, Dwight, &c." were unique, that they "are not to be taken as defining at all the actual posi-

52. Thomas K. Beecher to EB, Walnut Hills, November 22, 1845 (MHCL). Thomas is writing, he says, to convey the sentiments of LB, who is ill.

tion of the Board" and the orthodox clergy.[53] Beecher and most of his colleagues in Boston and elsewhere were not "indifferent to the sin and shame of slavery, and disposed to take the slaveholder's part against every earnest effort for abolition."[54] Beecher would have been quick to admit the existence of orthodox clergymen like Nehemiah Adams and Joel Parker (who had also been at Alton), whose pro-slavery sentiments were embarrassingly obvious, and worse, tolerated as respectable. Indeed, much of his anti-slavery activity was directed against their kind. But they were in the minority. As the American Board controversy suggests, there was a large body of clergymen, neither radical abolitionists nor the Finneyite Perfectionists whom such twentieth-century historians as Gilbert Barnes have used to attack the Garrisonian radicals, who considered themselves abolitionists, but "conservative abolitionists." In 1835 they had joined the American Union for the Relief and Improvement of the Colored Race; in 1840 they voted for the Liberty Party; they joined the American and Foreign Antislavery Society; they signed antislavery petitions and worked against slavery within the church; in 1845 they supported the American Board in Brooklyn. Of this group Beecher may be considered a representative.

Beecher was a representative of this same group in 1837–38, also, though the terms of its definition were not available then. As he pointed out in 1845, the Declaration of Sentiments he wrote for the Illinois society embodied his theory of organic sin without giving it a name. It was the expression of his conservative abolitionist sentiments. So,

53. A. A. Phelps, quoted by Leonard Bacon, "The Collision Between . . . ," *op. cit.,* p. 161.
54. Johnson, *op. cit.,* p. 70.

also, his re-creation of the Alton affair: when he wrote in the *Narrative* that not until 1835 had he found immediate abolition "philosophical," he meant that not until then had he developed satisfactorily the doctrine of organic sin (then still unnamed). In Alton, as Beecher points out again and again in the last third of his book, the "community" was at fault; it was a "sin," a communal sin, not to defend free discussion. "Who are responsible?" he asks at the beginning of Part II. The theory of organic sin, never named but always there, gives him the answer. Alton was a microcosm of the nation. Alton's sin was a national sin. Alton was a "test question for our whole land." "Deadly influences were at work; anarchical principles were eating out the very life of the body politic; and yet the nation was asleep," unaware of the sin in which it was inextricably involved. As a "nation," Beecher wrote, "we have long been sinking from the lofty ground of principle with which we began"; the "cursed love of gold has left to multitudes no standard of right and wrong but dollars and cents" and the "thirst for political promotion has left to others no criterion of truth but the opinions of the majority, however profligate." It was the nation, the organic political entity, that finally must be held responsible for Lovejoy's murder.

The proper answers to the rhetorical questions of the *Narrative*—"Is not a full discussion of this subject a part of the plans of God? Does not it belong to the movement of his providence in the present age?"—depend in part upon a right apprehension of Beecher's theory of organic sin. The "full" discussion of slavery was appropriate, indeed inevitable now, because, as Beecher would explain in 1845, the evolution of God's immutable principles of "honor and right" demanded it. The discussion was not proper before the nineteenth century; God's design had not progressed that far then. Now it had. The "signs of the times are not ambiguous," Beecher wrote in 1838; "they may easily be known." They signaled that, although slavery per se was not condemned in the New Testament (as Garrison would have it), the *principles* of Christianity required its abolition now. Who could "arrest the current of the universe?" If it was true that in Alton the "enemies of liberty have won the day," God would inescapably win the century. It was to this certainty that conservative abolitionists attached their hopes. It was what made abolition not only philosophical but "safe" as of the mid-1830s.[55]

10

In writing about "the actors in this scene" at Alton, the "theatre of a tragedy so bloody," then, Beecher was in fact writing providential drama. Behind that drama lay a theory of history which, like the theory of organic sin, was unnamed and implicit in 1837–38. The theory of history was not to become complete and explicit until 1849 when, out of the "painful experience of fourteen long years" in the West, Beecher delivered in Brooklyn the sermon *The Question at Issue* before the Society for the Promotion of Collegiate and Theological Education at the West.

World history, he said to the members of the society, occurs not only in time but in a place; there is a "main channel in which the destinies of the world have flowed." At one time the channel flowed through the Mediterranean nations, later through northern Europe; now it flows

---

55. EB, *Narrative*, pp. 109, 111, 113, 135, 151, 157.

through the United States, particularly the West. Or if, as everyone in the audience knew—to adapt the metaphor Beecher utilized in *The Conflict of Ages* four years later— all parts of God's universe are ordered like "wheels in some vast machine" to secure some preordained end, it is the West that is now the drive wheel. The West, then, is the main channel of history, the drive wheel of the universe, and (to return to the Alton metaphor) the stage on which the drama of time and timelessness is to be acted in this generation. It is therefore vital, Beecher said, that it be seen in proper perspective:

> Ideas of backwoodsmen, rude society, pecuniary mismanage-
> ment, religious enthusiasm and excesses fill some minds, and
> create an unintelligent prejudice against enlarged plans for the
> West; by others, the subject is seen under the influence of sec-
> tional feelings, or personal losses; and by others, it is seen in the
> general, and all plans to aid the West are helped without study;
> and sometimes those are the most aided that deserve least con-
> fidence. By few is the subject seen in its true glory, as a part of
> the plans of an infinite God, the most wonderful evolution of
> human society that he has ever caused on earth, and for the
> highest and noblest ends.

The West, in short, was the place where the infinite God's utopian blueprint for society would be realized.

For Beecher that was not a matter in dispute. The prac-tical problem, the real "question at issue," was not whether God (through Christianity) would control the destiny of the West. Certainly Christianity in some form would be in control. Methodism, Baptism, Episcopalianism, Mormon-ism, Roman Catholicism—all those (even though for Beecher some were only partial and some clearly spurious forms of Christianity) were practical possibilities. The question was not *whether* Christianity, but *what form* of Christianity. Would the Puritanism that is New England's contribution to divine history be able to "exert a controlling energy on the development of the West" and "become an element of immense power, to influence, modify and benefit every other element of civil and religious society"? Would the "leading features" of Puritanism—the rejection of infallible church authority, the testing of all principles by the Bible, the repudiation of the theory of grace by sacrament, the insistence instead on an "intelligent" regeneration by the Spirit, the emphasis on popular education so as to prepare the people for grace intelligently received, and the establishment of colleges to promote popular education and to educate the ministry—would these leading features prevail in the West if the agents of Puritanism remained "greatly in the minority"? Would Puritanism realize its "manifest destiny"? That was the question at issue.

Beecher was pleading that the society help history work out its inevitable pattern, a paradoxical plea not uncommon to his time, or for that matter to any time. He "sometimes feared" that his generation was "feeling less and less the impulse" which drove the early Puritans, that the "system" was "running down." He wanted the "mainspring," now "uncoiled," to be "wound up again." His listeners needed "only to gain a new historical and religious ardor; to go back to the original fountain-heads of thought and feeling; to penetrate to the depths of the great contest." We may assume that he thought one of the means of penetration would be his new system of the universe, to be published in four years. But if historical fact is to be consulted, the mainspring had already been rewound.

What Beecher thought of as inevitable, as historically determined, was being accomplished at the very time he was speaking. Already Puritanism—the two most congenial forms of which were Congregationalism and Presbyterianism—was dominating the history of the West (and thus world history). By 1849 latter-day Puritans had founded fifty permanent colleges, thirty-four of them since Beecher had been born. In the next decade they would establish twenty more—almost two a year. They were already, in fact, as Beecher was urging, helping "leaven the whole mass," exerting a "permanent" and "incalculable" influence on the West and the world. They had already, as one of our best historians has observed, made "the greater contribution," even though outnumbered.[56] Beecher himself was the living refutation of his fears.

Beecher's intense concern for a correct theory of history in *The Question at Issue* had appeared implicitly in the *Narrative*; the concern reappears in *The Conflict* and its sequel, *The Concord of Ages* (1860), Beecher's major theological works. In *The Papal Conspiracy Exposed* (1855) it became central.

"History is made up of two elements," Beecher wrote in 1855: "facts which transpire in this world and the relations of those facts to the universal system. . . . Each generation of men has its principles, ends, and aims; but no common intelligible human plan runs through the history of all ages. To discover such a plan we must pass into the

56. For the data, see Donald G. Tewksbury, *The Founding of American Colleges and Universities before the Civil War: with Particular Reference to the Religious Influences Bearing upon the College Movement*, Teachers College, Columbia University Contributions to Education No. 543 (New York: Teachers College, Columbia University, 1932), pp. 93–95, 121–122. For the observation, see Wright, *op. cit.*, p. 98.

invisible world" and study God's "designs." Beecher felt
this generation was living in an "age of [historical] light"—
if not "the age of perfect light," "soon to become so"; this
was "to be the age of true and impartial history." This
generation, located in the main channel of providential
history, at a climax in the "evolution" of God's design,
was destined to see straight and see true. When it did, it
would see history, both in and out of time, in Beecher's
image: the image of conflict. The West would be "the field
of Armageddon," the locus of "the Waterloo conflict of the
globe," of "the battle of the great day of God Almighty,"
of "one more conflict, and that the last." The systems of
good and evil, Beecher said, "are fast coming into their last
collision" in the West. And he was confident that

when the time comes, one final, sudden blow from God [and
Puritanism will] smite the brain [of the system of evil,] and its
convulsive dying agonies shall be felt in every land as a voice
from the throne shall proclaim, It is done! This work belongs
to God alone; it is his last and greatest work before he reigns
on earth.

The system of evil Beecher had in mind, as the *Narrative*
illustrates, was embodied in part in the proslavery monolith
that American society had become. But as in his 1827
Address, where his political and social attitudes became
clear only in the imagery of theological discourse, so in
The Papal Conspiracy Beecher revealed himself as social
architect primarily in the imagery of his attack on the
Roman Catholic religion. For him the Catholic "corporation" was then as always the "enemy of humanity," the
source of "spiritual despotism and of religious and civil
bondage." Its destruction was "essential to the coming of
an age of intelligence, liberty, and social purity." Never
would men "have true freedom," never would "society be

truly organized" until that was understood. Catholicism was the religious version of the monolithic society Beecher feared America was becoming; it was a model of the bad society. As Beecher said over and over again, any time the context allowed, the Catholic church was a closed corporation "invested with the monopoly of the grace of God, and of heaven and hell, to the whole human race, centralized by a universal spiritual monarch." Its "sources of profit" were the indulgences for sin it sold; all its "peculiar doctrines and practices" were wonderfully adapted to produce "immense pecuniary profit"; it was a "commercial confederation" carrying on an "immense trade," always seeking another source of revenue, by its very "structure" the "hotbed of ambition, pride, the love of money and power." Its downfall was represented in Biblical prophecy "under the symbol of the ruin of an immense commercial city."

The Catholic church, in short, provided the symbolic antithesis to Beecher's blueprint for the good society. As a system the church did not "tend in its ultimate results to simplify organization and reduce the expenses of government." On the contrary, it encouraged "extravagant centralized aristocratic systems." It had been, and always would be, "the great corrupter of all earthly governments." It had to be leveled to the ground before the good society could be built. How might a social architect create, "not the infidel or transcendental millennium," but the "true Protestant, scriptural" heaven on earth? How might he "reduce the world to such order that all human governments will become so simple that men will scarcely feel their existence"? How might he guide "self-governing freemen" in revivifying "this great nation, in which, for the first time, the great principles of civil and religious liberty have been developed on a scale adequate to the wants of humanity"? How might a social architect, in short, recreate the West and all of American society in the image of Puritan New England, so that the local government, like the Congregational church, becomes an autonomous unit, the national government nearly withers away and "the invisible government of God" and universe replaces it, and finally "Every thing . . . will be simplified"— how might he do this when the embodiment of evil, the spiritual corporation that had tried to dominate history, still existed?

Beecher's question and his conception of the Roman Catholic Church as the antichrist, as a satanic corporation, were not uniquely his. The image of a "papal conspiracy" to describe the growth and plans of Roman Catholicism in the United States belonged to the entire orthodox community's vision of the West, especially about the time Beecher went to Illinois. Even earlier, by the late 1820s, it had become clear to the orthodox community that the Pope was trying to subvert the civil and religious liberties of the country by taking over the West. Beecher became part of what one historian has called a Protestant Crusade, which manifested itself in the 1830s in debates (Breckinridge vs. Hughes, Brownlee vs. Powers *et. al.*, Fuller vs. England, Campbell vs. Purcell)[57] and in such popular

57. Ray Allen Billington, *The Protestant Crusade, 1800–1860: A Study of the Origins of American Nativism* (New York: Rinehart and Company, 1952), pp. 62–66. As a vice president of the Western Literary Institute and College of Professional Teachers, EB was probably present at the meeting in October 1836, when the group was addressed by Alexander Campbell, who devoted his lecture to attacking Roman Catholicism. Bishop Purcell of Cincinnati objected and subsequently, in January 1837, debated Campbell. See Billington, *op. cit.*, p. 65; Harveson, *op. cit.*, p. 91; EB, *The Papal Conspiracy*, pp. 125, 205; and Robert Frederick West, *Alexander Campbell and Natural Religion* (New Haven: Yale University Press; London: Oxford University Press, 1948), pp. 36–37.

books as Lyman Beecher's virulently anti-Catholic *Plea for the West* (1835); in the forties in such sermons as the one by Beecher on "how much the Catholicks are enslaved poor deluded creatures," reported in the diary of Mrs. Joseph Duncan, wife of the Illinois governor, or Beecher's "terrifick description" of the poverty of Catholic philosophy another time;[58] in open letters like the series of twelve from Beecher to Bishop Kenrick in the *Christian Alliance*, exposing Kenrick's "deliberate Jesuitical frauds, designed to hoodwink and delude";[59] in arguments such as that in Beecher's address to the Ladies' Society for the Promotion of Education at the West, proposing to counter the Catholics' "deliberate" attempt to "proselyte the West, by the power" of women's minds, "the ruling minds of a nation,"[60] and in his resolution at a meeting in behalf of the Society for the Promotion of Collegiate and Theological Education at the West—"*Resolved*, That in the coming conflict of the moral world" in the West the "descendants of the Puritans" should realize that schools are "engines of war";[61] and in the fifties in courses of sermons like Beecher's attacks on Roman Catholicism, in books like *The Papal Conspiracy Exposed*, and, as through all three decades, in comments and asides showing the relationship of nearly all Protestant projects to the crusade. Some observers, like Orestes Brownson reviewing *The Papal Conspiracy*, thought this "the quintessence of Evangelical acidity double distilled." But the Protestants themselves

58. Elizabeth Duncan Putnam, editor, "Diary of Mrs. Joseph Duncan (Elizabeth Caldwell Smith)," *Journal of the Illinois State Historical Society*, XXI, No. 1 (April 1938), 25, 32 (entries for January 10 and March 7,1841).

59. EB, *The Papal Conspiracy*, p. 98. See also Billington, *op. cit.*, p. 255.

60. "Dr. Beecher's Address," *History of the Formation of the Ladies' Society* . . . (1846), p. 9.

61. *Proceedings of a Public Meeting* . . . (1845), p. 4.

thought of the crusade as a fight for civil liberties; they were "sure" that the claims of the papal hierarchy were "inconsistent with political liberty, with self-government, with free institutions, with intellectual progress, and with the elevation of the human race."[62]

If applied consistently, the principles the Protestants enunciated in their attack on Catholicism would seem to commit them also to abolition. But men are not always consistent: the fact is that all anti-Catholic men were not also antislavery men. Still, there was more consistency than the radical abolitionists and their historians have supposed, and if Beecher's attack on the satanic corporation was not unusual, neither (in a lesser sense) was his conservative abolitionism. Only the process by which he arrived at his political position and his theoretical rationale for it were distinctly his. The *Narrative* he published in 1838 was more than a public and objective account of the Alton riots. It was a very personal book, drawing upon the imagery of cosmic drama and the "corporation," and, though not always explicitly, upon the theories of eminent holiness, organic sin, and providential history. Beecher wrote in his diary that he did not "hide any opinion."[63] But from the time he was twenty-four he had been hiding his personal, heretical revelations about the pre-existence of souls and a suffering God. Without these doctrines, Beecher thought, too many of the clergy were still unable to find an acceptably orthodox rationale for their conservative antislavery impulse. Would not a new definition of

62. Orestes Brownson, Review of *The Papal Conspiracy, Brownson's Quarterly Review*, 3rd ser., III (April 1855), 246; "The Romish Hierarchy," *North American Review*, LXXXII (January 1856), 114, 125–126.

63. EB, quoted in "Life," p. 136.

the "moral relations of God and Man"—the subtitle of
Beecher's next book—help resolve the conflict that pervaded the time: the conflict between impulses toward cosmic justice (which the Garrisonian radicals heeded) and
the evidence of man's depravity (which provided empirical
support for American orthodoxy)? Beecher thought so:
and just as politics had for him become a problem in theology, so, in finally revealing the doctrines by which he
had continuously rationalized his action, he would show
how for everyone theology had become a problem in politics.

It may not be clear at first to
the ordinary mind why slavery and
theology should go hand in hand, in
national affairs. But if we reflect
that theology is but another name
for the politics of the universe,
or the kingdom of God, the problem
becomes simple.

—Charles Beecher (1896)

Three:

The Politics of the Universe

11

ON August 27, 1853, Beecher finished the Dedication to *The Conflict of Ages* and sent it to the offices of Phillips, Sampson & Co., Boston publishers who had declined *Uncle Tom's Cabin* because they thought an anti-slavery novel would not sell well. The publishers had had most of Beecher's "system of the universe" "in press" since July.[1] Though nowhere made explicit in the text of *The Conflict*, nevertheless they may have been aware that this book also dealt with the slavery problem; that it, like the novel, was motivated in part by the slavery crisis, particularly the crisis of the early fifties; that in it, theology was related to abolitionist politics. If they did not know that by August 27, surely the Dedication, though only a little more explicit than the text, made Beecher's intentions unmistakable.

1. "Literary Intelligence," *Literary World*, XII (July 9, 1853), 551.

There Beecher pointed out that *The Conflict* contained a revisionist theological system that would provide his age with "the power intelligently to meet and logically to solve all of the great religious and social problems" that it was "called on to encounter in the great work of converting the world, and thoroughly reorganizing human society." A workable and "complete" system of the universe, as Beecher had explained also toward the end of the book, is more than a "natural want of the mind"; it is indispensable to an effective solution of social and political problems. All men are influenced by their view of the universe, "even those who affect to discourage such theories in others." The system that controls any given man—and the world is full of systems—may not have been developed by him, or even "consciously stated and adopted" by him. But he nevertheless feels its influence constantly. Such systems function like "elevated reservoirs of water," which impel the "little streams of water which are used in the varied business of daily practical life," but which are visited by few.[2] The reservoirs that fed the daily life of his time, Beecher felt, were polluted. The system he was offering in *The Conflict*, the purpose of which he was now clarifying in the Dedication, was intended to purify the source, and thus the life, of his culture.

On one level, *The Conflict* synthesizes the multiple themes with which Beecher had been publicly concerned in the past, as if the earlier writings had been but first drafts of parts of a larger whole. In the book, as in the *Hints*, one of Beecher's aims is the revival of real Christian experience; as in the baptismal studies, he seeks Christian unity; as in the 1835 *Six Sermons*, he contends that eminent holiness is crucial to the eventual reorganization of

2. EB, *Conflict*, pp. iii, 493–494.

society; as in his accounts of Roman Catholicism, he advocates the decentralized good society modeled on the New England past and attacks the "corporate" society; and, finally, as in the theory of organic sin written implicitly into the 1837 Declaration of Sentiments at Alton and the 1838 *Narrative* and stated explicitly in the 1845 essays in the Boston *Recorder*, he sees sin as not only individual but social.

On another level, as Charles Beecher observed, the book represents more than a public synthesis; it represents the culmination of Beecher's inner history. It is objectified autobiography; it provides a "virtual and vivid history" of Beecher's "religious experience, which moulded his whole life and work." At its very center is a theory of the pre-existence of souls—initially, we recall, a private revelation. We must not, consequently, as Beecher warned us in the book itself, think of *The Conflict* as a collection of "dry and dead dogmas," forgetting the "circumstances and trials" behind them, forgetting that the man who wrote was "once filled with the warm" stuff of life, forgetting that each man writes not only "for God and for man," but for "his age" as well.[3]

A book so decidedly the climax of a lifetime of public discourse and private experience has no beginning. It was undoubtedly begun sometime during the decade (1844–55) Beecher spent in Boston. But the circumstances surrounding its writing are not clear, and the best an examination of Beecher's most important activities during that time can provide is the context in which it was written. During that decade he was minister to the Salem Street Church; his sermons ("written discourses"), the church historian informs us, had a "tendency to the abstract and

3. CB, "Life," p. 209; EB, *Conflict*, p. 357.

metaphysical,"[4] perhaps even a tendency toward the speculations of *The Conflict.* He continued his preachments
against Catholicism and for Protestant education in the
West. His studies on baptism continued to appear, leading to a book in 1849. A stream of articles and lectures
poured from his study: "Remarks on Stuart's Commentary
on the Apocalypse" in 1847; "Influence of the Literature
of the Saracens" in 1848; "Life and Times of Leo the
Great" and "The Doctrine of the Trinity, Rational and
Scriptural" in 1849—all these in one of his favorite scholarly journals, the *Biblical Repository.* In 1845, the year of
the debate and essays on organic sin, he lectured on *Faith
Essential to a Complete Education* and wrote the decision
of an ex parte council trying the Rev. J. H. Fairchild for
immorality.[5] In 1848 he gave the annual address at the
anniversary of Mt. Holyoke Seminary (where Emily Dickinson heard him). During certain weeks of every year he
was almost totally engaged in preaching ordination sermons.[6] At times, his private correspondence was volumi-
nous; in 1847, for instance, he argued with his brother
Charles over Charles's sermon *The Bible a Sufficient Creed,*
and at least one of the letters in the series was twenty-five
pages long. In May 1849 he delivered a sermon before the
Pastoral Association of Massachusetts, and in June 1851 he
addressed the Home Missionary Society.[7] He lectured often

4. Stephen H. Hayes, "Historical Discourse," in *Memorial Volume of
Salem Church* (Boston: The Church Committee, 1874), p. 23.

5. See J. H. Fairchild, *Remarkable Incidents in the Life of Rev. J. H.
Fairchild, Pastor of Payson Church, South Boston* (Boston: The Author,
1855), p. 207 ff.

6. EB to HWB, Boston, September 28, 1848 (Yale).

7. See the reports in the *Congregationalist,* I, No. 2 (June 1, 1849), and
III, No. 23 (June 6, 1851).

in favor of the temperance cause, perhaps the most important occasion being his *Address to the Citizens of Massachusetts* given at the State Temperance Convention in September 1853.

The list could be extended indefinitely. But only one item seems as if it might offer a useful clue to the actual writing of *The Conflict*. In 1849, after being tempted by Henry Ward Beecher's invitation to "preach true revival sermons" in New York permanently as he had on occasion in the past, Beecher became chief editor of the *Congregationalist*, a new sectarian Boston weekly.[8] Although he had been told he was the only man in whom all the factions of Boston Congregationalism could find unity, an opening editorial (May 1849) promising to "stand on the broad ground of New England theology" led immediately to a friendly controversy. How was that theological tradition to be defined? The discussion that followed and continued through 1850 involved three of the most important orthodox theologians of the time, Leonard Woods, Bennett Tyler, and Nathaniel Taylor. Editorially, Beecher "considered" the entire course of New England thought, as three years later he would consider it in *The Conflict*. We may suppose the editorials were preparation for the book. But, as Charles Beecher indicates, "the most remarkable thing in the whole series of editorials is the absence of any allusion to pre-existence." This was, indeed, a "striking instance of self control."[9]

8. In September and October 1848, EB wrote at least four letters in reply to HWB (Yale), all dealing with the question of whether he should come to New York or stay in Boston as editor of the new paper.

9. *Congregationalist*, I, No. 1 (May 24, 1849). CB, "Life," pp. 190–191; CB's discussion of EB and the paper is extensive, pp. 158–160, 173–184, 189–192.

It is more striking, even mystifying, that on March 14, 1853, Beecher could write to an unidentified correspondent that he was "not pledged" to write a book. For five years he had been engaged in what Charles Beecher describes as "extensive" labors in libraries around Boston, undoubtedly doing research for *The Conflict*. Yet the letter was written only four months before the *Literary World* announced that the book was in the presses and ready for publication about the first of September.[10] Presumably, however, if we follow Charles Beecher's explanation, those "most intimate" with Beecher were aware that *The Conflict* was being written. And only they knew the "travail of soul" that gave it birth—the "Many hours" Beecher "lay prostrate on his face before God agonising in prayer." Only they realized that Beecher's "ambition, 'his idol,' " was to have the same effect on theology and politics that the shift from the "Geocentric to the heliocentric system of astronomy" had on science, to become the "moral Copernicus" of his generation. Presumably from their point of view, as from Charles Beecher's, it was "a noble ambition."[11]

In *The Conflict*, and later in *The Concord of Ages*

10. EB's anonymous correspondent—EB to ?, Boston, March 14, 1853 (BPL)—seems to be a southerner ("Allow me to answer," EB wrote, "in Yankee fashion."); he evidently asked questions about EB's notion of benevolence, right, choice, and Jonathan Edwards, and EB responded in four illuminating pages. It may be that the book EB said he was "not pledged" to write is a book on these subjects and that the comment is not meant to refer to *The Conflict*. But for some time before the publication of *The Conflict* there had been, in one reviewer's words, much "busy rumor" about EB's "novel theories and daring speculations"; see [H. B. Smith], "Preexistence of Souls," *Presbyterian Quarterly Review*, II, No. 8 (March 1854), 552–553. What else could EB have meant?

11. CB, "Life," pp. 89, 191–192.

(1860), laboring to correct his generation's various and inadequate systems of the universe, Beecher worked one image over and over again. It clarifies both the central problem in the book and the dialectical method of its solution. Suppose, Beecher said, that a community ignorant of steamships were told on good authority that "the wheels should be so adjusted that they would revolve in opposite directions." Experience would soon show that the boat, with the wheels so adjusted, "would do nothing but revolve incessantly round, without progress,—and, moreover," her "whole frame" would be "unnaturally wrenched and strained by this method of procedure." No doubt the community would repudiate the "traditional" and authoritarian directions it had received. Men would experiment; they would eventually try readjusting the wheels so that they moved in the same direction. The boat would then, of course, move "straight on in obedience to her rudder." Could "any amount of authority avail against this practical demonstration, taken from the working of the system itself"? "An argument of the same kind," Beecher said, coming to the point of his analogy,

and of no less power, would rationally arise from the practical workings of a system of theology, against any traditional adjustment of its parts, if it had been found, on trial, to cause its main moving powers, in like manner, to work against each other,—thus introducing perpetual internal conflict into the very vitals of the system.

It was, then, the "traditional adjustment" of the orthodox "system of theology" that concerned Beecher. Its two power wheels, working in opposite directions, were unnaturally wrenching and straining the church.

One "power wheel" on the orthodox steamship was its

"true and thorough statement of what is involved in the fallen and ruined condition of man." The second, moving in a circle opposed to the doctrine of depravity, consisted of a "full development of the honor, justice, and benevolence of God, in all his dealings with man." The first wheel, characteristically orthodox, explained human corruption. The second, characteristically Unitarian, had to be "so made" by the orthodox "as, in the first place, to free" God from the "charge of dishonorably ruining" man; and, in the second place, to "exhibit" Him "as earnestly and benevolently engaged in efforts" for man's "salvation, through Christ," after man had been "ruined" by his "own fault."[12] Beecher's problem in 1853, as in 1827 when he had his revelation, was to synthesize thesis and antithesis so that neither would overpower the other. Since 1827, but especially during recent years as he prowled the libraries of Boston, Cambridge, and New York, he had presumably been searching the theological past for "mode[s] of adjustment" other than pre-existence. In *The Conflict* he contended that by the manner in which it went about finding a solution, any theology—Universalism, Unitarianism, Transcendentalism, and Swedenborgianism, as well as the various forms of orthodoxy—might be defined. He felt that this was, in fact, a conflict of *ages*, that whole epochs and cultures could be characterized by the modus vivendi they accepted as a solution.

His own "fundamental idea"—namely, that "by supposing the pre-existent sin and fall of man, the most radical views of human depravity can be harmonized with the highest views of the justice and honor of God"—had been suggested numerous times, most prominently by Origen.

12. EB, *Conflict*, pp. 9–10, 16–17.

Like the Copernican theory of the solar system, though, it was put off, rejected, outlawed. For Beecher, the theological past had developed dialectically, in a pattern of near acceptance and rejection of his idea. At times, for example, men like Augustine (for whom Beecher felt profound admiration) "stood on the verge of truth"; but Augustine's doctrine that all men pre-existed in Adam had proven inadequate; there had been a "reaction" away from it.[13] History, in fact, was a series of actions and reactions like this, and Beecher devoted a hundred pages of *The Conflict* —pages highly praised by reviewers—to an analysis of such sequences. His reading of the past, however, was finally an exposition of the present. As such contradictory American philosophers as George Santayana and John Dewey remind us, men are forever trying to hypostatize their ideals and their problems onto the universe, as if giving them eternal and immutable reality provided comfort. That, no doubt, is what Beecher was doing. He was trying to project his solution to a cultural problem into the universe; he was hypostatizing his own inner conflict into history. On his evidence, we may be sure that men of the past did agonize as he did and that in some very limited sense the natural antagonism between the two "power wheels" of Christian theology has created personal and cultural conflicts in all ages. But it seems clear in retrospect —and one cannot be sure it was not obvious to Beecher as well—that the conflict between two principles that he writes about was the characteristic experience of *his* time; that it belonged particularly to *his* generation, which felt the conflict as an intensely personal one; that it was to be resolved in order that *his* society might be reorganized and

13. EB, *Conflict*, pp. 242, 246, 296.

the millennium arrive. Beecher himself seems to be insisting on the contemporaneity of the conflict.[14] The major portion of his book is devoted to a discussion of five characteristic "experiences" men (and especially Americans of his generation) have endured trying to resolve it.

He begins with the orthodox "experience," the essence of which is the belief in "the doctrine of real, responsible, punishable depravity in man, before voluntary action." The doctrine derives, as Beecher knew, from a certain kind of experience of which Jonathan Edwards's "abhorrence" of his own righteousness provides the representative type. How, Edwards asked, can one require that God be just, honorable, benevolent, in the sense that men mean those terms? Is not the difference between the infinite and the finite so immeasurable that to question God's sovereignty by questioning his justice approaches blasphemy? "The very thought," Edwards wrote in the *Personal Narrative*, "of any joy arising in me, on any consideration of my own amiableness, performances, or experiences, or any goodness of heart or life, is nauseous and detestable to me." Beecher thought Edwards "great" not only in "intellect" but in "piety and humility"; I suspect that in the late 1820s he loved Edwards, as he wrote in a letter then, because he was then undergoing the Edwardsean experience. As if he were writing out of personal insight, he described in *The Conflict* Edwards's experience as that of

one to whom God has shown, in its true light, the deep and unutterable pollution of that spiritual unchastity which is in-

14. H. Shelton Smith, in placing the beginnings of the conflict in America in 1750, would seem to confirm this point: *Changing Conceptions of Original Sin: A Study in American Theology Since 1750* (New York: Charles Scribner's Sons, 1955).

volved in that deep-rooted pride, which, like a cancer, seems to have struck its roots deeply into the human soul, and the extermination of which calls for so much providential discipline, and so many and so painful struggles.[15]

But by the beginning of the nineteenth century, even earlier, the Edwardsean experience was no longer satisfactory. If it accounted for human depravity, as the orthodox community demanded, it did not meet the demands of the new principles of honor and right. It forced a "reaction" into a second experience, which took the form of the Unitarianism that antagonized Lyman Beecher and that so greatly influenced Edward Beecher. "The existence of the Unitarian body," Beecher wrote in *The Conflict*, "is a providential protest in favor of the great principles of honor and of right." "It is an entire recoil from Old School theology to the other extreme." Beecher admitted that Pelagius and Socinus anticipated the Unitarians, and he noted the case of John Adams as an instance of eighteenth-century American Unitarianism. But the figure who dated the "reaction" was William Ellery Channing, who had influenced Beecher in the twenties. Channing, Beecher felt, had forced not only him but the nineteenth century to an inchoate awareness, not of the conflict of "ages," but of the cultural conflict of an age. His variety of Unitarianism had at least one quality in common with orthodoxy. Both, in Beecher's image, tried to "reconcile" the conflict by belittling the importance of one of the wheels of the theological steamship and magnifying the importance of the other.

In reaction, a third experience arose. It tried to hold "unmodified" and at once "the most radical facts" about

15. EB, *Conflict*, pp. 89–92. EB to [his uncle] Col. George A. Foote, New Haven, September 9, 1828 (Yale).

both human depravity and divine justice. It attempted to "take refuge" in the doctrine of universal salvation. To find psychological (and doctrinal) "relief" from the conflict, Universalists like John Foster and Hosea Ballou rejected, "on purely moral grounds," the idea of eternal future punishment. God, they thought, could thereby be vindicated from the charge of creating depraved "creatures" and then punishing forever the depravity He originated, for ultimately we all will be saved. Evil thus became temporary, a mere appearance, and God's plan as a whole honorable and just.[16]

As the Universalists were aware when they reviewed *The Conflict*, Beecher's attitude toward this third "experience" was at best awkward and ambiguous, and to explore his attitude briefly is to mark the thin line he continually walked between orthodox acceptability and some form of heresy. On the one hand, he sympathized with Universalism's attempt to embrace unmodified both basic doctrines; he sympathized with its concern not only for man's corruption but also for God's justice and involvement in revitalizing and reforming American society. And universal salvation was, after all, a solution, even though denied (Beecher thought in 1853) by the Bible. On the other hand, Beecher had feared as early as 1827 the ascendancy of the restorationist heresy, and one of his motives in writing *The Conflict* was to prevent it from gaining credence. To deny the eternal damnation of sinners, he felt in 1853, would destroy orthodoxy.[17] (Universalism, if accepted,

16. EB, *Conflict*, pp. 116, 124, 147, 153.

17. EB, *History of Opinions on the Scriptural Doctrine of Retribution* (1878), p. 295. EB's attitude toward the restorationist doctrine of Universalism fluctuated until his old age. In his 1878 *History* he repudiated in part his stand of the 1850s. No longer did he find that the Bible insisted

would also destroy Beecher's "fundamental idea"; pre-existence and after-existence were not, after all, so very different, and if one of the ideas worked, the other was unnecessary.) There had been another and more accept-able "reaction" from the exclusive concern of both ortho-doxy and Unitarianism with only one of the basic doc-trines. The 1837 split of the Presbyterian church into new and old school institutionalized what Beecher described as the fourth "experience" in the odyssey of his generation's inner life.

The new school constantly appealed to the principles of honor and right to "modify or correct certain parts of the Old School doctrine of the ruined state of man," and at the same time it made an "earnest effort" to "retain and in-culcate" fully the "real and essential facts of human de-pravity." Out of it developed the "theology of revivals." Those who sought this manner of relief from the conflict of their age held several beliefs in common:

---

on the eternal punishment of sinners; no longer did he contend that since Christian experience "reveals the malignant [and voluntary] nature of sin" (*Conflict*, p. 156), Universalism fails because it does not contain a satisfac-tory account of the will; no longer did he believe that the doctrine of pre-existence required as its corollary the doctrine of endless punishment. Were he forced to choose between eternal punishment and some form of univer-sal restoration, he said in 1878, he would have to accept the latter (*History*, p. 297).

On one point, however, he remained firm: if eternal punishment *were* to be sustained, it could not be on the grounds of the fall of Adam, as it was argued by almost the entire orthodox community. "I believe," he said, "that to punish endlessly men born as any form of that system [orthodoxy] represents, and placed in this world as men are, under satanic delusions and powerful evil social influences, would be an extreme of injustice and cruelty that would entirely transform the character of God" (*History*, pp. 296–297).

His final statement on the problem came when he was eighty-seven years old, in his note on "Lyman Beecher and Infant Damnation" (1890).

They deny the imputation of Adam's sin to his posterity. . . . They also deny the existence in man of a nature in the strict sense sinful and deserving of punishment anterior to knowledge and voluntary action. . . . As a natural result, they also deny the doctrine of the absolute and entire inability of the sinner to do the duties required of him by God.

Beecher felt that the fountainhead of new school doctrine was Jonathan Edwards's student Samuel Hopkins, who developed out of his teacher's description of a "sinful nature" the theory that "all sin and holiness consist in voluntary action, and that the essence of holiness is disinterested benevolence, and of sin is selfishness." The Hopkinsian theory, which rejected the doctrine of the imputation of Adam's sin, had been at the heart of Beecher's 1835 sermons on eminent holiness, and the new-school experience was, of course, the one Beecher inherited from his father. Arising out of the attempt to meet Unitarian objections to orthodoxy, "in many respects" new-school doctrine gave "great relief to the mind." Moreover, Beecher observed, it had effected an "incalculable amount of good." It had acted as a "penetrating and powerful . . . counterpoise" against the tendency of the old school to "paralysis and inaction"; it had "elevated" the level of piety and action in the orthodox community; it had generated "great intellectual activity." Under "the influence of its advocates, the modern system of benevolent enterprise came into existence and was matured and established."[18] Most antislavery men began as new-school Congregationalists or Presbyterians. Yet, notwithstanding its contributions, the new school had not, Beecher insisted, succeeded in uniting the Christian community. From it also there

18. EB, *Conflict*, pp. 160–167.

had been a reaction, one in which Beecher himself participated.

New-school theology, many felt, tended "to degrade our conceptions of free agency." Beecher explained that the "denial of a depraved nature" forced one either to accept "a doctrine of divine efficiency in the production of sin," which both "reason and the moral sense repudiate"; or to believe that "the cause of man's entire actual depravity is an innocent nature, and circumstances," which seemed preposterous. Moreover, the new-school theology, as a fourth "experience," satisfied neither the "zealous advocates" of honor and right, the Unitarians, nor the "thorough defenders" of innate depravity, the old school. For both, it was an unsatisfactory compromise, not a real synthesis. Was it then the case that no theological position, no "experience," could provide a resting place for the orthodox consciousness? To each of these experiences there had been a reaction. And to each reaction there had been a counter-reaction, in what seemed a circular and endless series. Could it be that "the conflict will be eternal"? The fifth "experience" consisted of precisely that fear, that the conflict had no final resolution. It differed from the other experiences in that it was peculiar to no sect; rather, it characterized everyone's movement in the nineteenth century from the Edwardsean experience to their particular revisionist position. Its defining quality was "the eclipse of the glory of God." It appeared when one assented both to the principles of honor and right and to the depravity of man, "yet without the perception of any satisfactory mode of modification and adjustment." One had the "oppressive and overwhelming consciousness of existing, apparently, under a universal system which is incapable of defence." One found himself in the great "dark valley" of religious experience. There was one solace: it was an experience characteristic of one's generation, and one did not endure it alone.

Beecher underwent such an experience in 1827, and admitted it in *The Conflict*, though he realized it was not an experience men, especially ministers, were "disposed to make public." "For a time," he wrote,

> the system of this world rose before my mind, in the same manner, as far as I can judge, as it did before the minds of Channing and Foster. I can, therefore, more fully appreciate their expression of their trials and emotions. But I was entirely unable to find relief as they did. The depravity of man neither Christian experience, the Bible, nor history, would permit me to deny. . . . Hence, for a time, all was dark as night.

Then Beecher began to make the major point of his book. "The transition in my own case," he wrote in a passage already quoted, was as if,

> when I had been groping in some vast cathedral, in the gloom of midnight, vainly striving to comprehend its parts and relations, suddenly before the vast arched window of the nave a glorious sun had suddenly burst forth, filling the whole structure with its radiance, and showing in perfect harmony the proportions and beauties of its parts.[19]

The "transition" Beecher describes was to a sixth "experience," one that had not yet appeared on any chart of characteristic nineteenth-century religious experiences, but one that Beecher hoped would make him the moral Copernicus who provided an effective solution to the conflict of his generation. The "glorious sun" which lit up the cathedral of Beecher's universe was not, of course, the sun

19. EB, *Conflict*, pp. 168, 181–191.

at the center of Copernicus' astronomical system; it was the "hypothesis" (that is, the revelation) of the pre-existence of souls. Beecher hoped that hypothesis would reconcile the two basic and conflicting doctrines of Christianity and provide an escape from the "dark valley" of his generation's religious experience.

Beecher's critics contended that the hypothesis of pre-existence was not original with him; they more than implied that he borrowed it from Indian philosophy, or from Origen, or from Julius Müller, a contemporary German Protestant theologian. But, as we have seen, certainly no one would wish to argue, least of all Beecher, that the general idea was new. As someone writing in 1860 said, the doctrine was "taught by Pythagoras, sung by Empedocles, dreamed by Fludd," believed by nearly "the whole world of Oriental thinkers," many of the Greek philosophers, and no small proportion of the early church fathers; that it was now being "contended for by Beecher" only put him at the end of a long tradition.[20] Beecher's originality lay, not in his doctrine, but in his use of it. The doctrine of the pre-existence of souls resolved the conflict of his time, at least theoretically. One ought, he argued, to accept the hypothesis because, like Newton's laws or like fixing a steamship, it worked. There remained none of those "obstinate facts" which, as Beecher was aware as early as 1824, "delight to deform systems" and "puzzle philosophers."[21]

20. William Rounseville Alger, *The Destiny of the Soul: A Critical History of the Doctrine of a Future Life* (14th ed. [1st ed., 1860]; Boston: Roberts Brothers, 1889), pp. 6, 476. Müller's book *The Christian Doctrine of Sin* (published earlier in German editions of 1838 and 1844) appeared in English translation (of the 3rd ed.) in 1853. It was sometimes reviewed jointly with *The Conflict* and often referred to when not being explicitly reviewed.

21. EB to Willard Fisher, Hartford, October 12, 1824 (Yale).

The hypothesis reconciled the facts of human depravity with man's (nineteenth-century man's) intuition that God *must* be just. Could other orthodox systems of the universe claim more?

Beecher could have made further claims for his hypothesis, but he did not, at least not in 1853. It met all the requirements for an effectively revolutionary orthodoxy. It allowed one to retain the orthodox sense of sin and human corruption, yet at the same time it gave cosmic comfort to the reform impulse—reformers could be doctors of society, of souls trying to recover their lost purity in a world Beecher imagined as a "moral hospital." To bring about such a reconciliation of orthodoxy and radical politics was Beecher's compelling motive in writing his book. He was first and always an orthodox servant of God, but he served God by seeking a theology potentially able to transform American culture in God's image (and his) of the good society. He hoped to free the orthodox community from its metaphysical (and thus political) paralysis: so that it could meet the challenge of the papal conspiracy in the West, the corporate society developing in New England, and, most of all, the slave power in the South; so that it could bring about the revolution that the new-school wing of the church had sought but not achieved, the revolution in the structure of society that would lead to—in fact would be—the millennium. Like Whitman he sought as his "ideal of the glory of these United States" that they be a part of a "Universe of gentleness, condescension, patience, tenderness, unity, upheld and invigorated by infinite power." On this, he wrote in his diary for September 20, 1860, he would concentrate everything, "all truth, all history, all science, all languages, all analogies, all illustrations, all powers of Style, all varieties of composition, all power of emotion."[22]

12

Though not so triumphantly provoking to the world at large as *Uncle Tom's Cabin*, which sold over two million copies the first year and was answered by some thirty books, *The Conflict* made a "comparable" stir in theological circles, noted later by Lyman Beecher Stowe and then by such popular periodicals as the *National Era, Harper's*, and the London *Times*.[23] It went through five printings in three months and seven "editions" in two years. Unlike Beecher's earlier books, all commercial failures, it earned royalties, about $700.[24] It was "reviewed and re-reviewed"

22. EB, quoted in "Life," p. 284.

23. Lyman Beecher Stowe, *Saints Sinners and Beechers* (Indianapolis: Bobbs-Merrill, 1934), p. 70. See also *Harper's Magazine*, VIII (December 1853), 138–139; *The National Era*, VIII (January 12, 1854), p. 7; and, for the London *Times*, CB to Mr. Lowe [Sampson Low?], Newark, New Jersey, December 8, 1856 (BPL).

24. Lyman Beecher Stowe, *op. cit.*, p. 149, says "five large printings." *The National Era* is quoted by Jacob Blain, *A Review, Giving the Main Ideas in Dr. E. Beecher's Conflict of Ages* . . . (Buffalo: The Author, 1856), p. 2, as saying fifth "edition" in three months. I have examined a "7th edition" (dated 1855). CB deleted his comment in the "Life" that the book "went through several editions." There was also an English edition, published by Sampson Low, HBS's English publisher. Except in the latter case, we should understand that these were "printings," not really new "editions." And even if each printing was only 1,000 copies, as in the case of Henry James, Sr.'s, *The Nature of Evil* (see below), the sale alone indicates unusual interest. For EB's royalties, see "Life," p. 232 (deleted by CB). To compare the sale of *The Conflict* to that of best sellers in the decade (defined as a sale of 225,000 copies), including *Uncle Tom's Cabin*, see Frank Luther Mott, *Golden Multitudes: the Story of Best Sellers in the United States* (New York: Macmillan, 1947), pp. 114–122, 307–308.

in lecture courses and from the pulpit like "showers that water the earth in time of drought."[25] Five books, two pamphlets, and a bewildering array of periodical essays, several extending beyond one issue and over one hundred pages—over 3,000 pages of fine theological print in all—were written expressly to deny, modify, or sympathize with Beecher's attempt to replace what he called "the bitter, rotting, corrupting curse of the doctrine of the fall in Adam" with the doctrine of pre-existence.[26] As Beecher observed in 1860, an "uncommon amount of eminent talent"—such men as Hosea Ballou (2nd), Moses Ballou, David N. Lord, Sylvanus Cobb, George Ellis, Henry Weller, Leonard Bacon, E. A. Park, Charles Hodge, Thomas Starr King, the elder Henry James, Oliver Wendell Holmes, James Freeman Clarke, and Ralph Waldo Emerson—engaged in a "great debate."[27] The bibliographical essay that appeared seven months after the book's publication came much too soon to be comprehensive.

As the bibliographer George Ellis was aware, however, beyond a certain point the problem was not quantitative. Insofar as possible (and taking into account Ellis's observation that a book like *The Conflict* has its effect "in a great measure secretly, through the channels which feed the minds of men"), one wished a count of the debaters less than an explanation of the debate: an explanation of its existence, its extent, its meaning, and its significance.[28]

25. H. B. [Hosea Ballou, 2nd], "The Great Moral Conflict," a Review of Moses Ballou, *The Divine Character Vindicated*, *The Universalist Quarterly and General Review*, XII (January 1855), 115.

26. EB, diary entry for September 14, 1860, quoted in "Life," p. 280.

27. EB, *Concord*, p. 389.

28. [George E. Ellis], Bibliographical Review of Reviews, *The Christian Examiner*, 4th ser., XXI (March 1854), 315.

First, then, and most obviously, the Beecher name, as before, explains a good deal. Though from a twentieth-century point of view the Beechers sometime seem reflexes of their society—purveyors of popular sentimentalisms instead of proponents of new truths—in their own time they were thought of as gadflies to the national consciousness, perhaps even as repositories of the national conscience now and then. As Thomas Starr King said in reviewing *The Conflict*, the Beecher name was so commonly associated with "some form of uncompromising utterance or uncanonical speculation" that the public was not likely to be "surprised with any new and startling theory" emanating from it. The early 1850s marked the climax of the family's achievement and fame. Lyman's collected works appeared in 1852. Catharine had recently published two controversial books, *Truth Stranger than Fiction* (1850) and *The True Remedy for the Wrongs of Women* (1851). Henry Ward had become phenomenally popular in Brooklyn. Harriet's first novel, *Uncle Tom's Cabin* (1852), was generally taken to represent the family response to the Fugitive Slave Law. And the controversy over Charles's *The Duty of Disobedience to Wicked Laws* (1851) had lost him his pastorate. All this served as an immediate prelude to *The Conflict*, which we may suppose was read initially because it was by a Beecher.

Once read, it surprised many readers, especially, as King said, serious ones. They were surprised that *this* Beecher, in whom previously the "conservative feeling and thought of the family-stock" seemed "concentrated," had written such a book. Edward Beecher had "always been reckoned a man of such substantial orthodoxy, such cool judgement, wide learning, and gravity of sense, as to stand for a

counter-weight to the unreliable impulses of his kindred";
he had been thought of as the "contribution made by the
family blood to established ideas," the family "pledge"
that it was not "theologically lawless"; by the "weight and
stamina of his allegiance" to orthodoxy, he had seemed to
atone for the "rhetorical and emotional friskiness" of other
Beechers. His book violated expectations. It "startled the
community" of serious readers because it revealed the inner torment that one of orthodoxy's prominent and stable
advocates had endured for twenty-five years.[29]

Second, and perhaps most complicated of the explanations, Beecher wrote as a conservative abolitionist. He dramatically admitted, even insisted that the psychological
and, in part, the social conflict of the Civil War generation
was the consequence of systems of the universe which, having evolved inadequately out of orthodoxy's inadequacy,
were inadequate to the demands made upon them—a situation everyone had felt but nobody fully realized. Beecher
not only had diagnosed, but wished to heal, the dislocation
between revolutionary hopes and reactionary theology in
his time. To be sure, his social intentions were not so explicit in 1853 as in 1860, when in *The Concord of Ages* he
would emphasize his belief that the "prevailing tempta-
tion" to accept the "law of force and injustice on which
slavery is based" was not "properly resisted by any adequate counterpoise in the character of God, as presented
in the common systems of Christianity." The orthodox
God, he would say then, seems "guilty of worse deeds than
those of any despots or slaveholders of any age"; He is

---

29. Thomas Starr King, Review of *The Conflict, The Universalist Quarterly and General Review*, XI (January 1854), 34–35. King's review was reprinted as a pamphlet.

"defended on no better principles." Without a new and "moral" God, it will be "utterly impossible" to give the "public mind that moral tone" which will inevitably lead to the destruction of all the "despotisms of organized force" that have for so long oppressed men.[30] In 1860 Beecher and his readers were thinking particularly of the despotism of slavery. I suggest that in 1853 most of the reviewers of *The Conflict*, though they tried to camouflage the anti- or pro-slavery clue to their response, were also very aware of the social issues Beecher's theology was meant to raise. What in their reviews often seems theological pettifogging or ecclesiastical politicking may be taken more precisely and more profitably, though of course only partially, as disguised response to social issues, particularly slavery and abolition.

Finally, and most extensively, out of the reviews themselves came the explanation of their multiplicity and significance. They offer superabundant, often explicit, confirmation that Beecher was right in thinking his was the characteristic experience of his time, in supposing that the experience of his generation followed an explicable pattern and sequence. In telling his personal truth he was telling everyone's.

But if nearly everyone assented to his perception of conflict, hardly anyone accepted his synthesis. Beecher found, as we may, no result of the publication of *The Conflict* more "striking or instructive" than its reviewers' "general development and elaboration" of their "theories of the universe." Their points of view ranged from Charles Hodge's reactionary old-school orthodoxy, through new-school orthodoxy, Universalism, and Unitarianism, to the senior

30. EB, *Concord*, pp. 465–466.

Henry James's radical Swedenborgian revisionism. (And in nearly every case, as Beecher would say in 1860, there was a correlation between the theology and the politics of the reviewer: certain attitudes toward the universe implied certain attitudes toward slavery, and vice versa.) Such an extensive "promulgation of opposing theories" provided for Beecher inescapable proof of "the reality, importance, and practical connection with real life" of the "miniature models" of the universe by which men organized their experience. By "real life," we may understand, he meant both the inner life of the individual and the public life of a society.[31]

As usual, there were personal and therefore partially irrelevant motives behind some of the reviews. E. A. Park, writing in the *Bibliotheca Sacra*, the scholarly new-school journal in which a number of Beecher's preliminary articles had appeared, protested that Beecher's "candor" failed where one would "least expect it to fail, in behalf of those with whom he has been thought to sympathize," that is, the new school.[32] Beecher's lack of "justice" in attacking his friends and praising his enemies was protested also in the *New Englander*, by Leonard Bacon, a new-school conservative abolitionist. Bacon hit as well upon a theme that would run throughout the reviews of *The Conflict*. The book, he said, by its "compressed thought," "vigorous diction," and clarity had commended itself "to the attention of many intelligent minds, who are not usually attracted by strictly theological publications." It influence, therefore, "is thus multiplied beyond computation." It not

31. EB, *Concord*, p. 212.
32. E. A. Park, "Dr. Beecher's Conflict of Ages," *Bibliotheca Sacra*, XI (1854), 187.

only would receive "the admiration of the most eminent scholars for its ability and erudition"—particularly for the historical outline of the conflict, never surpassed for "breadth and accuracy, by any history of doctrine"—but its influence on the theologically uninitiated would be incalculable. The "great peril" was that Beecher had insisted that other reconciliations of the conflict, including that of new-school orthodoxy, were "absolutely false." If, as Bacon supposed, "droll conceits and ridiculous images" were being fashioned in "witty brains" to "pelt" the doctrine of pre-existence and thus demolish it, would that not leave with nothing all those who took *The Conflict* seriously? If Beecher's only alternatives were pre-existence or doom, and if pre-existence were not acceptable, what remained but doom?[33]

Beecher had no objection to the reviews by Park and Bacon, who were, after all, friends presumably saying as much favorable about *The Conflict* as conscience would allow. But in other new-school reviews the tone was more disconcerting. Both the New York *Evangelist* and his own journal, the *Congregationalist*, reverted to what Beecher called "pious ignorance" in meeting his arguments. "We say there is a solution," said the *Congregationalist*, "but it is unrevealed, and we submit to remain in ignorance." Beecher saw ominous portents in the new tone because it was the same as that of the old-school reviewers, especially Charles Hodge. Hodge's critique in the *Princeton Review*, Beecher asserted (quite incorrectly), represented the only "serious and formal effort" to reply to his book.

Hodge had at first in half-serious irony hailed *The Con-*

33. [Leonard Bacon], Review of *The Conflict, New Englander*, XII (February 1854), 160–163.

flict "as an ally," just as the Unitarians would later, but for very different reasons. Beecher "concedes," Hodge said,

that the Old-school doctrine as to the nature of sin, and the natural state of man, is the doctrine of the Church, of the Bible, and of Christian experience. This is much. These admissions, coming from such a [new-school] source, cannot fail to produce a strong impression.

The new-school reviewers had seen Beecher's real alternatives as pre-existence or doom. Hodge saw them as pre-existence or old-school orthodoxy and, rejecting pre-existence, found Beecher, nominally a new-school man, willy-nilly supporting the old-school side of the orthodox debate. He was, of course, distorting Beecher's point. Beecher did not "concede" the old-school doctrine of the nature and extent of sin; he asserted it. To illustrate his position he could appropriately have cited a now-famous review in the *Literary World* of August 1850, in which Herman Melville, writing of Hawthorne, contended that "no deeply thinking mind" can be free from "visitations, in some shape or other," of the "Calvinistic sense of Innate Depravity and Original Sin." The problem in Beecher's book was to go *beyond* the weak old-school attempt to justify sin and evil, to try to square man's depravity with the principles of honor and right. If Hodge had a "better cause," Beecher wrote, "he could afford to rise above such verbal quibbling."

But the irony and quibbling were only a preface to Hodge's real objections. He execrated at length the "unbelieving spirit" which underlay Beecher's image of God. Beecher's "grand design seems to be to bring down God's nature and dispensation to the level of human comprehension," setting up "the standard of human judgment as the rule by which God is to be judged." Beecher's constant mention of God as "being subject to law," as being bound by the principles of honor and right, "just as though he were a creature," outraged Hodge. "This mode of thought and expression," he said, "is not only highly irreverent, but incompatible with the true idea of God." God, he insisted, "cannot be bound." Beecher was settling wrongly the "old alternative, God or man." One or the other must be sovereign, and it could not be man. "The first and most indispensable condition of piety," Hodge concluded, "is submission—blind, absolute, entire submission of the intellect, the conscience, the life, to God." "The Lord reigns."[34]

Just as *The Conflict* was written to "revolutionize the world" by developing an orthodox system of the universe compatible with the reform impulse disturbing Beecher's generation—thereby resolving the conflicts within the orthodox church—so the old-school responses to the book, their "false and paralyzing" conception of God as well as their assertion of "pious ignorance," were written to deny Beecher's system and the reform impulse metaphysical validity. For Beecher, to repeat, the phenomenon was disturbing primarily because it was not confined to the old school, from which one might expect it. The new school, too—the group from which he expected to draw his support for social reform—retreated to the pious plea of ignorance. Is it not "wonderful," he asked, "that the leaders of the conflicting parties of the orthodox are so unwontedly unani-

34. The *Congregationalist*'s comment is quoted by EB, *Concord*, pp. 350–351. For the identification of Hodge as the reviewer, see *Concord*, p. 385; see also pp. 389, 397. [Charles Hodge], Review of *The Conflict*, *Princeton Review*, N. S., XXVI (January 1854), 96–97, 126, 135, 138. Hodge presumably also wrote the preliminary notice: see *ibid.*, XXV (October 1853), 687–690.

mous and harmonious in their retreat to the domains of mystery"? Their syllogisms, unreliable though they may be, unhappily agree: God, not man, must rule; God is mystery; God's rule is therefore mysterious. If in the universe there is injustice—the institution of slavery, for instance—it ought to be accepted and submitted to. It derives from God's mysterious will, and will ultimately result in good.[35]

Such antireform motives lurked in varying shades of visibility behind the other orthodox reviews. After objecting on much the same grounds as Hodge to Beecher's apparently blasphemous image of God, *The Christian Review*, an orthodox Baptist journal, insisted that there was probably "no such thing as pure individualism," as the reformers thought and as Beecher in his one-hundred-page analysis of the doctrine of the fall in Adam seemed to think. To contend for pure individualism—as opposed to the unity of the race in Adam's fall—is to suppose that men alone are capable of deciding their own destiny, that men can do without God—which is atheism. The theory of preexistence springs from "pantheism"; it is "inexpressibly ludicrous" and "intensely horrible"; the "whole thing," the reviewer observed as if it were the final radical heresy, "is a transcendental speculation." To be sure, the reviewer admitted, we must all fear the bottomless abyss of darkness and despair into which one falls when he loses his faith in the mysterious God. We must do Beecher "justice." His "very rashness and dogmatism" have an "air of nobleness and generosity" and at the "hazard of his reputation" he has thrown himself into what appears to him to be "the imminent deadly breach" in order to save "the very citadel

35. EB, *Concord*, pp. 292–293, 351.

of truth." But finally, since the book denies that mystery is "involved in all things," Beecher must be taken as an enemy, not an ally; he offers an "immense concession to the Unitarians."[36]

David N. Lord, editor of the orthodox millennialist *Theological and Literary Journal,* continued the anti-reform motif in the longest periodical review of Beecher's book, writing that *The Conflict* was "utterly false and revolting," that it bespoke a "wild hallucination, rather than sobriety of mind." Lord took great pains to "refute" Beecher's pre-existence hypothesis and his position on the nature of sin. He attacked Beecher's pride in "arraigning the Infinite One" at the "bar of his intellect" and scoffed at the "principles of typology" Beecher employed in interpreting scripture metaphorically. He proceeded to show that Beecher's theory was "wholly unsupported by evidence; that it is in the most open contradiction to the Scriptures; that it has no adaptation to the end for which he advances it; that it involves the most awful accusations of God." He asked, in summary:

What faith can be put in the reasonings, what confidence can be felt in the judgment of one, who is so utterly regardless of the laws of logic; who is the victim of such shallow and fanatical delusions! The whole idea, indeed, of seeking a solution of the difficulties of the present system by a theory of pre-existence, is a consummate self-contradiction and absurdity. . . . A maniac might attempt such a task; a man of sense surely would not.

The violence of Lord's language may suggest that the real issue was not simply a logical one, however. As Lord put it, whether Beecher's views were true or false "is a

36. Review of *The Conflict, The Christian Review,* XIX, No. 75 (January 1854), 108, 113, 117–118, 124–125.

question of infinite moment." Lord took the refutation of Beecher so seriously because, if Beecher's map of the universe was right, his was wrong. His own solution to the contradictions of orthodoxy involved a vision of the millennium, in which this world and "myriads and millions" like it served as God's "great experiment." The universe was a gigantic testing ground where a "vast display" of the "heart of man natural and regenerate" was being made. After multiple tests, all things would be "made new" and a reign of bliss would "extend through the vast round of a prophetic millennium, or three hundred and sixty-five thousand years." The testing cycle would then resume briefly until God rang in eternal "blessedness." The "present dispensation" was thus explained "in the office it fills as a necessary preparative."[37]

Lord's wildly speculative resolution of the conflict of his age was much like that of Universalism in that it looked to a future event to justify present misery. But it differed from Beecher's resolution, and from the one Universalism offered, at a critical point: Beecher and the Universalists proposed a cosmology laden with nineteenth-century concepts of justice, of "honor and right," and demanded that men act politically as if they were made in a just God's image; Lord meant to lead men to accept the present dispensation as a necessary, and therefore good, prelude to the future. Beecher and the Universalists urged reform, even revolution; Lord's system was a mask for his repudiation of the reform impulse.

The reviews of Park, Bacon, Hodge, *The Christian Re-*

---

37. David N. Lord, Review of *The Conflict,* in two sequential issues of *The Theological and Literary Journal,* VI (April 1854) and VII (July 1854), 584, 607–615; 57–58, 64, 72, 85–86.

view, and Lord do not exhaust the orthodox responses to *The Conflict.* Professor H. B. Smith of Union Theological Seminary, in a review in the new-school *Presbyterian Quarterly Review,* accurately predicted that, far from "adjusting" the conflict of the age, Beecher's book would "only be the signal for a renewal of hostilities on the same old battle-ground";[38] the old-school *Presbyterian Magazine* could not agree that Beecher's "freak of the imagination" was a "harmless piece of folly," as others had said, and put Beecher at the end of a long line of "opposers, skeptics, and madmen" who have "stumbled, and fallen into absurdity";[39] the editors of the *Puritan Recorder* (old-school competitor of the *Congregationalist,* which Beecher had earlier and privately described as "dull" and unrepresentative of New England Congregationalism) "fundamentally and perseveringly misrepresented" the book to the point that Beecher felt compelled to resign from the *Congregationalist* to avoid discrediting it;[40] and the New York *Observer,* the *Independent,* the *Evangelist,* and (for a second time) the *Congregationalist* were all negative. All fit to some degree the ideological pattern established by the major reviews.

38. "Pre-existence of Souls," *Presbyterian Quarterly Review,* II, No. 8 (March 1854), 590; quoted in "Life," pp. 216–217, where CB attributes the review to Smith. CB's summary judgment of the review, deleted in the manuscript, was that, though presumably "over fifty pages coming from a New School man," it was "more old-school than the Old school"; EB's judgment, more general, appears in *The Concord,* pp. 568–569, where the journal is mistakenly called the "Philadelphia Quarterly."

39. Review of *The Conflict, Presbyterian Magazine,* IV (January 1854), 38–39.

40. EB to HWB, Boston, October 5, 1848 (Yale). EB, Letter of Resignation from the *Congregationalist,* December 9, 1853, reproduced in "Life," pp. 225–226.

Beecher felt that only one or two orthodox reviewers, at most, "professed to answer" his arguments and that even those were "exceedingly hasty, limited, and superficial," not to say "utterly inconclusive." But perhaps his father described the situation more perceptively when, in one of his lighter moments, he admitted his son had "destroyed the Calvinistic barns" but hoped Beecher would not "delude" himself into thinking that the animals would go into his "little theological hencoop."[41] None of the reviewers on the orthodox farm, as even a brief survey indicates, wanted to enter; they balked. But on other farms, those of the Universalist and Unitarian liberals, for example, or even the Swedenborgian radicals, the hencoop appealed to many. With a little modification here, a paint job there, it might do.

13

What is there "peculiar" about *The Conflict*, Hosea Ballou, a Universalist reviewer, asked, "to put all our tongues and pens in motion, and to keep them in motion?" Why have the Universalists responded in what seems so "disproportioned" a fashion?

Ballou was asking his question in response to the book he was reviewing, Moses Ballou's *The Divine Character Vindicated*, itself a reply to *The Conflict*. He was as well reminding his readers of the many short Universalist reviews that had lately appeared (as, for example, a review in the *Ladies' Repository* where Beecher was anecdotally compared to a spiritualist medium); of the series of essays

---

41. EB, *Concord*, pp. 347, 404; LB, quoted, but undocumented, by Lyman Beecher Stowe, *op. cit.*, p. 70.

(later collected in a book) by Sylvanus Cobb in *The Christian Freeman,* the journal of which Cobb was editor; and of the "exceedingly brilliant" pamphlet by Thomas Starr King, Theodore Parker's friend. Ballou's answer was that *The Conflict* came as a "disclosure," as "testimony to a fact known, and grievously felt, and no longer endurable." It "lays bare" in the "very core of our common Orthodoxy" the "same intolerable conflict" the Universalists had often "logically proved" and the orthodox as often "denied." Now here, in Beecher's book, the conflict is "at length frankly and solemnly avowed as a fact of actual experience." Beecher's "full utterance" of the groan of a generation long "conscious of intolerable offence in their theology" demonstrates conclusively that "Somehow and somewhere, the Creed is at war with the Divine Perfections. So much may now be regarded as fact, rather than a mere conclusion from reasoning."[42]

The Universalists, then, viewed with satisfaction "the novel spectacle in New England, now, of a man clinging with a masterly grasp, to all the fundamentals of Orthodoxy," yet strengthening the position of "those who rebel against it." Beecher's "ardently zealous" advocacy had ironically dealt orthodoxy a blow "beneath which it reels as it has seldom done under any heretic's arm." Beecher

---

42. Hosea Ballou, *op. cit.*, pp. 115–116. Moses Ballou's *The Divine Character Vindicated, A Review, &c* (New York: J. S. Redfield, 1854) was reviewed also in *The Christian Review*, XIX, No. 77 (July 1854), 468; in *Harper's Magazine*, IX (June 1854), 135; and in the *Presbyterian Quarterly Review*, III (December 1854), 525–526. For the anecdote about the spiritualist medium, see the *Ladies' Repository*, XXII (January 1854), 237. Sylvanus Cobb's book, *Review of the Conflict of Ages, by Edward Beecher, D.D.: and an Exhibition of the Gospel Harmony* (Boston: The Author, 1854), was reviewed, *ibid.* (March 1854), 358. King's pamphlet, *op. cit.*, was also reviewed, *ibid.* (April 1854), 397.

had done exactly what Leonard Bacon feared. By positing "Orthodoxy *plus* pre-existence," as King wrote in the most able of the liberal reviews, "or, as the alternative, a hopeless wrestle with the noble elements of human nature," Beecher had destroyed what he was trying to save, for pre-existence could be accepted by only one in fifty thousand, and about one in a million of "even the Orthodox." He had inadvertently proven, the Universalists thought, the validity of Universalism.[43]

The Universalists, disapproving of Beecher's defense of eternal damnation, were not alone in their interest in Beecher's handling of life after death, the area of their solution to the conflict. Jacob Blain and Robert W. Landis were also interested. But if the Universalists thought Beecher's advocacy of the traditional doctrine of damnation unacceptable, Blain, a Baptist minister from Buffalo, who in 1856 wrote in pamphlet form *A Review, Giving the Main Ideas in Dr. E. Beecher's Conflict of Ages and A Reply to Them and to His Many Reviewers*, thought Beecher did not go far enough in the other direction. Blain was a "destructionist," one of about a hundred such clerical advocates in the United States. As if he had heard Lyman Beecher talk about the Calvinist barns, he rejoiced that Beecher's book had appeared, "for, to use a comparison, the Doctor has, with a giant hand, torn down the old house, and as his new one affords no shelter, many, seeing they are houseless, will, by re-examining the Bible, set about erecting a new and better one, and cease to patch up the old deformed fabric." Blain's pamphlet nearly became an outright defense of Beecher's "magnanimous and far-reaching mind" against all his reviewers. Plainly, so far as Blain was concerned, Beecher had hit upon the

43. King, *op. cit.*, pp. 36, 68.

clue to the times. Blain quoted "friends" who said so; he cited approvingly reviewers who said so; he proved that his hero Albert Barnes also experienced Beecher's "anguish of spirit"; he insisted that many, like Beecher and Barnes (and Blain), have "struggled with traditionary opinions and feelings . . . for years, and searched to learn from the Bible God's purpose as to the existence of evil." Beecher, however, had only come close to the "real" solution. Had he "used his discriminating mind to discover which the Bible teaches, endless woe, or destruction, he would have found the latter to be the fact." Blain could "but hope he will employ his logical powers in this way ere long."[44] Robert W. Landis, a Presbyterian clergyman from Ionia, Michigan, thought, unlike the Universalists and Blain, that Beecher had been foolishly complicated. He could not see how a man of Beecher's "confessed ability," after twenty years' work, had failed to realize that any intelligent antagonist could "sweep the theory" of pre-existence "utterly away, root and branch." Why, he asked in his "handbook" study of *The Immortality of the Soul and the Final Condition of the Wicked Carefully Considered*, bring "forth into galvanic reviviscence the old incarnate-devil theory" from the "putrid charnel-house in which it had long lain entombed" when a simple affirmation of the Biblical doctrine of eternal punishment would suffice to resolve the conflict?[45]

Though Blain and Landis shared with the Universalists a concern for Beecher's treatment of the afterlife, their attitude toward reform, particularly abolitionism, cannot

44. Blain's title continues: *to which is Added, the Bible Meaning of the Word Hell. Also, Two Hundred Texts Quoted, to Show the Nature of Future Punishment. Op. cit.*, front cover advertisement, pp. 1, 20, 29–31.

45. New York: Carlton and Porter, 1859; 5th ed.; New York: Carlton and Lanahan, 1868, pp. 22, 23n.

be defined by reading their reviews. Between the Universalists and the orthodox, however, the differences were not merely theological quibbles over the "right" interpretation of Beecher. It was no rhetorical accident, we may be sure, that when Moses Ballou, in his four-hundred-page Universalist Vindication of God from Beecher's supposed aspersions, noted that for "ages on ages has a false theology interposed like a dark cloud between the human soul and the sunlight of Divine Love," he clarified the imagery of light and dark by pointing out that "Crouchingly and servile as a whipped slave have men crept" to the altar of the orthodox God. Nor was it rhetorical accident when, in objecting to Beecher's analysis of Romans, Thomas Starr King compared it to "hoisting the proem of the Declaration of Independence over a slave-auction."[46] Images such as these appear frequently throughout the Universalist commentary on Beecher's system. It cannot be accident that all the Universalist reviewers, agreeing with Beecher's chart of his generation's experience, were antislavery men and universal reformers. They identified orthodoxy with political paralysis and regarded Beecher's attempt to revitalize orthodoxy, therefore, as well-meaning but futile. To celebrate Beecher's analysis of orthodoxy's inadequacy, then to deny his attempt at revision, was to strike a blow for one's social and political, as well as one's theological, ideals.

Like the Universalists, the Unitarians saw the significance of the book in its source. That the "new exposure" of orthodoxy's contradictions and inadequacy should come from a "faithful and esteemed" orthodox minister, a Beecher, was immensely important. It demonstrated from the inside that orthodoxy was "fast losing its hold upon the

---

46. Moses Ballou, *op. cit.*, pp. 163–164. King, *op. cit.*, p. 61.

convictions of all classes of society," even its leaders. George Ellis, editor of the Unitarian *Christian Examiner*, thought the book so important that he was willing to propose that one half of the $50,000 the Unitarians were raising to circulate their own books be spent instead on "dissemination" of *The Conflict*.

Ellis admitted that *The Conflict* had deficiencies: three of them, to be precise. The hypothesis of pre-existence, he said first, while it might "relieve" orthodoxy's theoretical problem, could not be believed and therefore would not, in fact, ease the agony of the orthodox experience. Second, the world could not properly be conceived as a "moral hospital," as Beecher wished; the world was rather a great school in which God "educate[s] us morally"; and no teacher, not even a divine one, would be so foolish as to attempt to educate the totally depraved. Finally, then, Beecher sought "recourse to that same plea of mystery" he ostensibly attacked, in a total depravity which did not exist. But even with its deficiencies, Ellis said, perhaps because of them, *The Conflict* awarded a "triumph" to Unitarianism. It was "the most important contribution which has been made for years to our religious literature." No one could fail to be impressed with Beecher's presentation of the "terrific power of evil as exhibited in the social and organic relations of men, in governments, in cities, families, society, and business"; nor was Beecher's attempt to solve "great religious and social problems," noted in his Dedication, less impressive. If Beecher finally failed, he nevertheless had made clear the increasing awareness in orthodox ranks that a solution was desperately needed.[47]

47. Ellis made the proposal to spend Unitarian money on disseminating *The Conflict* in his later bibliographical survey, *op. cit.* His own review appeared in *The Christian Examiner*, 4th ser., XX (November 1853), 394–395, 408, 417, 419, 422, 425.

The liberal Universalist and Unitarian reviewers' responses to *The Conflict* disturbed the orthodox community, and the more the liberals took Beecher as an inadvertent ally, the more the orthodox reviewers felt it necessary to defend his orthodoxy. The *Congregationalist,* no doubt sensing that in defending its former editor it was defending itself, in an article attacking Thomas Starr King said that the liberal reviewers were superficial, that they swam "continually in a surface current, without ever diving into the deep sea of thought." *The Conflict* would never "convert the world" to pre-existence, and, though when "skimmed" by a "sketchy pamphleteer" it might seem decidedly liberal, finally it was a "very unsafe book for heresiarchs to put into the hands of either Universalist or Unitarian . . . accustomed to deep and serious thought"—if, that is, there were any of that kind. The book describes an inner conflict, the *Congregationalist* article continued, "the yawning gulf of whose demand will take in a thousand petty and unsubstantial theories like those of the lexicography and metaphysics of the modern 'liberal' schools, and still yawn as before." When one was able really to sympathize with the experience of evil that Beecher described, the orthodox paper concluded, he would be a "hard man" to satisfy with a soft theology, certainly not with Unitarianism or Universalism.[48]

Beecher no doubt agreed with the *Congregationalist*'s critique of liberalism, as indeed he had probably agreed in part with the liberals' rejection of orthodoxy. Each reviewer, to this point, had taken the predictable and characteristic position his theology and politics implied. But a final group of reviewers was more difficult to assimilate.

48. Quoted in "Life," pp. 221–222.

Though the ideology of their response was similar to that of the liberals, they were for the most part members of no religious institution, defenders of no church's vested interest. And often orthodoxy had for them distinctly attractive virtues.

Hiram Parker's *The Harmony of Ages* perhaps best illustrates the strange, unpredictable mixture of idea and emotion part of this group represents. Parker, a doctor of medicine and for years a member in good standing of the Baptist church in Lowell, Massachusetts, wrote against Beecher's theology out of conviction, not out of professional necessity; he said he had no idea of publishing a book when he began, but a book was finished in the summer of 1855 and published in 1856.[49] The theory it contained, wrought out in opposition to Beecher, was unorthodox, eccentric, amateur, and in its stylistic obscurity and disorganization nearly incomprehensible. In general, it offers insight into the chaotic and incoherent systems into which the conflict of Beecher's generation forced some men.

Specifically, Parker found "perfectly absurd" and a "subterfuge" Beecher's attempt to reconcile the "character of God with the condition of man" through pre-existence. He could agree that man and society were depraved. He could even assent to Beecher's rejection of the doctrine of the fall as an explanation of evil, for, like Beecher and

49. The full title of Parker's book is *The Harmony of Ages: A Thesis on the Relations between the Conditions of Man and the Character of God* (Boston: John P. Jewett and Company, 1856). I quote below from pp. iii, v, 4–5, 8–10, 43, 47, 126, 241, 268, 328. Biographical information on Parker is available in *Old Residents Historical Association*, II (1888), 442–443, according to Mr. Hugh F. Downey, librarian of the City Library of Lowell, Massachusetts, who kindly provided me with it.

others, he had his own explanation. Evil and sin, he said, entered the universe through "transmission." The theory of transmission would explain "those phenomena which are now regarded as mysteries, and reduce the now dark problems of nature to that simplicity" we all seek.

The theory had three stages. First, the mental and moral "condition" of parents "at the time of conception" is transmitted to the offspring. Second, the "mind of the mother" exerts an "influence on the foetus during uterogestation." Finally, the education of the offspring may modify his genetically inherited "predisposition." Thus, each "generation is responsible for the influence which it exerts on the next succeeding one, in transmitting to it the tendencies of its constitution." This, Parker contended, provides a better explanation of the existence of evil than pre-existence. Like O. W. Holmes's medicated character, the snake-bitten Elsie Venner, Parker's characteristic man was predisposed to evil (but not necessarily evil, since not God but the previous generation, and specifically parents, are at fault; and they may by an act of will "transmit" good as well as evil, though they do not). Such an argument naturally led Parker to deal with the first generation, and the first parents, Adam and Eve. Adam entered Paradise totally innocent; "something" in his environment led to the fall; the fall was fortunate: the "world," Parker said, "is better than it would have been had Adam never been subjected to a test for the development of his character." God is not, therefore, to be blamed; He is to be praised. And the "only difference between Adam and his posterity consists in a farther perversion of the faculties of his descendants, who inherited the tendencies of their perverted constitutions"—"inherited" them, that is, in the same way biological characteristics are inherited.

Parker felt that by developing the theory of the genetic transmission of morality he could show there never had been a conflict between God and man in the first place; the *real* "conflict of ages" was among theologians (even though he himself felt the conflict and described it in another part of the book). His system, able to explain the "predisposition" of a man to drunkenness, provided a rationale for the temperance movement. It also implied a solution to the slavery controversy: if Caucasians and Africans intermarried for five generations, the color and features of both would be modified; intermarriage would not violate but, on the contrary, would preserve the "harmony of the laws of nature." The theory, in short, seems on the one hand to be a medicated version of orthodoxy (the practical difference between "transmission" and "imputation" is slight) and on the other hand, like Beecher's book, to be motivated by the reform impulse. It illustrates, in a way that Beecher's book does not, the fantasies which some segments of the nominally orthodox (in Parker's case, Baptist) community conceived in order to justify at once their traditional vision of evil and their sense of urgency about social reform.

Beecher himself had admitted in *The Conflict* that certain aspects of human depravity are "transmitted by the material system." But, he said, as if trying to pre-empt Parker's argument, the central elements of *"a sinful spirit,"* namely "pride, selfishness, self-will, envy, and the like," do not "rise and sink in successive generations"; nor was it "reasonable" to suppose it in the "power of matter, or any law of generation, to originate or to remove them."[50] In a sense, then, Beecher had unknowingly anticipated

50. EB, *Conflict*, pp. 543–544. For a discussion of the transmission theory, see H. Shelton Smith, *op. cit.*

Parker's theory, just as he had knowingly anticipated the sectarian objections to his theory and the alternate solutions he rightly suspected would be offered. He had shown that they were, and would continue to be, inadequate; there would invariably be a justifiable reaction to them. He did not, however, foresee two other independent book-length reviews of *The Conflict*, both by Swedenborgians, both remarkably provocative.

Henry Weller's *The Conflict of Ages Ended* appeared first in successive issues (from July 1, 1854, to June 15, 1855) of his Swedenborgian journal, *The Crisis*. Copies were sent to Beecher from Indiana, where they originated, so that if they failed to do him justice, Beecher could comment before the book was published.[51] Weller was sure, however, that objections could "hardly occur" (and evidently rightly so; Beecher said nothing of Weller in *The Concord*) because the book was meant, not as a critique of, but as a "Succedaneum" or substitute for *The Conflict*. Weller wished "no controversy with the book itself." He would "descend to no verbal criticisms." He would "merely take certain leading principles" that Beecher had "fully and forcibly enunciated" as the "groundwork" for a "new construction of the entire question," hoping to "lead the way to a termination of the conflict."

51. The title of Weller's book continues: *A Succedaneum to Beecher's "Conflict of Ages," in which the Great Question of the Moral Relations of God and Man is Treated upon New and Catholic Principles* (LaPorte, Ind.: J. S. Weller and Brothers, 1855). I quote below from pp. 13, 20, 53, 59–60, 69–70, 80, 274–279. We may take the manner of Weller's publication of his differences with EB as representative of one important way that word of the new system was spread. Weller, like Sylvanus Cobb, both serialized his book in his own journal and offered an extensive summary of *The Conflict*. He realized that he would "reach numbers who will not see the work of Beecher's" (p. 46).

Like Beecher, Weller too had gone through agonizing inner experiences. He also had been "perplexed beyond measure, and utterly lost in the conflicting claims" of orthodoxy and Unitarianism. He had felt himself "tossed between two contending forces" without a way to "escape" the "dilemma"—until, that is, he discovered Swedenborg. But he had not discovered Swedenborg for twenty years, during part of which time he remained with the Unitarianism he had been brought up in. He had "retained" Unitarianism's "doctrines and philosophy" until what then seemed a "brighter light dawned," namely "The Church of God," commonly known as "Free-thinking Christians." The "cold, external and artificial condition" of Unitarianism had led a "number of ardent, enterprising young men to come out" from it and to try to "place religion in life, rather than in outward forms and ceremonies." They "organized upon the simple laws collected from the New Testament." Their "entire object" was to be a "living" church, each member to "devote himself to his own and his brother's improvement." And it seemed in the "enthusiasm of a new effort" that the new church would be the "instrument of regenerating the world."

But the new church, Weller wrote describing his own reaction, erroneously held that human nature began neither evil nor good (the *"equally balanced* system"). Its theology could not explain the "slumbering passions," the "conflict and division" that periodically seemed to deny the group's "great hopes" for "improvement in the general state" of society. The theology "placed its main reliance on human principle and power" and "ignored" the elementary and "great facts of human depravity." As a consequence, the new church, dedicated to changing the very structure of society, sank "into a mere worldly business organization." Out of it came only "shallow reforms," and Weller felt obliged to abandon it. He felt he must return somehow to the "deep radical religious feeling" embodied in the orthodox church. Only that could be worthy of one's "reverence and admiration."

Sanctified by so many associations of piety and learning as cluster around the institutions of the great orthodox church—its *frame-work* still towers majestically heavenward. There is a power somewhere, which modern off-shoots from the parent stem have not inherited. And this power lies in the deep abasing views of human ruin, which lead the soul to an unlimited refuge and trust in God, instead of the flimsy and self-sufficient human schemes and inventions with which our modern reforming churches abound. . . . it is, I say, refreshing to turn to these remnants of a great decaying church, from the sickening cant of human greatness[,] the dignity of human nature, self-culture, self-made men—architects of character and fortune and destiny—all exalting the mere creature, and putting the great Creator in the back ground.

Weller, in short, came to feel the same sense of need for theological reform that Beecher felt, though he arrived at that feeling from the opposite direction, by way of Unitarianism. Orthodoxy's sense of human depravity was necessary, but as his experience as a Unitarian and a freethinker had made him particularly aware, so too were the "principles of Divine equity and honor" Beecher was seeking. Those very principles, however, had become the "lever that broke up the crust of New England orthodoxy, and upheaved its elements with a convulsion that has shook its foundations, and scattered its landmarks so that its own conservators scarcely know where to find them." Where, then, if neither the new principles nor the old orthodoxy alone would do, and if it was in fact the new which broke up the old, might one find the synthesis he so desperately needed?

Surely not, Weller argued, in *The Conflict*. Beecher offered something only a "little better or more endurable" than the orthodoxy he attempted to supersede. He took an "intellectual, mechanical, sensuous view of the governing principles of the conflict." Despite the fact that Beecher's "struggles" were the "type" of the intellectual and emotional struggles of the age, despite Beecher's sincerity and effort, despite his extended discussion of "experience": despite all this, the "life-part" of the book was but an "undercurrent," there only for the purposes of "logical combat." Beecher's primary intention was to "get a *logical* consistency." His pre-existent "panacea" was an "unquestionable failure," in short, because it did not really appeal to the experience of men. The only satisfactory synthesis was to be found, not in Beecher, nor in the systems of Universalism, Unitarianism, new-school orthodoxy, and the rest—all sincere and the result of profound inner struggle—but in Swedenborg. Weller, able unlike Parker to put his perceptions in convincing language, argued brilliantly that orthodoxy survived (revised and satisfactorily) only in Swedenborgianism. There, original sin became "selfhood" (much like Hopkins's "selfishness"). And all the "depraved social organizations" of the world became "developments of the first great and only evil,—that of man appropriating to self what belongs to the Lord."

At about the same time Weller's book appeared, another Swedenborgian critique of *The Conflict* made much the same point. The elder Henry James's *The Nature of Evil* was finished in January 1855 and published during the spring of that year. The Baptist *Christian Review*, having followed the great debate for several years, thought James's contribution, which "propounds 'a new orthodoxy' " to replace the old one, a "philosophical and theological curiosity." James Freeman Clarke in a long and excellent review in the Unitarian *Christian Examiner* praised it as "a remarkable book by a remarkable man."[52] James's friend Emerson evidently also offered high praise, though unfortunately his letter to James has been destroyed at just the crucial place. James replied to Emerson on June 18, 1855:

What you say of my book is only another installment of your unequalled generosity, and I am not taken in. I have only to hear the book [*The Nature of Evil*] named by you, to feel at once how desperately faulty its form is. But I am past regrets on this score. I will do better in [the] future. But I have one astonishment to give you, which is, that the whole edition—1000 copies—is exhausted. To think of a book of that dullness as to subject, and that *thereforeiness* as to treatment, being sold to this extent in four months, gives one new hope in humanity.

The faulty form James mentions probably refers to his habit of "chromatizing," as Emerson described his style in another letter.[53] *The Nature of Evil* is a 348-page "letter"

52. Review of *The Nature of Evil*, *The Christian Review*, XX (1855), 299. James F. Clarke, "James on the Nature of Evil," *The Christian Examiner*, 4th ser., XXIV (July 1855), 116.

53. For Emerson's letter to James (May 4, 1855), see Ralph Barton Perry, *The Thought and Character of William James: As Revealed in Unpublished Correspondence and Notes, Together with His Published Writings* (Boston and Toronto: Little, Brown and Company, 1935), I, 78–79. For James's reply, see I, 81. Emerson's letter about James's "chromatizing" was written June 25, 1855; see Perry, I, 81–82. Responding earlier to a letter from another friend, James had written: "your frank and cordial approbation was nothing short of charming. . . . No soul but you has broken silence in that way, and I have a feeling of intense intellectual solitude. . . . the beast that is in all of us begs to be fed upon the rabble's applause. . . . I

to Edward Beecher in which James, as usual, plays all the notes on his philosophical piano one after the other, without giving them the standard expository form a large composition requires. The relatively large sale of his book may be explained by its place in the great debate: it was the latest addition to a popular controversy. But it was also James's best book to date. His earlier writings, as James himself said in 1855, represented "little more than a hearty outcry against established and insensate error, and a prophecy of advancing knowledge."[54] In *The Nature of Evil* James for the first time shaped what his famous children called "father's ideas" into a coherent system. Commentators on James, probably because they have not read the book in the context of the debate of which it was a part, have missed the point.[55] That James admittedly first forged his characteristic position as a critic of culture in response to *The Conflict of Ages* provides a dramatic instance of the general truth that the radical religionists of the nineteenth century invariably emerged from, and in opposition to,

---

fancy that our valorous defenders of Orthodoxy mean to give the book the go-by. However some of the larger periodicals may ultimately see fit to notice it. I shall go on to give them a richer dose next time. The subject of this book was someway too narrow, and when I came to prepare it for the printer, I was obliged to crowd out much matter which ought to go forth. . . . I shall try *The Church* next time, in all the breadth of its meaning." H. James, Sr., to S. G. Ward, March 16, 1855 (Houghton Library, Harvard University, quoted by permission of the Harvard College Library). The sale of *The Nature of Evil* as reported three months later may have made James feel less isolated and more encouraged to continue.

54. Henry James, Sr., "Preface" to *The Nature of Evil Considered in a Letter to the Rev. Edward Beecher, D.D. Author of "The Conflict of Ages"* (New York: D. Appleton and Company, 1855), p. 7.

55. The most important commentators are Austin Warren, *The Elder Henry James* (New York: Macmillan, 1934) and Frederick Harold Young, *The Philosophy of Henry James, Sr.* (New York: Bookman Associates, 1951).

some form of orthodoxy. Had not orthodoxy existed in the form it did, the Universalists, the Unitarians, and the Swedenborgians may have had to invent it.

As if to make the point, James began his critique of *The Conflict* by offering his "unfeigned sympathy" for Beecher's "intellectual struggles."[56] He could personally testify that Beecher's "theologic experience reflects that of numberless thousands." This book, of course, was not the place for full personal testimony, but if Beecher could have read James's *Autobiography* and letters, he would have found verification. As James wrote in the *Autobiography*, as a boy he did not really believe orthodoxy's "puerile and disgusting caricature of the gospel," but in being forced to endure "its authoritative imposition" he was scarred for life. At the same time, he found a partial truth in orthodoxy's sense of evil: "I believe Jonathan Edwards *redivivus* in true blue," he wrote Emerson, "would . . . make the best possible reconciler and critic of philosophy" today.[57] Like Beecher, then, James was attempting to revise orthodoxy, in this case into Swedenborgianism, not so much to escape it as to embody in it his sense of right.

Also like Beecher, James disliked everything about Unitarianism except its sense of social and cosmic morality. He wrote in the middle of *The Nature of Evil* that there were three modes of Christianity: Roman Catholicism, Protestantism, and Unitarianism. The first, "regarding Christ's work as insufficient to reunite man with God," interposed the "priestly viaticum." Protestantism, in rebellion against

56. James, *The Nature of Evil*, pp. 9–10.
57. Henry James, Sr., *Autobiography*, reprinted in F. O. Matthiessen, *The James Family* (New York: Alfred A. Knopf, 1948), p. 23. James to R. W. Emerson, New York, May 11, 1843, quoted by Matthiessen, p. 43.

such pretensions on the part of the church, made Christ not a redeemer of all men, as for James he was, but a redeemer only of "sanctified sinners." Protestantism turned Christ's universal redemption into "an exclusive possession of certain persons who are diligently exercised with religious hopes and fears, and hence into a religio-legal basis upon which one man is approved and another condemned by God." "Unitarianism may certainly be pardoned for rejecting a gospel so niggardly as this," James commented. But not content, Unitarianism denies the fall of man (and man's corruption), makes Christ into a mere higher Socrates, and "approximates man to God, by vacating Christianity as a *supernatural* method of salvation." All of which, for James, is tantamount to curing the hunger for a just universe "by pronouncing starvation impossible, and the demand for nourishment premature and illusory." Unitarianism, in short, "pours its consecrating oil upon the natural selfhood, and bids it aspire to immortal bliss"; it deifies morality and the self, a deification which for James was the essence of all evil. Even a doctrine like the pre-existence of souls was better than that.[58]

For James, doctrines like the pre-existence of souls and aberrations like spiritualism were the "inevitable logical fruit of the old Theology." Beecher's intentions were praiseworthy; James too wanted at once to liberate orthodoxy from its doctrinal caricature and to "calvinize" liberalism into a deeper perception of the evil of "moralism" (that is, an excessive valuation of the self). But the established theology to which Beecher still held "excludes any rational solution of the problem as to the nature and origin of Evil." Its "cosmological method," James said,

58. James, *The Nature of Evil*, pp. 165–173.

"unspiritualizes the Divine existence and operation, by reducing God to the dimensions of nature, or making creation a physical phenomenon." Its method finally is that of natural, not revealed, religion, and as such it cannot solve the problem of evil: if creation is merely a physical act of God, "the phenomena of the moral world become strictly unintelligible"; it becomes "instantly clear" that God alone is responsible for evil, and no theory of pre-existence which merely pushes back the time of God's responsibility can vindicate Him. Moreover, the established theology, as naturalistic, cannot provide a rationale for revolution. The idea which "incessantly stimulates political revolutions and reforms" is the idea of the "equality of man" in a justly governed universe. If one, for instance, puts a "merely pecuniary value" on his fellow-man—as slaveholders do on Negroes—one shuts himself "up in hell," to be sure, but naturalism justifies his act. One is neither a "good man" because he obeys the "behests of any government under the sun" nor a bad man because he disobeys. He is good or bad "exclusively" as he obeys or disobeys the "needs of society, the sentiment of human fellowship." The established, naturalistic theology cannot logically provide for these definitions of good and bad. "Your own book," James said in his book-length letter to Beecher, "may not literally prove the *last* gasp of that theology, but clearly, gasping is the only function that remains to it, until it is decently and tenderly interred out of human remembrance on the shelves of disused libraries."[59]

59. James, *The Nature of Evil*, pp. 12, 19–20, 90–91, 94–97, 111, 207. As early as the 1827 *Address*, EB had tried to protect himself from James's point that pre-existence cannot solve the problem of evil, by limiting God's power in the "moral universe." He may have replied cogently to James, but did not.

In suggesting that orthodoxy as he and Beecher knew it was ripe for burial, James was anticipating, if only a little. In fact, by the end of the Civil War, though most of them were still writing, not only Beecher but nearly all those participating in the great debate were to see their work relegated to the shelves of disused libraries. The miniature models of the universe that seemed so important to the public before the war, after the war seemed unrelated to the realities of American society. Disused and dead as they may be, however, *The Conflict* and the documents of the debate clarify a major cultural condition without which the Civil War, as we know it, would have been unthinkable. Beecher's concern, as nearly all his reviewers sensed, was to free the American church from its paralysis in confronting social corruption, particularly slavery. In the language of the twentieth-century historian Stanley Elkins, he was aware that the church as a "source both of organized social power and internal discipline" had in the thirties and forties undergone a "relentless process of fragmentation," that as an institution it was consequently unable to contribute much to the peaceful solution of the slavery controversy.[60] But Beecher was also aware, by virtue of his own experience of the relation between theology and political action in his time, that in part the church was fragmented precisely *because* it was attempting to respond to the slavery problem. The nature of the traditional orthodox theology blocked the church, as an institution, from performing its proper mediating function. To revise orthodoxy for revolution, or at least reform, such men as Beecher's liberal and radical reviewers found they could

60. Stanley M. Elkins, *Slavery: A Problem in American Institutional and Intellectual Life* (Chicago: University of Chicago Press, 1959), p. 28 ff.

do no less than reject it. In rejecting it they found ironically (and perhaps tragically) that they had lost their only
practical chance to save their society from schism and war.
The problem of the church and slavery—as nearly all of
Beecher's critics agreed in response to his analysis of his
generation's inner experience—was a problem of "systems
of the universe," ultimately a theological problem, inter-
mediately a biographical problem. Beecher, like the liberals attempting to rationalize action against slavery and
"thoroughly reorganize human society," but unlike them
attempting it while remaining orthodox, perhaps revealed
most clearly the irony of his generation's condition.

14

The irony in Beecher's case was compounded by his contribution to his sister Harriet's inadvertently divisive antislavery novels, *Uncle Tom's Cabin* (1852) and *Dred* (1856).
Perhaps, finally, that contribution was the most significant
and enduring consequence of his attempt to make politics
a matter of theology and theology a matter of politics.

Already, of course, the search for Mrs. Stowe's sources,
particularly her sources for *Uncle Tom's Cabin*, has been
penetrating. We have learned that Uncle Tom's prototype
was Josiah Henson; that Simon Legree's life counterpart
was described to Mrs. Stowe by her brother Charles, who
had lived for a while in Louisiana; that the models for the
Shelby family and Eliza lived in Kentucky, to which Mrs.
Stowe had on occasion traveled from Cincinnati; that Augustine St. Clare was drawn in the image of Lord Byron,
one of Mrs. Stowe's childhood idols; that Mrs. Stowe read
Theodore Weld's *American Slavery As It Is* (1839), the

major abolitionist compendium of facts detailing the evils of slavery; that she read Francis Trollope's antislavery novel, *The Life and Adventures of Jonathan Jefferson Whitlaw*, as well as Richardson, Defoe, Cervantes, and Scott.[61] The source list may be continued to great length. Mrs. Stowe herself tried to continue it in her 262-page *A Key to Uncle Tom's Cabin* (1853), written (with the help, I believe, of Edward Beecher) to prove the "truth" of her "pictures" of slavery.

But all inquirers into sources have been oblivious to what seems an obvious coincidence: namely that, at the very moment Mrs. Stowe in Brunswick, Maine, was hurrying through weekly installments of *Uncle Tom's Cabin*, her brother Edward was agonizing in his Boston study (to which, during the agony, Mrs. Stowe sometimes came) over the book he hoped would provide a revisionist theology for orthodox social action, particularly against slavery. Given that coincidence, perhaps a refocusing of the official account of the genesis of Mrs. Stowe's first novel may serve to redirect the search not only for her sources but for her meanings as well.

After leaving Edward Beecher's house in Boston, where she had met Henson and talked over the Fugitive Slave Law, Mrs. Stowe returned to Maine, where she received a letter from Beecher's wife: "Hattie," wrote Isabella Beecher, "if I could use a pen as you can, I would write something that will make this whole nation feel what an accursed thing slavery is." Mrs. Stowe read the letter to her

61. Charles H. Foster, *The Rungless Ladder* (Durham, N. C.: Duke University Press, 1954), pp. 13–22. In my comments on HBS here, as earlier, I depend heavily on Professor Foster, especially his chapter on *Uncle Tom's Cabin*, pp. 12–63.

children, crumpled it in her hand as she rose to her feet, and swore to write something—if she lived. A few months later, in February 1851, attending communion services at the First Parish Church in Brunswick, she had a vision of the scene that later became the flogging of Uncle Tom by Sambo and Quimbo at the direction of Simon Legree. She put this first "picture" on paper that night, and about a month later, with Calvin Stowe's blessing, she began to write the novel that would for the next year appear in weekly installments in the *National Era*. She told Beecher later that she wrote as if inspired by God, as if she were only His scribe. When the installments appeared as a book on March 20, 1852, *Uncle Tom's Cabin* sold 3,000 copies the first day, 20,000 in three weeks, and between two and three million in a year. Mrs. Stowe became the most celebrated novelist of her time. In some magical (though not, as she thought, divine) fashion, she had been able to shape the multiple fears, images, superstitions, and sentiments of her culture into significant form. After 1852, to think about slavery without thinking in the language and imagery of her novel would be impossible. She had defined by coalescence the terms of the public and political imagination of her time, insofar as it imagined slavery.

If this was one of her major achievements—if, that is, she defined the terms in which her society subsequently imagined slavery—then the appropriate questions to ask about her antislavery novels deal primarily, not with immediate sources (who was the prototype for a given character? how much did she know about slavery first hand? where did she get her facts?), but with the terms of her meaning: How did she understand slavery? Was there, implicit in her imagination and her novel, a theory to which she subscribed?

Charles H. Foster has shown in the best study of her books that in part Mrs. Stowe's attitude was as theory unarticulated, personal, and feminine. The leitmotif of *Uncle Tom's Cabin* is the separation of mother and child, or more generally, the separation of the family unit, as if the anguish and religious uncertainty that followed Mrs. Stowe's loss of her son during the 1849 cholera epidemic in Cincinnati were being exorcised in the writing of her novels. If the separation theme, by implicitly denying the validity of the southern defense of slavery as a patriarchal, beneficent institution, contributed to the abolitionist theory Mrs. Stowe was promoting, the contribution may well be biographical accident. Again, as Professor Foster has also pointed out, if she did have a theory, its "masculine bite" is clearly provided by Augustine St. Clare, whose economic analysis of slavery is reminiscent, if not of Marx, then at least of Orestes Brownson's essay on "The Laboring Classes" (1840). It may be that she found her theory, as Professor Foster suggests, in Brownson. After all, Augustine St. Clare, like Brownson, is a Roman Catholic; his theories sound more like Brownson's than those of any other American thinker Mrs. Stowe might have read; and St. Clare (surely not, as James Baldwin has influentially contended, Miss Ophelia) is, on the theoretical level of the novel, Mrs. Stowe's mouthpiece. But even such a minor matter as St. Clare's first name, Augustine, seems to point elsewhere. It was, we note, St. Augustine whom Beecher in *The Conflict of Ages* praised as the "master spirit," the "centre of revolution and of light."[62] Was it a clue to the source of her

62. EB, *Conflict*, p. 259. For Baldwin's reading of *Uncle Tom's Cabin*, see "Everybody's Protest Novel" in *Notes of a Native Son* (Boston: Beacon Press, 1957), pp. 13–23.

theory, as well as something of a family joke, when Mrs. Stowe had Augustine St. Clare in Chapter 19 of *Uncle Tom's Cabin* suspect that his father, a born aristocrat, had been in "some pre-existent state" part of one of the "higher circles of spirits"? Have we not, moreover, been directed by the official account of *Uncle Tom's* genesis to a more likely source of abolitionist theory, through which Mrs. Stowe tried to see everything? Should not the facts that it was at her brother's home she met Josiah Henson, that it was Mrs. Edward Beecher who wrote her the catalytic letter, that it was Beecher she told about God's writing the book, lead us to explore further her relation to her elder brother?

By Mrs. Stowe's retrospective account, Beecher was one of the two people (the other was her sister Catharine) who "most strongly influenced" her in her formative years. Beecher, we recall, had written her about a suffering God during the two years she, as a student in Hartford, was struggling toward conversion. She found in his God exactly what she needed. She wrote Beecher that he could "feel" as she did, that he could "speak of Him! There are few, very few, who can." "Somehow or another," she said, "you have such a reasonable sort of way of saying things that when I come to reflect I almost always go over to your side."[63] The evidence that she not only went "over" but stayed on Beecher's "side" on this matter is, though circumstantial, impressive.

The image of God she promoted in both of her antislavery novels, in *Dred* (1856) as well as *Uncle Tom's Cabin*, was that of the Man of Sorrows, not that of the tra-

63. Quoted by Charles Edward Stowe, *Life of Harriet Beecher Stowe* (Boston and New York: Houghton, Mifflin and Company; Cambridge: Riverside Press, 1890), pp. 22, 47–48.

ditional, orthodox God of dispassionate implacability. A God who suffers with them provides solace for the Negroes in *Dred*.[64] God also suffers and sorrows in two crucial chapters in *Uncle Tom's Cabin*—the second of which, on other evidence, one can be reasonably sure Beecher influenced. In Chapter 38, Tom, like Beecher in 1827, has a vision of "one crowned with thorns, buffeted and bleeding." In Chapter 12, "Select Incident of Lawful Trade," Mrs. Stowe in her own voice urges "Patience! patience! ye whose hearts swell indignant at wrongs like these. Not one throb of anguish," she promises, "not one tear of the oppressed, is forgotten by the Man of Sorrows." It may be that the source of Mrs. Stowe's God was the popular sentimentalism of her time, or perhaps Henry Ward Beecher, her favorite brother in the late forties and early fifties, whose God also suffered. In an 1885 analysis of Henry Ward's theology, Edward Beecher observed that on this "most fundamental doctrine in the whole range of theology" the brothers were in agreement. Both would subscribe to Edward Beecher's statement "that God so loves his creatures that he is capable of joy in their obedience and of sorrow and suffering from their sins, and that he is not only capable of suffering, but that he has suffered and still suffers for their redemption and moral renovation." As Beecher went on to point out, it was only during the nineteenth century that this view had been "fully and consistently held by an individual here and there"; all current, official statements denied it. Beecher had been developing the theory of a suffering God since his 1827 revelation, most fully in *The Concord of*

---

64. See, for example, *Dred: A Tale of the Great Dismal Swamp* (Boston and New York: Houghton, Mifflin and Company; Cambridge: Riverside Press, 1887), p. 191 (Chapter 16).

Ages. It came much later to Henry Ward, Beecher reports, by a "similar" "spiritual disclosure." We may be inclined to doubt, however, Beecher's assertion that the brothers "thought and acted independently" on this matter. As Charles Beecher observed in a footnote, it is "probable" that Beecher had "indirectly more influence" on Henry Ward than he was "aware."[65] Perhaps, then, even if Mrs. Stowe did not take directly from Beecher her "views of God," if Henry Ward was more recently influential, or if the popular sentimentalism of the time made such a God convenient, Beecher was in all cases seminal.

As Beecher so often pointed out, certain views of God imply certain views of society, and certain views of society imply certain attitudes toward slavery. For Beecher all these matters had come to a head in 1837–1838 at Alton. For Mrs. Stowe, Alton was nearly as central—as both a personally felt and symbolic event. When Lovejoy was mobbed and murdered defending his press, rumors that Beecher too had been killed came to Cincinnati, where the Stowes and Beechers were laboring for the West (and where James Birney a year earlier had received much the same reception as Lovejoy). Mrs. Stowe wrote to Frederick Douglas that she was always proud that Beecher was "to the last the bosom friend and counselor" of Lovejoy.[66] Frequently and sometimes a little irrelevantly, as if it pre-

65. The 1885 analysis is reproduced in "Life," pp. 451–482; for my quotations, see pp. 454–456. CB continued his footnote to observe that the same view was held by Catharine, William, and HBS. He then deleted the observation.

66. The letter to Douglas is quoted by Annie Fields, *Life and Letters of Harriet Beecher Stowe* (Boston and New York: Houghton, Mifflin and Company; Cambridge: Riverside Press, 1898), p. 135. For the rumor of EB's death, see the ninth paragraph of the 1878 Introduction to *Uncle Tom's Cabin.*

occupied her, she mentioned the Alton affair: in her introduction to the 1878 edition of *Uncle Tom's Cabin*, in the long, self-justifying letter to Frederick Douglas, and in *Men of Our Times*. She adopted as her version of the affair the account in Beecher's *Narrative*, which she quoted at length in Part IV, Chapter iii ("Martyrdom") of the *Key*. *Dred*—which more obviously than *Uncle Tom's Cabin* shows Beecher's extensive influence on her imagination—is on one level an allegory of Alton. The mob, as in the *Narrative*, is "infuriate." Father Dickinson is Lovejoy transposed. Clayton, in many biographical respects clearly an exact representation of Beecher, plays Beecher's Alton role. And as if to confirm the point, Dickinson's wife is compared to the "wife of Lovejoy."[67]

Uncle Tom's Cabin was not, like *Dred*, centrally concerned with Alton, but one of the most remarkable footnotes in literary history can be attributed to the affair. In a footnote to Chapter 12 of the serial version of the novel, Mrs. Stowe named the Reverend Joel Parker as the man who said that slavery has "no evils but such as are inseparable from any other relations in social and domestic life." Parker protested to Calvin Stowe that he had said no such thing. The ensuing "comedy of errors and cross-purposes," recounted in detail by Mrs. Stowe's biographer Forrest Wilson, ran from May through October 1852 in the public press.[68] Speculations about where Mrs. Stowe saw the Parker statement, and particularly about why she insisted on using and retaining it, have been unconvincing.

---

67. See especially in *Dred* the chapters "Lynch Law" (Chapter 48) and "More Violence" (Chapter 49).

68. Wilson, *Crusader in Crinoline* (Philadelphia: J. B. Lippincott, 1941), p. 309 ff.

In the context of Mrs. Stowe's relation to Beecher at the time, it now seems possible, even probable, that the footnote got there because of him.

Since 1837 Joel Parker had been one of Beecher's most despised enemies. Parker had been the leader of the Colonization Society in Alton and Beecher felt that his rabble-rousing speeches at its meetings had led directly to the violence of the Alton mob. Beecher blamed Parker, more than any other single man, for the death of Lovejoy. And he named Parker in the *Narrative*, though most of the time he avoided naming antagonists. May we not suppose, then, that Mrs. Stowe's chapter "Select Incident of Lawful Trade" was one of the "Several numbers" Isabella Beecher tells us were written in Beecher's Boston study,[69] that, as was her habit, Mrs. Stowe read it to him and he suggested the passage to her? Certainly we are justified in surmising that something like that took place. Not only was Parker an implacable enemy, but Beecher as editor of the *Congregationalist* and the antislavery scholar of the family, was most likely to have known of the passage.[70] The supposition gains plausibility, even seems confirmed, when we learn that, in the aftermath of the Parker episode, Beecher helped Mrs. Stowe dig up evidence to refute Parker's disavowals as he was helping her write the *Key*. Mrs. Stowe wrote Henry Ward (who was mismanaging the New York end of the Parker controversy) that Beecher was "exhum-

69. Quoted by Charles Edward Stowe, *op. cit.*, p. 145.

70. In December 1854, for example, Salmon P. Chase wrote EB, presumably asking the nature of the argument behind a proslavery speech in Congress. EB replied fully, and added to his explanation both questions and suggestions of his own. EB to the Hon. S. Chase, Boston, December 21, 1854 (Library of Congress).

ing all sorts of inconvenient declarations and arranging them in most uncomfortable proximities" and was "up to his chin in documents which he reads and makes more of with that grave thoughtful smile peculiar to him." The documents included not only the back files of the Philadelphia *Observer*, in which many of Parker's proslavery statements had been published, but also a "great abundance of declarations of Synods. Presbyteries and ecclesiastical bodies of all denominations." All seemed "in their way considerably striking."[71]

Mrs. Stowe's appropriation of her brother's God and her enduring interest in the Alton affair, especially as it appears in the allegory in *Dred* and in the Parker footnote to *Uncle Tom's Cabin*, provide considerable evidence of Beecher's influence on her attitude toward slavery. Other facts point in the same direction.

For example, in December 1850, a few months before beginning her first novel, Mrs. Stowe wrote Beecher's wife asking what "folks in general" were saying about "the slave law" and attacking the "stand taken by [orthodox] Boston ministers universally, except Edward," as if the Boston Beechers were not only a chief source of her antislavery information but also something of a model. In the same letter she echoed the *Congregationalist* when she described the Fugitive Slave Law as "incredible, amazing, mournful."[72] In fact, she often echoed the *Congregationalist*, and the December 1852 masthead listed her as a "special contributor." If we adopt Charles Beecher's "principle" that a newspaper is a "book published in successive

---

71. HBS to HWB, November 1, 1852 (Yale).
72. Quoted in Fields, *op. cit.*, pp. 130–131.

annual volumes" by the editor, the paper should be included in the list of Beecher's works.[73]

Beecher's "grand volume" had announced in its first issue that it was interested in the "great work" of Christianity in "regenerating human society"; that it belonged to the "party of progress"; that its "mission" would not be "fulfilled till idolatry, caste, slavery, political despotism, intemperance, impurity and all other abominations of sin are swept from the face of the earth."[74] But for all that— and for all Beecher's intensity—its position on slavery was moderate, as Mrs. Stowe's would be. At the beginning (late 1849, early 1850), it did no more than "earnestly" oppose the extension of slavery. When, toward the end of 1850, Beecher sought a new assistant editor, he wrote privately that "we fear an ultra antislavery character."[75] His situation was difficult, as was that of all the conservative, clerical abolitionists. Charles Beecher describes it in this way:

Lovejoy had fallen a martyr. Dr. G. Bailey's paper had been mobbed in Cincinnati; the Liberator had fulminated against Slaveholders. Confessedly till 1829 the advocate of gradual Emancipation Mr. Garrison now thundered "Let Southern oppressors tremble! Let their secret abettors tremble. Let all the enemies of the persecuted blacks tremble!" Wendell Phillips was spreading a burning ungent of Spanish flies on the inflamed South. Abolitionism was a blister-plaster to the Nation. How

73. "Life," p. 179. *Congregationalist*, IV, No. 49 (December 3, 1852). John R. Adams has provided the best account of HBS as "Magazinist"—*Harriet Beecher Stowe*, Twayne's United States Authors Series No. 42 (New York: Twayne Publishers, Inc., 1963), pp. 109–122—but he has nothing to say about her relation to the *Congregationalist*. I have been unable to attribute to her any articles in the paper.

74. Quoted in "Life," pp. 176–177, from the *Congregationalist*, I, No. 1 (May 24, 1849).

75. EB to E. A. Park, Boston, November 25, 1850 (BPL).

was it possible to be a true antislavery editor, without being a disunionist, and denouncing the constitution as a league with death and a covenant with Hell; and the churches as "a brotherhood of thieves?" How treat slaveholders politely without being called "a dough face," "a manstealer," "a pirate?" The editor of the Congregationalist like Michael the Archangel disputing with the devil durst not bring a[n] accusation against him, but said "the Lord rebuke thee."

Beecher's initial problem, in short, was that he "loved the Church tho' he saw the guilt."[76]

Given the context Charles Beecher describes, it should be no surprise that near the end of 1850 the paper's specific response to the Fugitive Slave Law, so important to *Uncle Tom's Cabin*, was ambiguous. On the one hand, its stand seemed strong: it lamented editorially that New England, "in the persons of many of our Northern statesmen," stands "apologizing" for itself, as if "asking pardon, that we have ever been guilty of regarding freedom as something more valuable than slavery." Two days after the bill became law, the paper continued to find it "exceedingly trying to the patience" to observe the "fatal facility" with which politicians yielded themselves "to the advocacy of wrong." It hoped, "notwithstanding all the unfavorable indications," for a "gradual but steady growth" of "true" antislavery sentiment in the country as a result of the law. Presumably this was written by the same quasi-editorialist who in March had said he did not wish to be "mealymouthed" in the matter of the law. He was then "entirely willing" to "take the ground of open disobedience." Some laws "stand in such direct opposition to the law of God" that every man with an "enlightened conscience" will

76. CB, "Life," pp. 182–183.

break them "just as often as they come his way." But, on
the other hand, was it the same writer—was it Beecher—who
on November 1 said he had "no sympathy" for either of
the extreme responses to the law?

On the one hand, there is the burning zeal and fervid, impas-
sioned declamation of the downright out and out opponents of
this law, and of slavery in all its forms and features; men who
will listen to no argument about the matter, but with all the
energy of their souls, and the terrible earnestness and force of
a rhetoric which sweeps all before it in its glowing, burning
track, denounces [the law and slavery]. . . . On the other hand,
we meet with the most profound indifference and apathy . . .
on the part of many whose cooler and more cautious tempera-
ment leads them to regard with distrust the movements of reform, or whose commercial and pecuniary interests and political prejudices so far prevail . . . as to render them insensible.

Was it Beecher who, the next week, then distinguished
between setting oneself "in direct and open *resistance*
to the execution of the law," which he would not do, and
refusing one's "aid and sanction to the carrying out of its
provisions," which he would do?[77]

Whether the distinctions and the unsigned editorials
were Beecher's or not, on Charles Beecher's principle he
was responsible for them. He may well have written them.
Their middle-of-the-road ambiguities, at once antiradical
and antislavery, were perfectly consistent with his conservative abolitionism. More to the point here, the very
same ambiguities were central to the theory of slavery and
society implicit in Mrs. Stowe's novels, neither of which,

77. *Congregationalist*, II, No. 15 (April 12, 1850), No. 38 (September 20,
1850), No. 12 (March 22, 1850), No. 44 (November 1, 1850), No. 45 (November 8, 1850).

contrary to popular opinion, may properly be read as a program for radical abolition.

Mrs. Stowe probably found the specific materials and perspective for *Dred* in still another series of articles by Beecher, published much earlier, in 1844. On January 25, the Boston *Recorder* reprinted one of a series of essays then currently appearing in the *Watchman of the Valley*, not by Edward, but by Henry Ward Beecher. The younger brother had insisted on the duty of ecclesiastical bodies to discuss the "moral bearings of all questions which affect the religious welfare of society," that is, the question of slavery. On February 29, then again on March 7, a correspondent signing himself A. B. and described by the editors as a "venerable and distinguished" clergyman attacked Henry Ward. Soon after, a series of seven articles appeared in the same Boston *Recorder*, written by Beecher in rebuttal of A. B., but signed merely Y. Z. Two aspects of Beecher's rebuttal help clarify the theory Mrs. Stowe adopted in her novels, especially *Dred*.

First, in response to A. B.'s standard defense of slavery— which we may call the argument from the good life of some slaves—Beecher's tactic, unlike that of most abolitionists, was to admit the "facts." He did not bother to deny A. B.'s contention that some slaveholders were often kind to their slaves or that some slaves were better off than free laborers. He asserted in his second article, rather, that the cause of which the good life of some slaves was the effect was not slavery as a social system. Slavery, he pointed out, was "but one system, operating simultaneously with many others," such as Christianity, political and social institutions, conscience, honor, humanity, and a regard for the opinion of others. It is therefore not enough "merely to prove that certain facts co-exist with the system of Slavery, in order to decide on its tendencies and moral character." One must show that slavery as a system is their immediate cause, that they are its "natural and designed results," that they are not the result of "some of the antagonist systems that co-exist" with it (such as Christianity); the apologist for slavery, in short, must show that the good life of some slaves is a consequence of slavery as a system, not, as Beecher supposed and emphasized, "*in spite* of it."

Beecher's carefully conceived causal distinction and his cool, dispassionate tone were disarming, and Mrs. Stowe adopted both the distinction and the tone in her fiction. She could grant so much to the South in her novels; she could in conscience take pains to show slavery and slaveholders at their best, because she had accepted Beecher's analysis. Beecher's argument provided a theoretical means by which she could flatter the South by admitting its honor and goodness—by, say, celebrating the goodness of the Shelbys and the St. Clares and the Claytons—without for a moment feeling or suggesting that slavery was good. Slavery, she could argue, was merely ameliorated by good southerners. Even at its best, it was bad. It was not the cause of the good life of the slaves. Their good life, whenever it existed, was a result of the ameliorating offices of good men with conscience, and in spite of slavery as a system.

In his fourth article, Beecher illustrated the point—the logical "end of the system" and the terrible "means necessary to gain that end"—by the testimony of a "witness to whom none can object." Judge Thomas Ruffin's credentials were impeccable, acceptable to even the most committed apologist for slavery, because he despised what he called the "false and fanatical philanthropy" of the abolitionists. No abolitionist could have so damned slavery, however, as Ruffin inadvertently did in an 1829 decision from the bench of the North Carolina Supreme Court. Ruffin decided that the patriarchal analogy (the argument that slaves, like children, are protected by law, an argument often appealed to by southern apologists and one that compelled Mrs. Stowe's imagination) was not legally applicable, that the aim of slavery was the "PROFIT of the master, HIS SECURITY, and the public safety," not the good of the slave. All else must be sacrificed to these ends.

This decision, probably taken at first from the context of Beecher's articles and later documented more fully, provided Mrs. Stowe with a theory of slavery to write against in *Dred*. As she observes in her Preface, she put Judge Ruffin's statement into "the mouth of one of her leading characters"; the decision climaxes the ideological argument of the novel. It is altogether probable that, just as she began *Uncle Tom's Cabin* with a vision of Tom's death, she began *Dred* with the idea of Judge Ruffin's decision and wrote up to and away from it (even to choosing her setting, North Carolina, because of it).

I mean to suggest, then, that since at least 1837 Mrs. Stowe had been vicariously in the midst of Beecher's theoretical discussions of slavery and society, that her novels were created not only out of emotion but also out of ideology, and that her source for the ideology (though inseparable from the matrix of her family, time, and place) was primarily Edward Beecher. More specifically, I find at the center of her novels, more clearly in *Dred* than in *Uncle Tom's Cabin*, the theory of organic sin which

Beecher proposed as a rationale for conservative abolitionism in 1845, the year after the Judge Ruffin articles. With
that newspaper controversy, again, Mrs. Stowe was personally involved. It will be recalled that in his 1845 articles Beecher directed his attention to Amos Phelps, secretary of the American Antislavery Society, and that at the
American Board debate from which the articles grew, Calvin Stowe had argued on Beecher's side. Phelps, then,
instead of replying to Beecher, decided to attack Calvin
Stowe and did so in a series of twelve public letters published in the Boston *Recorder* as soon as Beecher finished
his series in the same paper. Phelps called his series "The
Bible Method of Prof. Stowe and the American Board."
Calvin Stowe responded only briefly. May we suppose that
his wife Harriet made the Stowe family rebuttal, though
six years later and in a manner different from the expository dialectic of her brother and husband?

I do not mean to imply that she never made her point
in expository prose. The theory of organic sin seems to
have conditioned everything Mrs. Stowe wrote about
slavery, even such minor productions as her chapter on
Garrison in *Men of Our Times*. Caught like Beecher between admiration and disapproval, she wrote in 1868 that
the radical abolitionists "represented the pure, abstract
form of every principle as near as it is possible for it to be
represented by human frailty." But the radicals, Mrs.
Stowe thought, in calling slaveholders, "no matter of what
rank in society, of what personal amiabilities and virtues,
man-thieves," insisted on a severe moral syllogism which
involved "many instances of individual and personal injustice."[78] Her concern for the term "man-thieves" is pre-

78. HBS, *Men of Our Times; or Leading Patriots of the Day. Being Nar-
ratives of the Lives and Deeds of Statesmen, Generals and Orators, Includ-*

cisely the same as Beecher's and Calvin Stowe's in their controversy with Phelps. Like her husband, and especially like Beecher, she felt that often ultimate blame should philosophically rest upon the political (organic) unit that allowed slavery, not upon the individual who suffered under its laws and often resisted them. Like her father when he wrote Beecher praising him for the 1845 articles—and like many others in the forties and fifties—in *Dred* she would call the sin "national," not organic.[79] But by the more common term she meant all that Beecher meant by his term, nothing less.

Whatever the medium, whether exposition or fiction, the doctrine of organic sin was present. It explains character and action in *Uncle Tom's Cabin* as well as in *Dred*. It provides an ideological context for Mrs. Stowe's sincere disclaimer in the preface to *Uncle Tom's Cabin* of "any invidious feeling towards those individuals who, often without any fault of their own, are involved in the trials and embarrassments of the legal relations of slavery." In this disclaimer she was following Beecher at Alton, who we recall was almost alone in insisting during the debates that the Illinois abolitionists not "bring a false accusation against any man, and not . . . blame any one for not doing impossibilities." The object of most of the others was "not to admit of any exception" to the classification of the slave-

---

ing *Biographical Sketches and Anecdotes of Lincoln, Grant, Garrison, Sumner, Chase, Wilson, Greeley, Farragut, Andrew, Colfax, Stanton, Douglas, Buckingham, Sherman, Sheridan, Howard, Phillips, and Beecher* (Hartford: Hartford Publishing Company; New York: J. D. Denison, 1868), pp. 192–198.

79. See particularly *Dred*, p. 293 (Chapter 25). The widespread description of slavery as a national sin may be seen quickly in the excellent anthology edited by Louis Ruchames, *The Abolitionists: A Collection of Their Writings* (New York: Capricorn Books, 1964), e.g., pp. 135, 148, 191.

holder as man-thief, as in all cases sinful. Beecher felt their position was false; to adopt it would be paradoxically to weaken the "power" of the abolitionist argument "on the conscience."[80] It is, to repeat, this same kind of peculiar restraint, this resistance to making inclusive denunciations, that is the single most remarkable aspect of Mrs. Stowe's ideology in *Uncle Tom's Cabin*. Mr. Shelby at the beginning of the novel, for instance, is a "fair average kind of man, good-natured and kindly"; he is led to sin, not particularly because of his individual corruption, but because the "portentous shadow" of law, of political and social institutions, allows him to buy and sell a man as if he were a thing. The denial of the "oft-fabled poetic legend of a patriarchal institution" depends on our seeing Mr. Shelby as an organic sinner, as a man (unlike Simon Legree, a New Englander) not finally responsible. So also may we understand Senator Bird, who finally does help Eliza escape, and St. Clare and even Miss Ophelia, who contributes to the argument by wanting to own Topsy only so that she might "have a right to take her to the free States, and give her her liberty."

As seems inevitable with such a theory, the tendency (if not the intention) of which is to absolve individuals, Mrs. Stowe was not consistent. When a "young man" on the boat taking Tom to Legree's plantation says that "it is you considerate, humane men, that are responsible for all the brutality and outrage wrought by these wretches" and that if "it were not for your sanction and influence, the whole system could not keep foot-hold for an hour," he is speaking also for Mrs. Stowe. She was wrestling with an old problem, the problem of whether the responsibility for sin is to be placed squarely on the shoulders of individual

80. EB, *Narrative*, p. 40.

men or whether it is to be attributed to something larger—organic social units, for example, or God.

Consciously, I believe, she followed her brother in deciding that society was finally to blame for the sin of slavery. (If she had gone further in this dialectic with Beecher—who in *The Conflict of Ages* laid the blame again on individual men in their pre-existent fall, not on collective man or God—she would have been able, like Beecher, to reconcile her occasional inconsistencies. The theory of the pre-existent fall allows for individual responsibility and, at the same time, depravity, yet remains potentially a hopeful doctrine: God, after all, feels sorrow at the fall and puts us in the world to expiate our wrongs.) But she also wanted to encourage the George Shelbys in their activist pledge to "do *what one man can* to drive out this curse of slavery" from the land. The theoretical problem was to reconcile the idea of organic or national sin with the dramatic and emotional need one felt to blame individuals. This was a reconciliation that Mrs. Stowe never fully achieved, perhaps because practically, as her fiction showed again and again, one man (or one woman) could not do very much. " 'Can I break their chains?' " asked George Harris at the end of *Uncle Tom's Cabin*. " 'No,' " he answered his own question, " 'not as an individual.' " What "can any individual do?" Mrs. Stowe asked in her concluding remarks. Her answer was that he can *"feel right,"* pray, and accept Negroes in the North. But in the South itself, in the organically diseased society, as especially Edward Clayton in *Dred* (like Edward Beecher at Alton) learned, one could do nothing significant; he could do no more than escape. Escape is not revolution.

For both Beecher and Mrs. Stowe the theory of organic sin began in optimism. If one declined to define as sinners individuals who wished to, but could not, change their society, one's restraint might encourage them in further action. But at the very moment one enunciated the hope for action, significant action seemed impossible. What *could* one man do? Did the theory not really provide an ideology for pessimism? Locked in their contradictions, Mrs. Stowe and Beecher, as well as some of the conservative abolitionists they represented, continued nevertheless to act as if the contradiction did not exist. With Beecher's help (to the extent of writing large parts of it, if my stylistic suspicions are correct), Mrs. Stowe wrote the *Key* to her first novel. Just as he had preached against the deportation of Tom Sims, a fugitive slave, in April 1851, so we may feel certain that in 1854 Beecher opposed the rendition of Anthony Burns, another fugitive slave.[81] In such opposition, Beecher was finding his colleagues to be, not the orthodox clergy of Boston, but the radical abolitionists he had so often resisted.

To be sure, when Harriet proposed that the united clergy of New England protest the proposed Kansas-Nebraska bill, Beecher gathered signatures for two weeks in New England and New York. He went to places like Hartford, saw all the "brethren" there, and wrote back that they "accord heartily" with the plan to "concentrate all possible force, at once against the passage of the Nebraska bill by sermons, remonstrances and public meetings." After he returned to Boston to "propose and execute" his petition there, he could say he had contributed much to collecting the 3,050 clerical names that appeared on the document presented to Congress on March 1, 1854. Perhaps he had even written it: it protested the bill "in the

81. Wilson, *op. cit.*, pp. 260–261.

name of Almighty God" as "a great moral wrong" which exposed the nation "to the righteous judgments of the Almighty." (Three months later the bill passed, and not even the similar petition sent by the clergymen of Chicago and the Northwest—perhaps instigated by Beecher—did much good.)[82]

But one suspects that, like Mrs. Stowe—who came to terms with Garrison in 1852—Beecher was coming to some kind of entente with his real allies, the radical abolitionists —for example, Theodore Parker and Wendell Phillips, whom he joined about this time in organizing a society to rescue delinquent girls.[83] One finds him invariably at consociation and board meetings attacking proslavery clerics, and his irritation with the "brethren" begins to show in his writing. He would never, of course, go all the way with Garrison. In 1868, for example, he (along with John P. Gulliver and his colleague from Illinois College J. M. Sturtevant) accused the "Boston abolitionists" of denouncing "evangelical Christianity" unfairly.[84] As late as 1882 he was still denying Garrison, suggesting that the church was slow to arrive at Garrison's immediatism because Garrison "seemed to them to be a firebrand and a denunciator." But in the same letter commenting on Oliver Johnson's biography of Garrison, he acknowledged the churches' error in taking the "course of the Apostles in their day as a law for all ages," that is, in not moving from

82. Wilson, *op. cit.*, p. 401. EB to Leonard Bacon, Hartford, February 16, 1854 (Yale). The petition is printed in David Christy, *Pulpit Politics; or, Ecclesiastical Legislation on Slavery, in Its Disturbing Influences on the American Union* (Cincinnati: Faran and McLean, 1862), pp. 598–599.

83. Henry Steele Commager, *Theodore Parker: Yankee Crusader* (2nd ed.; Boston: Beacon Press, 1960), p. 177.

84. See *Garrison*, IV, 250n.

the fact of God's toleration of slavery in the primitive church to its absolute unacceptability in the nineteenth century, the age of reform and providential revolution. The church, he said, did not notice "the evolution of truth in subsequent times and the condition of the world and the principles avowed by our nation."[85] His abolitionism was becoming less conservative, more like that of the radicals—which may explain his and Mrs. Stowe's contradictions. The cause of the change, it seems clear, was the intransigence of the church, its resistance to reform, its inability to act in the face of the central social problem of its time. And, as Beecher would say for the rest of his life, the key to the church's paralysis was its theology.

15

When *The Conflict of Ages* appeared in 1853, Beecher was fifty years old and at the prime of life. His remaining forty-two years, though fruitful, would be years of defeat and considerable bitterness. He resigned from the *Congregationalist* on December 9, 1853, for example, because of the "undeserved popular odium" surrounding him, which he felt would "almost of necessity result in injury" to the paper of which he was senior editor.[86] After helping his sister with the *Key* and the clerical protest against the Kansas-Nebraska bill, he resigned also his pastorate at Salem Street Church and in 1855 retreated to Illinois. In September he went to "survey" Galesburg, preached two Sundays, and decided to move to the town which was to

85. EB to CB, August 21, 1882, quoted in "Life," p. 446.
86. EB, Letter of Resignation from the *Congregationalist*, December 9, 1853, in "Life," pp. 225–226.

Illinois what Lawrence was to Kansas: it was known locally as the Abolition Hole. There were other attractions there as well. About one hundred miles straight north of Jacksonville, Galesburg was the home of Knox College. It was "also the center around which the universalism of the West" was trying to converge, and thus a place where orthodoxy needed "strong leaders." Moreover, Beecher thought that from there he could "exert influence" on the theological seminary to be established in Chicago.[87] And he did. He was one of the six lecturers appointed when the school opened in 1856. In Charles Beecher's judgment, Edward Beecher's lectures on church institutions (the thesis of which, from notes that have survived, seems to have been that institutions must "be polarised by Christ's spirit, and vitalised by his life") were a "real work of genius," "prophetic," "poetic," "inspired."[88] Still, according to the secretary of the seminary, G. S. F. Savage, his appointment was made only "with the understanding that he should not teach his views on pre-existence," just as, one presumes, he was enjoined from preaching pre-existence from the pulpit of Galesburg's First Congregational Church.[89]

Beecher remained in Galesburg sixteen years, with frequent interruptions to return east for special events. In March 1858 he attended the second family reunion in

87. For the quotations, see EB to ?, Chicago, October 4, 1855 (Yale) and EB to HWB, Boston, November 13, 1855 (Yale). See also Hermann R. Muelder, *Fighters for Freedom: The History of Anti-Slavery Activities of Men and Women Associated with Knox College* (New York: Columbia University Press, 1959), p. 1.

88. CB, "Life," pp. 295–297. CB is here relying upon and quoting from a set of lecture notes taken by EB's son Frederick in 1858–1859. The notes are at MHCL.

89. Savage to CB, undated but probably 1895–1896, quoted in "Life," p. 292.

Brooklyn. No sooner had he returned west than a storm blew the church steeple through the roof, forcing him east again that summer for money. In February 1859 he returned to Boston to speak at the semi-centennial celebration of Park Street Church, where he had held his first pastorate. In 1863 he hurried to Georgetown, Massachusetts, to defend his brother Charles against charges of heresy. In 1865 he was one of the leaders at the National Council of Congregational Churches, held in Boston in June. And so the pattern continued into the 1870s. All the time, of course, he was also engaged in Illinois in the work of the Lord. He preached a sermon on "the holiness of God" before the Illinois General Association in 1856. He began his weekly lectures at Chicago Theological Seminary in 1859, traveling about three hundred miles round trip each week. In 1862 he reviewed a collection of English Broad Church essays, *Essays and Reviews,* in a series of fifteen articles for *The Independent.* He played a leading role in the Gale-Blanchard fight for control of Knox College. And he performed his daily ministerial duties with diligence, though the church record for 1870 describes him as deficient in one respect—his "abstraction," his failure to recognize "brethren and sisters of the church" when he met them in the streets and elsewhere. The church clerk, paraphrasing Beecher's reply to the criticism, said that it was a habit "which he, in some measure, regrets. But, then, it is a family trait; and this concentration of thought, for such it is, has its advantages, as well as attendant evils, and but for it he could not have achieved what he has in the circumstances."[90] We cannot be sure of the achievement Beecher meant as he responded to his dissatisfied parish-

90. Records of the First Congregational Church, Galesburg. Entry for December 22, 1870.

ioners, but perhaps he meant in part his writing *The Con-cord of Ages* amidst the activity of his first five years back in the West.

Beecher had conceived of *The Conflict* as a "profoundly philosophical" yet "popular and easily apprehended" book. By 1859–1860 the "first excitement" over its publi-cation had passed and the time for "sober second thought" had come. Yet, for all that had been said in opposition to his system and "with all due respect" to his "opponents," he felt "constrained to say" that he saw "no reason to change" his views. Once he brought all the reviews of *The Conflict* together for analysis, he saw that

to answer them would require a wearisome amount of contro-versial detail. But, on reflection, I [also] saw that almost all the objections to my views had their roots in false conceptions of God, and erroneous views of his system growing out of them. I determined, therefore, entirely to avoid controversial detail, and to concentrate my energies on the great organic law of the universe, as growing out of a true conception of God, and to apply it to that perfect organization of earthly society and of the universe which lie in the future.[91]

The "true conception of God" outlined in *The Concord* had been growing in Beecher's mind at the same pace as his thoughts about the traditional doctrine of the fall— at least since his exchange of letters with Harriet Beecher in the twenties. It had appeared briefly in *The Conflict*, and some reviewers had noted it. But in 1853 Beecher had been first concerned with the nature of man's depravity, with the theological source of the moral and social conflict of his time. Only another full-length study could describe the source of the inevitable future "concord" of the uni-

91. EB, *Concord*, pp. v, 407, 410.

verse. Beecher's central purpose in *The Concord*, then, was to describe God fully as suffering, limited, sorrowing for fallen humanity, sympathizing with our inability to be perfect but powerless to prevent our compulsion to sin.

For Beecher, however, the "true conception" of God was not only a matter of fact and Biblical interpretation, though those were important. He knew that His "character operates on us according to our conceptions of it, and not according to its intrinsic reality." A society's conception of God provided its "organic power." Therefore, the false and ruinous conception of God in American Protestantism was demonstrably the source of our "corrupt despotic organizations." "Why, at this day," he asked,

> are Slavery, Romanism, and other corrupt systems, so powerful? Why, even now, are the fear of human organizations, and the worship of human power, more extensive and influential principles of action than the fear and worship of God? Why is the whole social system still in disorder?

The facts, Beecher said, "cannot be denied." What, then, is the explanation? It is that there has been a "fundamental error" in our conception of God. Were our conception true, and had we acted according to it, the millennium would have arrived. Consequently, it was "no small issue, which of these opposite Gods and universes" were true, and more, accepted as true. The future of American society and the world depended on it.[92]

In *The Concord* Beecher insisted again and again that he was not concerned to engage in a "dry and heartless discussion, like the abstractions of metaphysical philosophy." Rather, he was trying to bring about "a fundamental

92. EB, *Concord*, pp. 17, 26–27. EB was contrasting the sovereign, absolutely powerful, orthodox God to his own, but we may also include in the contrast all the other versions of God that existed in his time.

revolution" in the "spirit of society," a "reconstruction of the whole social system." The revolution would come when men saw and imitated a God whose dominant characteristics were honor, self-denial, sympathy, not a God who was "heartless, unfeeling, arbitrary, unjust." Then the "idea of progress," so dear to men, would be actualized. The traditional orthodox denial of God's suffering led to a "denial of the great divine organic attractions and sympathies by which the holy universe is held together." It substituted "infinite, unconditioned and mysterious force" for harmony. God as "mysterious force" did not allow for the "spirit of service," but until that spirit prevailed, the "insane love of money, and desire of selfish accumulation" would control the United States; the "diseased desire to monopolize and accumulate" would become plague; "tendencies to luxury and self-indulgence" would grow. The "false intellectual theory" of God blocked "heroic activity" in the church. It would continue to corrupt theology, darken the universe, and produce "a conflict between theory and experience." Only new truth, a new image of Deity, could furnish a proper "counterpoise" to the decline of American society.[93]

While the primary purpose of *The Concord* was to provide a new truth, it also had to convince Beecher's critics, especially his orthodox critics, by rebutting their reviews of *The Conflict*, at least implicitly. Beecher said that he had been "little moved" by the wholesale enmity of the church toward his system. But the anger of his attack on his reviewers was barely controlled and surely kept him from placating them. The "battle of ages," he wrote, has been "against corrupt organizations." The force behind the organization has been Satan and his dupes, and the "false

93. EB, *Concord*, pp. 90–91, 174, 191, 463, 471, 559–560.

sentimentality" of the reviewers in rejecting automatically
the hypothesis of pre-existence and defending their particular narrow tradition illustrated the point. Their rigid-
ity moved Beecher to what was, for him, verbal violence.
Is it "not enough for me to agree with God's elect in their
truths?" he asked. "Must I agree with them in their errors
and inconsistencies, also?" Must we forever be burdened
by the unbearable weight of "old formulas"?[94]

Though we need not follow Beecher's dialectic as he
answered his reviewers, the new tone of the 1860 volume
requires comment. Beecher had become less self-effacing,
less humble and conciliatory—more certain of his vision in
print. He no longer seriously referred to his system as a
"hypothesis." The new tone did not, however, grow out
of certainty that the system would triumph in his time,
though he was always hopeful that, being right, he would
eventually be vindicated. He became less restrained, I
think, because he had been frustrated in his attempt to
become the Copernicus of his generation, and he felt he
had nothing to lose. His diaries for 1860 bulge with self-
analysis, with reviews of his "past life," with "thoughts and
prayers" about "the influence of my book on the church
and on the world." Rejected by the church and by those
outside the church as well, he found himself "thrown entirely upon God." He reflected on the covenant with God
he had agreed to thirty-five years ago, as a tutor at Yale:
"to suffer all that God should please in order to make Him
and the Universe happy in the highest degree." His reflection led him to analyze how he had "been rejected by those
whom I regard as his true people, and whom I love," and
how he had "borne shame" for God's sake, and how he had

94. EB, *Concord*, pp. vi, 9, 44, 370, 505.

"labored intensely and painfully in an arduous intellectual and moral work" which had "taxed" him to his limits, yet in return for the "travail" of his soul he prayed only for one reward: "the power through the Holy Spirit to give holiness, and excellence and salvation, to those for whom I have suffered."

Men, Beecher brooded, were "weak, timid, limited in intellect"; they accepted thoughtlessly "the works of Satan around them erected in ages past." If his system was true, as he was sure it was, it was not so much he as his opponents who would be "rejected and dishonored" by God. As if he could no longer contain himself, he wrote that God must "redeem" the universe, "the Sun, moon, and stars, the air the light the heat, the clouds the rain the electric fire, the ocean the mountains the continents . . . the human body, all, all he will redeem. He will redeem this continent, he will redeem this great West." He prayed that his emotions and energy would no longer be "repressed thro' fear of errors," that he would find somewhere in the depths of his being the "fulness of emotion" and almost "infinite power" it would take to make the world over in his vision. He reflected that a nation, like a man, could be evil "if misdirected by pride and ambition and false glory," as his nation in his time was. What it needed was a "true ideal" to which its "creative power" might give form. The "intellectual problems involved" were "vast, and difficult, and tax the mind," but they must be solved, if not in his time, then sometime.[95]

95. EB, extracts from diary entries for September 5–20, 1860, quoted in "Life," pp. 273–285.

At last the discussion . . .
began, and notwithstanding various
protests, it was so limited in time
as to make it a mockery, and to
render certain great errors and
injustice, in the Result.
    —Edward and Charles Beecher (1863)

Epilogue:

The Result Tested

16

CULMINATING about the time Beecher's major books were being written and reviewed, the revivalism of the 1840s and 1850s occurred, not in the rural areas as did the 1740 and 1800 Awakenings, but this time in the cities, in the midst of a financial crash. During the five months from February to June 1858, the kingdom of God seemed finally about to be realized on earth.[1] But taking our cue from Henry Weller—who lamented in conventional tones that the times were really "flippant," "shallow," and "external," that religious conflict was "feebly felt" and "lightly regarded"—we may regard the new evangelical intensity as, like Indian summer, illusory, a last glow of heat before a long cold spell.[2]

1. Timothy L. Smith, *Revivalism and Social Reform in Mid-Nineteenth-Century America* (New York and Nashville: Abingdon Press, 1957), p. 63 ff.
2. *The Conflict of Ages Ended* (La Porte, Ind.: J. S. Weller and Brothers, 1855), p. 100.

Orthodoxy was in fact drying up at the very moment it seemed on the verge of flooding. It was becoming more like a tributary creek than the mainstream of American culture. If the one-hoss shay that Jonathan Edwards built and that had lasted so long and served so well was not wearing out all at once in the mid-1850s, as Oliver Wendell Holmes thought, it was at best becoming anachronistic. By 1860 Beecher was intensifying his attack on the "spurious religious experience" of his time, but even he seemed to fear, even acknowledge, that his analysis of American experience had only historical, not present and immediate, validity.[3] In 1865, at a meeting of the National Council of Congregational Churches, his former Illinois College colleague Truman Post joked at his expense about "those who present complete systems to us."[4] By 1874 Beecher had been not so much refuted as bypassed; in describing his ideas as "theological antiquities," Elizabeth Cady Stanton was expressing the verdict of post–Civil War America.[5] And by 1896, Charles Beecher felt that the world would no longer read Beecher's "immortal works" if it could, "and could not if it would."

The World is in its literature, arts, science, politics, religion as Christ declared it would be before his second advent. Men in millennial days will look back on our battle-ships, and machine-guns, and armies, as men now look back on extinct monsters of ante diluvian times; or upon the Savage festivities of cannibal-

3. EB, *Concord*, p. 289.

4. *Debates and Proceedings of the National Council of Congregational Churches, Held at Boston, Mass., June 14–24, 1865* (Boston: American Congregational Association, 1866), p. 290 ff.

5. Chicago *Tribune* (October 2, 1874), quoted by Paxton Hibben, *Henry Ward Beecher: An American Portrait* (George H. Doran Company, 1927; New York: The Readers Club, 1942), p. 196.

ism. The range of human thought in Spiritual things is inconceivably low. The power of reason, except in material things, [is] extremely feeble. The Soul's insight concerning Eternal realities [is] dim.

As Beecher's brother charted the history of the last third of the nineteenth century, in short, it was as if Beecher belonged to "another age."[6]

For both Edward and Charles Beecher, the last third of the century began with Charles's 1863 heresy trial, completely omitted from the "Life" of Beecher, yet surely a central motive in the writing of it. The trial indicated, though everyone involved would have doubted it, that orthodoxy as the Beechers knew it belonged to an age now gone and, moreover, that orthodoxy's difficulties with slavery and abolition provided a key explanation for its decline.

In 1853 no one would have been surprised had *The Conflict* provoked a heresy trial. Thomas Starr King went so far in his review as to imagine the "singular spectacle" a dialogue between Beecher and his prosecutor would be:

"Do you believe in the Trinity?" "Yes." "Do you hold to universal sinfulness?" "Yes." "Do you accept the doctrine of total depravity?" "Yes; I hold to complete corruption of nature antecedent to all volition." "Do you believe in eternal punishment?" "Yes" [in later years, Beecher would have qualified this answer]. "Do you acknowledge this world as a final state of probation?" "Yes." "Do you hold strictly to the atoning mission and death of Christ?" "Yes." "Do you believe that faith in the atonement, and a consequent regeneration by the Holy Spirit, open the only avenue of salvation?" "Yes." "Do you believe that Dr. Bushnell is a heretic?" "Yes."

6. CB, "Life," pp. 316–318.

"Surely," King commented at this point, Beecher must be "acquitted by acclamation." But let us "imagine one question more."

"You hold then, firmly to the Orthodox system of theology as organized in the prominent Confessions?" "No; I believe that every one of its theories of forfeiture involves God, and his whole administration, and his eternal kingdom, in the deepest dishonor that the mind of man or angel can conceive, by the violation of the highest and most sacred principles of honor and right, and that on the scale of infinity and eternity."

King found Beecher's last answer "savory" and declined to imagine the "expressions" and "perturbation of the council" when Beecher then told them that only pre-existence could give the "tumbling arch" of orthodoxy "symmetry and strength."[7] King in 1853 was only imagining. Who would have supposed that ten years later, not Edward but Charles Beecher would face such a council, respond to such questions, and be convicted?

Born in 1815, twelve years after Edward Beecher, Charles learned of his older brother's pre-existential hypothesis in 1829 and wrote in 1896 that he had "never doubted it" since.[8] In 1834, though only a senior at Bowdoin College, he came to Lane Seminary to join Henry Ward and others in attempting to fill a class depleted by Weld's revolt. He read Jonathan Edwards on the Will and sank into the "midnight of fatalism." For six years afterward, he knew the "inevitable unhappiness produced by fatalism on any mind of Christian nurture." He tried to escape to New Orleans (where he collected some of the material that later appeared in *Uncle Tom's Cabin*) but in his retreat

7. Review of *The Conflict*, *The Universalist Quarterly and General Review*, XI (January 1854), 68–69.
8. CB, "Life," Preface.

from orthodoxy he found only what his father called a closer "communion with suffering." He became a family cause, a subject of weekly prayer, and finally, though still "perplexed," a Presbyterian minister.[9] In 1844 he was ordained pastor of the Second Presbyterian Church of Fort Wayne, Indiana, and in 1846, at the dedication of a new church, he preached the two sermons by which he made his first public contribution to "Beecherism," later published together as *The Bible a Sufficient Creed*. In 1851, as all the Beechers began their return east, he left Fort Wayne to reorganize the Free Presbyterian Church of Newark, New Jersey, into the First Congregational Church. But after he delivered his sermon attacking the Fugitive Slave Law, *The Duty of Disobedience to Wicked Laws*, that same year, his clerical colleagues expelled him from Newark's ministerial association. His reform activities had made him "odious to the conventional pillars of society."[10] In 1853 he served as secretary to Mrs. Stowe on her triumphal tour of Europe, taking a position as professor of Rhetoric at Knox College on his return. Beecher was undoubtedly instrumental in bringing Charles to Galesburg in 1856, and Beecher's prominent role in the Blanchard-Gale struggle for control of Knox College probably caused Charles's departure the next year.[11] In November 1857 he was in-

9. *Autobiography*, II, 461–466.

10. Lyman Beecher Stowe, *Saints Sinners and Beechers* (Indianapolis: Bobbs-Merrill, 1934), p. 338.

11. See CB to ?, Galesburg, Illinois, February 19, 1857 (BPL). The Blanchard-Beecher faction (the Congregationalists) lost. One Presbyterian opponent described EB's address (attacking "the moral assassination of Blanchard") as being distinguished for "blasphemy and a fiendlike malignity," "wholly fabrication containing not one word of truth," "sixteen columns of coarse vituperation"; he said EB was a "sanctimonious hypocrite," "disgorging venomous scurrility" with the "sneaking cowardice inherent in the character of a slanderer." All of this will suggest the intensity of the

stalled as pastor of the First Congregational Church of Georgetown, Massachusetts, where in 1863 he was tried for heresy.

Charles said he had believed in pre-existence and a suffering God since he was fourteen. At times he was more fervid than his temperamentally conservative brother. A lengthy correspondence followed the publication of Charles's *The Bible a Sufficient Creed* (1846, 1847), for instance. Beecher wrote conservatively in his letters that because he had "neither printed nor preached" his system he was "uncommitted"; that certain Biblical passages might be interpreted literally; that Charles, in contending that Satan, an archangel, could "fall" only if he were tempted, illuminated merely a " 'subjective absurdity' " in the Christian fable; and that Charles was offering the " 'eloquent plea of an advocate,' " not engaging in a " 'calm & candid' " attempt to " 'comprehend all the length & breadth & highth & depth of the great theme [of] the origin of evil and the relations of its great Author to the System of God.' " Charles replied that Beecher had indeed committed himself ("Have you not over & over again preached the *principles* which logically contain all things— & the *results* which you logically drew from the central truths"); that Beecher's whole system depended upon his metaphorical explication of Romans 5:12 (and on that explication also depended all Beecher had said "against Rome, & concerning prophecy & the philosophy of History"); that Beecher's rejection of Charles's theory of Satan's fall as mere "subjective absurdity" was like rejecting his own perception of the absurdity of a benevolent God

struggle. Quoted by Earnest Elmo Calkins, *They Broke the Prairie* (New York: Charles Scribner's Sons, 1937), pp. 192–193. See also Hermann R. Muelder, *Fighters for Freedom* (New York: Columbia University Press, 1959), p. 339.

"creating the present system under the aspect of *the fall in Adam*" (which absurdity was also subjective, ironically shared by Beecher with "all infidels"); that finally Beecher's response to his tone more than anything else tended to "destroy" his "confidence" in Beecher and all his "results" (the dispassionate tone, Charles explained, implies that one can finally explain God and universe, which is prideful presumption).

As Charles said in the 1846–47 correspondence, he thought his brother had a "daring" and "powerful" mind; but sometimes he may have felt the need to push Beecher a little in the direction Beecher's own principles indicated. On a few matters Charles pushed very hard. In that same series of letters, Beecher, again conservatively, had tried to distinguish the " 'important truths' " from the " 'erroneous, or one-sided statements' " in Charles's two sermons. He agreed with Charles that the Bible alone, without the various man-made, partly fallacious, sectarian "creeds," was enough creed for Christians. But he objected to Charles's conclusion that the "substitution of any other creed" besides that of the Bible is "one step in Apostacy." Charles replied that once Beecher accepted the major premise, he must accept both the conclusion and its implication—namely, that American Protestantism was now apostate. Beecher's distinction between the " 'reception of a particular creed' " as the " 'basis of Organisation' " in Protestantism, but not the " 'ground of salvation,' " Charles said firmly, would not do at all.[12] We may presume that with this Beecher finally agreed: when Charles defended in 1863 his right to preach pre-existence and made use of

12. CB to EB, Hartford, June 16, 1846 (SL). CB to EB, Fort Wayne, September 7, 1847 (Yale). CB's side of the correspondence is all that survives, but internal evidence suggests that EB wrote at least three letters, perhaps more; and CB quotes and paraphrases EB extensively.

his 1847 argument to support the right, Beecher, serving as Charles's advocate at the trial, adopted the anti-institutional, ultimately anarchical defense Charles had begun fifteen years earlier.

Involved deeply in his brother's system of the universe, Charles followed closely the reviews of *The Conflict*,[13] especially the English reviews (the book was published just as he returned from England), and particularly the review in the London *Times*, to which he eventually wrote a lengthy letter of rebuttal. Charles thought the *Times* critic had "failed to apprehend the true spirit" of Edward's book. He had neither appreciated its "noble design" nor estimated "justly its deep importance and power." Nor had he understood the extent of its influence and popularity in America, which Charles outlined. Charles wrote as a Beecher, whose "honored name" the *Times* reviewer had wrongly thought sullied by *The Conflict*. He corrected a number of "wrong impression[s]" in the *Times* summary of the book. He argued against the reviewer's "strictures." And, most important for our purposes, he for the first time publicly identified himself as his brother's admirer.[14]

The step beyond admiration was soon forthcoming. Charles told the ministerial council that came together in 1857 to affirm his "settlement" at Georgetown that he

13. "Life," pp. 227–228.
14. CB to Mr. Lowe, Newark, December 8, 1856 (BPL). CB addressed his letter to Mr. "Lowe" and wanted his letter to the editor (which he enclosed) inserted in the "Christian Times." He was probably in error on two counts. The name is Sampson "Low," the English publisher of HBS's books and of *The Conflict*; the paper must be the London *Times*. The letter is probably in response to reviews of the English edition of the book: thus its date. It is possible that HBS promoted publication of an English edition when she was in England. It is also possible that CB's letter was either not published or not sent. See also Forrest Wilson, *Crusader in Crinoline* (Philadelphia: J. P. Lippincott, 1941), p. 425 ff.

believed in pre-existence. Though one minister objected privately, Charles was easily installed: "as it was not deemed a proper ground of suspending Dr. Edward Beecher," said the Reverend John Pike of Rowley, "so it was not for denying his brother installation." Six years later, Pike and others who had installed Charles would vote, in effect, for his conviction and expulsion from their midst as a heretic.[15]

Their reversal is partly to be explained by Charles's increasingly public advocacy of Edward Beecher's heresies. In March 1860, Charles preached *The Divine Sorrow* to his Georgetown congregation. Three friendly parishioners asked him to publish the sermon so that, as they said, it might be studied more carefully. Others, however, took "Great exception" to Charles's thesis that God "in his intellect" and "emotions" can be known because ours are a "miniature likeness" of them, that God sorrows and suffers like men. For proof, Charles appealed to the Bible and to the "more full presentation of the scriptural argument" in *The Concord,* just published. Denying that his theory was a speculation, denying that it was "degrading to God," Charles suggested rather that the orthodox doctrine of "impassibility" was degrading. Look at orthodoxy now, he said, its "churches divided, disputing, quarrelling, full of mammon, having a name to live, but dead, unable to cope with infidelity, debauched by slavery, torn by intestine feuds." Look at the situation:

Private Christians must, indeed, be humble; but public corporations may be proud and overbearing. The laity must be careful about lying and slander, but the religious press may

15. *The Result Tested,* pp. 13–14, 38 (Appendix M). All subsequent quotations in this section, unless otherwise noted, are from this source.

freely admit both for the glory of God. Obscure village saints and village pastors, nay, even metropolitan bishops, must be careful not to speak heresy; yet, aside from their own selfish schemes of denominational aggrandizement, none can be more contemptuously indifferent to orthodoxy than the defenders of orthodoxy.[16]

Is not such a situation to be explained, he asked as if paraphrasing his brother, partly by orthodoxy's denial of God's suffering? And, if not by that, then by causes Charles announced six months later, on September 9, in a sermon delivered at the opening of the Essex North Conference and also published. In *The Antichrist of New England* Charles attacked the "New England naturalistic school," the Unitarians, an attack which, of course, appealed to his orthodox audience. But surely he antagonized the audience when he pointed out that the Unitarians were still powerful only because of the "concessions" of orthodoxy; that in their appeal to mystery and irrationality the orthodox had virtually conceded that the Bible was irrational, as the Unitarians insisted. And when, echoing the *Conflict* and *Concord*, he denied the traditional interpretation of the fall; when he insisted that it be "unanimously confessed" that God suffers, that "the body is pure and purifying, the spirit alone defiled and defiling; that the whole physical system is essentially reformatory"; and more, when he demanded that orthodoxy turn to the new system of the universe for guidance–then surely he became a marked man.[17]

16. CB, *The Divine Sorrow: A Sermon Preached in Georgetown, Mass., March 18, 1860* (Andover, Mass., 1860), pp. 3–4, 17–18.

17. CB, *The Antichrist of New England. A Sermon Preached at the Opening of the Essex North Conference, Haverhill, Mass., Sept. 9, 1860* (Boston: Crosby, Nichols, Lee and Company, 1860), pp. 19, 23–24.

The "opposers" in his congregation subsequently employed a stenographer to take down his weekly discourses and had several of them published in the *Traveller*. Immediately after the sermons appeared in print, "and with every indication of a concerted plan," they were brought to the attention of the Congregational Association to which Charles belonged in an attempt to "procure a sentence of virtual disfellowship." But the Association—and both Beechers later thought this very important—"with no sympathy for pre-existence, refused in the most significant manner to declare it a fundamental error." The next summer, then, on June 12, 1863, the "opposers" adopted a new strategy. They requested that Charles call a traditional Congregational council "to investigate our affairs and give such opinions and advice as their wisdom shall dictate." His congregation by then was so split—the request of twenty-seven of the sixty-three male members of the church called the division "unhappy"—that he consented. A council of local ministers, with Edward Beecher traveling from Galesburg to serve as Charles's advocate, convened on August 15 and 16 and reconvened to approve its *Result* on August 22.

Pursuing and arguing the details of the council's deliberations is not crucial to the point: the council's failure to allow Edward Beecher's system a place within the orbit of orthodox possibilities—its insistence on a rigorous orthodoxy—marks the moment when orthodoxy (here Congregationalism) in effect admitted its inability to revise for social change.

The Beechers themselves argued the case in *The Result Tested*, their joint pamphlet "testing" the *Result* of the council. They pointed out that historically the touchstone of orthodoxy for Congregationalists had been the Bible, not a creed, and that the "genius" of Congregationalism had been "to base all ecclesiastical power on spiritual life in the individual soul." Councils traditionally only advise; they do not judge. To insist—as this council did in its *Result*—that Charles Beecher taught doctrines "vitally and fundamentally erroneous" and that therefore the pastoral relations between Charles and his congregation ought to be terminated "without delay": this was not only to usurp its authority but to symbolize the death of the orthodox (Congregational) tradition. The Beechers attacked with all the sarcasm at their disposal the council's "suggestion" that, if Charles had held his ideas "as academic theses . . . which he could and would conscientiously keep in abeyance," and had not (as Edward had not) preached them, the council would have arrived at "very different results." Does this mean, the Beechers asked, that

A Congregational minister is a man to whom the church lets out the job of creed-preaching by contract. So much creed—so much money. The business of the minister is *to prove to people that what they already believe, so far as dried in the creed,* is right, to the dot of an i, the cross of a t. *Not*—to teach. Not to bring out of his treasure things new and old. He is "under contract by his settlement to preach the creed," but he may believe fundamental error on every point, "as academic theses." He may laugh in his sleeve at those stupid gulls, who imagine he is under contract to *think.*

The Council [then] has no objection to heresy, however damnable, provided it is "brought in privily.". . . The world would like to know about this.

And, naturally, the Beechers were willing to tell the world: if this is Congregationalism, if this marks the real state of modern orthodoxy, they felt, orthodoxy is no more than a Protestant version of papal totalitarianism.

On one level, then, *The Result Tested* is an attack on the ecclesiastical and theological "establishment" of Congregationalism. But the Beechers insisted that heresy trials such as this were seldom completely about theology. If the trial in Georgetown were only about a heretical system of the universe, why was Charles Beecher installed in the first place? And why was Edward Beecher not tried? The Unitarian journal, *The Christian Examiner*, in a review of the Beechers's pamphlet, posed the real questions we must ask about the trial. Is it not well-nigh "impossible" that "points so wholly abstract and ideal should make the matter of serious controversy at this day"? Must we not look rather to "a variety of personal considerations, which can be but imperfectly understood outside a limited circle" for the explanation of the trial's real meaning?[18]

The Beechers argued in their pamphlet and Charles pointed out in a series of letters to Leonard Bacon that there were two "real" reasons for the heresy conviction.[19] First, Charles was a Beecher, and it was common knowledge that he was editing his father's *Autobiography* (published in 1863–64).

Those who know the ecclesiastical history of New England for the last half century, and of that theological faction which has been incessantly whetting the scalping knife, and sounding the war whoop [against the new school] . . . ; those who know that it is substantially the same party that made covert war on Dr. Lyman Beecher all through his Boston ministry, and pursued him with relentless animosity to the West, and which persecutes the children hated for the father's sake as for their own; those

18. "Some New Attempts at Conformity," *The Christian Examiner*, LXXV (November 1863), 387, 389.

19. CB to Leonard Bacon, Georgetown, Massachusetts, July 3, 1863 (Yale). The quotation following, however, is from *The Result Tested*, p. 23.

who know any thing of the antecedents of that faction [that is, of the old school], and of the master spirits of this Council, will find it impossible to doubt their complicity before the fact, in the conspiracy against the ecclesiastical life [of Charles Beecher.]

The old-school–new-school war, in short, was still on, covertly but intensely. Now, however, the differences were less differences of principle than of personality and warmed-over animosities.

Second, probably "few communities" could be found, according to the Beechers, in which the antislavery and reform agitation of the forties and fifties was "more radical, or the difference of sentiment more marked" than Georgetown. When Charles Beecher arrived in 1857, the community was already divided. To be sure, the division was along theological lines; but theological and political lines in the first half of the nineteenth century were often almost exactly the same. So it was in Georgetown. Although not every opponent of Charles's conservative predecessor was "progressive nor every supporter conservative, nevertheless the parties on the whole were of opposite sympathies and tendencies" politically. Charles had come to the community "under the auspices of those who had demanded, and against the wishes of those who had resisted church action against slavery." When he spoke in *The Divine Sorrow* of "churches divided, disputing, quarrelling" and "debauched by slavery," his parishioners were no doubt aware he meant, at least in part, the Georgetown church. When, then, in *The Antichrist of New England* he urged all Congregationalists to "beware of suffering social reform to become the monopoly of the destructives," that is, the Unitarians; when he "humbly" hoped he spoke the "honest conviction of the New England churches" in saying that "slaveholding is a sin"; and when he charged the Congrega-

tionalists to work for the immediate abolition of slavery—
he must have been aware he was taking his ecclesiastical
life in his hands.[20]

What was perhaps Charles's most divisive act, however,
occurred on December 23, 1860, early in the sequence of
events leading to the trial. On December 14 President
James Buchanan had called on the people of the North to
observe a day of "fasting, humiliation and prayer, for the
sin of opposition to slavery" and for thus provoking the
rebellion in the South. Charles Beecher preached against
the proclamation, and with the marked exception of twenty-
three members (all of whose names were "found on the
recent petition for a Council"), the congregation adopted
resolutions refusing to comply with Buchanan's request. If
the Beechers were right, these resolutions were the
"stepping-stone" to the heresy trial. They charged that the
"President of the United States is in treasonous conspiracy
with rebels to overthrow the government"; they urged that
"the only amendment which the age demands" is not, as
Buchanan recommended, an amendment to the Constitution that would allow the rebels to submit, but "an express
repudiation of the slave construction of the rendition and
representation clauses of the Constitution"; and finally,
the resolutions observed that the proclamation of a fast,
while "verbally pious," was "an act of hypocrisy and spiritual usurpation in the highest degree insulting and detestable." Surely this provides the clue to the real meaning of
Charles Beecher's heresy conviction. As in 1851, he had
offended the "ecclesiastical copperheadism of New England," and he must pay the penalty.

The trial at Georgetown, then, was more than a test of

20. CB, *The Divine Sorrow*, pp. 17–18. CB, *The Antichrist of New England*, pp. 30–32.

the "orthodoxy" of Edward Beecher's system, considered purely as theology—if there can be such a phenomenon as "pure" theology. It was a test of orthodoxy itself. As a minister Charles Beecher was eventually vindicated. He was elected in 1864 to represent Georgetown in the Massachusetts legislature. Though the disaffected "opposers" left to build their own church, the majority of his congregation stood by him, ready to withdraw from "fellowship" with other Congregational churches rather than lose their pastor. Ultimately, a few years later, the local Congregational conference rescinded the council's "verdict" and Charles again became a Congregational minister in good standing. But personal vindication is not the same as ideological viability. As Charles Beecher said of *The Conflict*, success takes many forms and has many ironies. Charles's personal vindication may well mark a second stage in the decline of orthodoxy as a socially viable theology. After the Civil War, it is clear, theology no longer counted for much; therefore heresies were no longer significant. Orthodoxy's moment had passed. It would not revise itself in the 1840s and 1850s; now revision no longer mattered. Church and society had entered into a new kind of relationship, and the equation that might describe the relationship would hardly include the old theological problems. Charles Beecher said thirty years after his trial that *The Conflict of Ages* might make "good millennial reading"; but at the end of the century, few would be interested in either its author or its subject. As Charles began to look for a publisher for his long, devoted "Life" of Beecher, he prophetically observed that it would never see print in his "life-time—if ever."[21] He was nearly right.

21. CB to Scoville [Beecher], Georgetown, Massachusetts, January 27, 1899 (Yale).

17

Charles's "Life" was not the only major Beecher document to go unpublished, nor was the Georgetown trial all that it omitted. Beecher's historical novel, *Cornelia, A Tale of the Second Century under the Reign of Marcus Aurelius*, probably written during the decade of the eighties, never saw print, though the state of the manuscript indicates it was ready and meant for publication.[22] That Charles Beecher does not mention it is the more remarkable because in Beecher's mind *Cornelia* may very well have replaced the autobiography he at one time contemplated. Like the plan for the unwritten autobiography, the novel was surely meant to popularize Beecher's reflections on the relation between religion and society without demanding the "exhausting thought" of *The Conflict* and *Concord*.[23]

Traditionally, of course, the orthodox community tended to deny the value of fiction, supposing it a minor and corrupting form of writing. But Harriet's novels and Henry Ward's *Norwood* (1867) had been successful and influential. To the question Beecher posed in a post–Civil War lecture—has fiction accomplished "more evil than good"?—the whole family would have answered, as Beecher did, "decidedly no." Beecher agreed that the "tons of trashy yellow literature & newspaper stories" overwhelming his time were poor "mental nutriment." "False ideas of life

22. The manuscript obviously underwent extensive revision: chapters were added and rearranged; the pagination became complicated (e.g., from p. 35 through 35a–35z, 35aa–35zz, etc.); pages were glued together at the appropriate places; false starts were deleted. But the arrangement is neat and the handwriting clear; in general the manuscript appears ready to proceed to editor and printer.

23. EB to CB, April 11, 1890, quoted in "Life," p. 517.

& its duties have undoubtedly been formed, expectations, never to be realized, raised, & the great cause & end of our existence here, misrepresented." But all chaff has its wheat, and to "blot out the novel, or fiction" would be to "obliterate one of the more eficacious & powerful means ever employed for exposing & assailing moral evil, especially for the overturning of cruel laws & oppressive legislation." Beecher cited as examples not only the case of *Uncle Tom's Cabin* and the Fugitive Slave Law, but the cases of Bunyan, Dickens, Scott, Cooper, Thackeray, and others, as well. Clearly, if his sense of the value of fiction was narrowly moralistic and social, it was also intense and reasonably well informed.[24]

Beecher's circumstances during the 1870s and 1880s, however, lead us only in the most indirect way to *Cornelia*. In 1871 Beecher left Galesburg, where he had passed what were in some respects the "pleasantest and most fruitful" years of his life, to return east. Apparently his immediate motive was purely personal: his son George, disabled with rheumatism, needed care in New York. In New York he acted for two years as assistant editor of the *Christian Union*. His essays commented on the gamut of contemporary events and were usually written from his special perspective. (For example, his essay in the issue of February 14, 1872, on "The International," suggested that if all the

24. "Has more evil than good been accomplished by ficticious [sic] writing?" (MHCL; probably delivered in the 1870s). EB would have answered his question differently in 1849. Speaking to members of the New England and California Trading and Mining Association on January 25 of that year, he urged that they take "unwearied pains to cultivate and enlarge" their minds. "You cannot read too much," he said, "in well selected works on history, chemistry, mineralogy, natural philosophy, agriculture, mechanics, political economy, government, and above all, Morality." To which he added: "The more you read of such works and the less of novels, the better."

"atheistic and infidel principles" could be eliminated and the "true Christian ideal" understood, then the international labor movement might be a blessing to humanity.) When, however, Oliver Johnson became proprietor and editor of the paper, Beecher was out of a full-time job. He bought a house on Macon Street in Brooklyn, joined Plymouth Church, and in effect, retired, becoming counselor and friend to his brother Henry, now the most famous preacher in America.[25]

His role as confidant and advisor to Henry was not altogether a new one. Several surviving childish letters from Henry to Edward attest that he had served in that capacity when Henry, ten years younger than he, was a boy.[26] Later, in 1848, at Henry's urging, Edward had considered a position in Brooklyn, though he finally became editor of the Boston *Congregationalist*. Their correspondence then was extensive; it continued, if at times sporadically, from then on. In the 1860s, for instance, when Henry's sermons were appearing weekly in the *Independent*, Beecher wrote him from Galesburg about his dislike for the editorial policies of the paper and received in reply a "confidential To be returned" denial of responsibility. In 1866 the younger brother was grateful for an unspecified personal service Edward performed in Chicago. In 1867, visiting the East, Edward stayed with Henry; the subject of their conversation during a memorable walk in the woods was Herbert Spencer and evolution. Shortly after, upon reading one of Henry's published sermons, Beecher was moved to pro-

25. "Life," pp. 351–357. See also the Records of the Parkville Congregational Church, at 18th Avenue and East 5th Street, Brooklyn, where for a few years beginning in 1885 EB served part time as pastor.

26. See HWB to EB, Mt. Pleasants (Amherst), July 11 and August ?, 1829 (Yale).

pose that they discuss by correspondence their mutual "trial[s] of faith"; neither of them had been able to find someone in whom he had enough confidence to unburden himself.[27] Henry was not the scholar Beecher was, and whenever he needed help—as, for example, in explanations of Hebrew, at which Beecher was expert—he turned to his elder brother. According to Charles Beecher, he had a "deeper respect not to say reverence for Edward, than for any living man."[28] And the elaborate estimate of Henry's orthodoxy—written by Beecher for the Funk and Wagnalls biography a few years before Henry's death in 1887, but not published—reveals that Beecher in turn took his younger brother's theology very seriously.

In such a context, it is no surprise to discover that Beecher played an "important part" in the transactions of the Congregational councils called in 1874 and again in 1876 to inquire into the affairs of Plymouth Church.[29] The councils grew out of the infamous affair between Henry and Mrs. Elizabeth Tilton, made public on November 2, 1872, by the Woodhull sisters (who hoped that the scandal would "burst like a bomb-shell into the ranks of the moralistic social camp," which it did) and continuing through a public trial and in newspapers over the country.[30] In nearly all the accounts of Henry Ward Beecher's activities, both then and later, the seldom-named, shadowy figure at his

27. HWB to EB, October 8, 1866; EB to HWB, Galesburg, October 29, 1866; EB to HWB, Galesburg, February 25, 1867; EB to ?, Galesburg, December 23, 1867; HWB to EB, December 27, 1867 (all at Yale).

28. CB, "Life," p. 447.

29. CB, "Life," p. 357 ff.

30. Victoria Woodhull, *Woodhull & Claflin's Weekly* (November 2, 1872), quoted by Hibben, *op. cit.*, p. 248. For a full account of the scandal, see Robert Shaplen, *Free Love and Heavenly Sinners: The Story of the Great Henry Ward Beecher Scandal* (New York: Alfred A. Knopf, 1954).

side, usually described only as "his brother," was Beecher, who "stood like a rock before Henry when Slander assailed him."[31]

Whether, in retrospect, Beecher's support of his brother should be construed as wholly laudable may be suggested by one of a massive heap of documents dealing with the case. The document is a long letter from Isabella Beecher Hooker, Beecher's half-sister (younger by nineteen years) and a suffragette friendly with the antagonists in the scandal—the Woodhull sisters, Elizabeth Cady Stanton, and Susan B. Anthony. The letter refers to a "hurried" conversation between Edward and Isabella in which Beecher had said that "if H. is guilty [of adultery] he ought not to make confession." This seemed to Isabella the height of male and, indeed, Christian hypocrisy. She expressed her "astonishment." If Henry was guilty, as Isabella seemed sure he was, he ought to confess and divorce his wife.[32] The question, of course, is exactly that: whether Henry Ward Beecher was guilty, and if so, to what degree. A fully satisfactory answer is unavailable; the truth is shrouded by rumor, by lies, by the reticence of a divided New England family. And the record of Edward Beecher's relation with Henry provides no entree into the mystery. The letter from Isabella Hooker, however, serves at least to indicate that in some respects Edward Beecher in the 1870s was a pious anachronism; his decision to defend Henry Ward Beecher no matter what, was a decision for which there might be only explanation, not a satisfactory defense.

In any event, and more directly relevant to *Cornelia*,

31. CB to Eunice Beecher, Georgetown, February 25, 1895 (Yale).

32. Isabella Beecher Hooker to EB, Hartford, January 16, 1873 (Library of Congress).

the ultimate issue of the Congregational councils was for
Beecher, at least publicly, again the issue of Charles Beecher's trial by council at Georgetown: does a Congregational
church owe primary allegiance to the traditions of Congregationalism or the truths of the Bible? In the 1840s,
Charles Beecher had evidently convinced him of the validity of the latter position. In Georgetown in 1863, his
defense of Charles depended heavily on the argument that
the Bible was the final and only court of appeal for Congregationalists. He made his most complete statement of
the position in April 1865 in "The Scriptural Philosophy
of Congregationalism and of Councils," written at the request of the *Bibliotheca Sacra* as part of a series representing the views of various denominations.[33]

There he argued that the purpose of the church—"to
bring civil government, the state, commerce, political
economy, the arts and sciences, and the schools, under the
influence of God, so as to pervade them with the influence
of his law and the gospel, and thus to make them a harmonious and consistent part of his kingdom"—could best,
perhaps only, be achieved by a system of "free, independent, self-governed, local churches." Hierarchy, which
at best made for a spurious, external unity, begot division;
real unity, real holiness, real vitality could be promoted
only by the congregational principle. The "grand peculiarity" of Congregational councils, therefore, was that they
were to function (Beecher noted with restraint that the
practice was far short of the ideal) without introducing
the hierarchical principle; they were advisory, regenera-

---

33. In accepting the request to write the article—EB to ?, Galesburg,
March 16, 1863 (BPL)—EB promised to write so as to avoid "playing the
part of an advocate," even though that would be "difficult."

tive, creedal only insofar as the Bible was creedal. Only when the congregational principle was realized would the church's purpose on earth begin to be realized. "Now that God has smitten slavery unto death," Beecher said, "he has opened the way for the redemption and sanctification of our whole social system, which was before impossible." Beecher's plea was that the churches should begin to see the validity of the congregational principle and, by that, begin the regeneration of society he sought.

He argued the same case in 1874 and 1876. To support it, he was forced to return once more to the early centuries after Christ. If Christianity was congregational before the Roman Catholic Church, should it not become Congregational again? The search for evidence was, in a sense, no more than he had carried on before: in the historical argument of his essays on "Organic Sin," in the section on the history of doctrine in *The Conflict*, and in his lectures on Christian institutions at the Chicago Theological Seminary (in which he "traced the progress of Society from the earliest times").[34] Each time, however, the issue was slightly different.

In 1878 Beecher again returned to the same period, this time in a new study: *History of Opinions on the Scriptural Doctrine of Retribution*. In the *History*, which appeared serially in the *Christian Union* before it was published as a book, Beecher was inquiring into the afterlife and the doctrine of eternal punishment, just as in *The Conflict* he inquired into pre-existence and the doctrine of depravity. As he saw it, God's honor was involved in both cases. If God through Adam's fall had created men depraved, He was culpable; if He then punished men eternally for what

34. CB, "Life," p. 296.

they could not help, He was also culpable. Only pre-
existence and a pre-existent fall could justify human depravity and at the same time absolve God from blame. In
the same way, only pre-existence could justify eternal
punishment, which could not be "defended" as it was by
the "orthodox generally; that is, [by] the doctrine of the
fall in Adam."[35] Beecher felt that if the church would not
accept the only basis on which endless punishment could
be justified, namely pre-existence, then he must align himself with the restorationists.

But he was not, in the *History*, so much arguing his case
as finally true, as he was arguing that it was respectable,
part of the great tradition, held by men eminent in the
church. His book was a history of *opinions*. As a consequence, he immerses us in the world of the church fathers,
some of whom play a role in *Cornelia*. It seems clear that
he was already considering a historical novel. Just as "every
painting" must have a "background and a ground-color as
indispensable to set forth the leading figures to be represented, so in an historical painting of past ages there is the
same necessity. There must be an historical background
and ground-color, or the actors of history cannot be truly
presented or seen." But even in the *History*, and certainly
in *Cornelia*, Beecher did not heed his own charge to historians to avoid carrying the "feelings and opinions of this
age back to the early ages." A passage in the *History* fore-
shadows the analogy in *Cornelia* between the burning issue
of his time and the situation of the early Christian martyrs. "In our war with slavery, for the life of our country,"
he wrote, "a common interest and common danger united
all who were willing to fight for their country. There was

35. EB, *History*, p. 296.

a readiness to subordinate all else to a great common interest and common danger. So was it during these early ages in the Church."[36]

All of this leads to the observation that *Cornelia* was a novel about a small group of men and women whose sense of God, whose theology, whose eminent holiness compelled them to resist the corruption of their society. *Cornelia* was not an allegory, but if the situation sounds like Alton all over again, we may suppose it was meant to. Beecher was impressed by the analogy between pre–Civil War America and the Roman Empire in 170–180. He expressed the analogy in many terms in *Cornelia*: in terms of personal religious crisis, theology, politics, social structure, institutions, slavery, war, history, the relation between the masses of men and intellectuals, ethics, the state of belief and skepticism, the breakdown of philosophical systems. In each case, he thought, America could be understood by understanding Rome, and he set the scene of his novel accordingly.

Reading all the primary sources in the original languages and all the standard secondary sources of his time (primarily Gibbon, W. E. H. Lecky, and Gerhard Uhlhorn, his favorite) led him to suppose that, like America between 1830 and 1860, the Empire in the decade beginning in 170 "had attained its highest development"; its "decay" as yet "had not commenced." Marcus Aurelius—the "best Emperor" that ever lived—had surrounded himself with men of talent and intellect. Beecher made those men part of the essential background of his novel, gathered them together at a banquet at the home of the heroine in Chapter II, and described them: Marcus Cornelius Fronto ("the

36. EB, *History*, pp. 168–169, 172.

Cicero of our day, and former teacher of Aurelius"), Rusticus (another teacher, and a leading Stoic philosopher),
Celsus (whose polemic against the Christians was the first
to endure), Lucian (whose dialogues of the gods everyone
had read), Galen the physician, and two of the "founders
of legal science," Gaius and Papinian. For these men, the
intelligentsia of the Empire, the Stoic philosophy served as
a guide to value and virtue, much like orthodoxy in America. Aurelius especially, not only in the *Meditations* but in
his actions as Emperor, represented for Beecher the best
that Stoicism could achieve.

But at the moment of apogee, the signs of impending
decline were clear, especially in religion. The rigors of
Stoicism were not for the masses, and, as Rusticus under-
states the situation in *Cornelia*, there had been a "great
decline of the worship of the [ancestral] Gods." In their
place the Empire had adopted an eclectic polytheism, im-
porting many of its gods from the Orient. Like Lecky,
Beecher saw a "broad chasm" developing between the
Roman moralists and the Roman people. On the one hand,
the Stoic system of ethics was magnificent in the "range
and beauty of its precepts, the sublimity of the motives to
which it appealed, and its perfect freedom from super-
stitious elements." On the other hand, Roman society was
"almost absolutely destitute of moralising institutions, oc-
cupations, or beliefs, existing under an economical and
political system which inevitably led to general depravity,
and passionately addicted to the most brutalising amuse-
ments."[37]

One of Beecher's central tasks in *Cornelia* was to explore

37. William Edward Hartpole Lecky, *History of European Morals from
Augustus to Charlemagne* (1st ed., 1869; New York: George Braziller, 1955),
I, 291.

the way in which Christianity bridged the chasm between the ethics of Stoicism and the degeneracy of the Empire, in a time when the "established religion" was "entrenched in all the usages and profitable business of society" and had become corrupt, worldly, and inadequate to the age's real needs.

The early action of the novel describes the conversion to Christianity of Cornelia and then Valerius, patrician supporters of the doctrine of Epictetus and Aurelius. Cornelia hears Valerius speak at a rhetorical contest, which he wins by speaking "nobly on the wants of our country, and of our duties to her in this crisis." The "crisis" is the invasion of the barbarians from the north, which had forced the Empire into years of war and which, with the plague and Christianity, has provided the traditional explanation for historians of the decline of Rome. Valerius joins the army. But before he leaves, he meets Cornelia; they fall in love, and their crisis becomes an inner one: the quality of their love (for Beecher, the key term to explain the spread of Christianity in the second century) makes Stoicism and the epistemological skepticism Valerius had previously espoused seem inadequate. "Perhaps it may seem incredible that any man," Beecher commented, "could so bewilder himself and paralyze his mind in Greece or Rome. But almost an identical train of thought can be quoted from an existing American philosopher of no small pretensions and celebrity." The American philosopher, whom Beecher quotes, is Emerson, as if Emerson represented to him the ultimately skeptical position one must reach before he can begin to travel a new road leading to common sense and Christianity.

Valerius leaves for the army. But Cornelia too finds herself "conscious of intellectual and moral impulses" which "shake" her "philosophical system" to its "foundations" and make it seem a prison. At first she finds no solution to her inner conflict, though she studies Skepticism, Epicureanism, and most of the minor "systems" of her time. Only when she discovers through the slave Blandina that Christianity has Love as its central doctrine does she find her way out: "This is what my heart has longed for!" she says. "God is represented as law, and right, and wisdom, and power, and in some sort benevolent—we are bound to obey him—but that he is really sympathetic, affectionate, tender, I never felt—." She tells her friend Julia that she finds herself "in a new world" where all her "darkness" and "doubts," all her "uncertainties" have "passed away."

In charting Cornelia's conversion, Beecher drew upon his experience in 1822, over sixty years earlier, with his sister Catharine. Like Catharine, who wrote Lyman Beecher inquiring why his theology did not square with her experience, Cornelia in her doubt writes to Marcus Aurelius and finds inadequate the Stoical consolations he offers, especially when she learns that Valerius has been captured. Also like Catharine, Cornelia's question is about immortality, which Aurelius regretfully denies. She writes:

If those who . . . have lived in intimate communion with the Deity perish . . . does it not prove the Deity himself either weak or unworthy? On such principles, how could there be a permanent & exalted system of intelligent beings ever increasing in knowledge & goodness? The attainments of every age are lost at death. Nothing remains but a ceaseless round without progress. Can a view so dark be true?

Beecher tells us that Cornelia's love is "shadowing forth an infinite system in which it is perfected"—Christianity.

Events move quickly after Cornelia's conversion, though

the pace of the novel is slow. Through the slave Blandina, Cornelia meets other Christians in Lyons, particularly Pothinus the Bishop. She studies Christian manuscripts. Scenes shift quickly: to the war and a description of the famous battle in which, according to Christians, God took a hand; to Valerius' complicated escape; to comic relief in the person first of soldiers and second a Christian family; to a description of the "simplicity" of Christian life and worship, its "brotherly love and friendship"; to several chapters giving the details of formal Christian worship. By the middle of the novel, then, we are prepared for the martyrdom to come, which Beecher describes by extrapolating from the famous Letter of the Churches of Lyons and Vienne (177). His narrative focuses on Blandina, the slave who has converted Cornelia and who appears in history as the most heroic of the Lyons martyrs. Beecher asks: Why was such a good woman tortured? He answers:

The reason is obvious. There was a combination of the interests of two great systems, polytheism, & slavery against her.
    Nothing enrages a slaveholding community more than independence of spirit in a slave. . . . Lamentable, but sublime situation! The despised slave is lifted to view of the ages as the champion of individual rights, on which human freedom is founded . . . the heroine of her age, in the war for religious & civil liberty.

Clearly here, as in the section immediately preceding when mobs attacking the Christians seem suspiciously like the mobs who attacked Elijah P. Lovejoy in 1837, Beecher was writing not only about Christianity and society in 177, but also about abolitionists and slavery in pre–Civil War America.

    At this point in the novel, Beecher's immediate problem was to bring about a denouement. His solution was amateurish. Cornelia, under a death sentence, is spirited away by Valerius and Claudius, her one-time suitor. Felecia and Phlegon, the lower-class equivalents of Cornelia and Valerius in the novel, escape to a cottage in the mountains. Later, Cornelia goes to Aurelius to try to persuade him to tolerate Christianity. He agrees, and Blandina's becomes the last of the persecutions in Lyons. Five years later, in a short final scene, Cornelia and Valerius are shown in a Christian community in the mountains, "forming the nucleus of one of those mountain churches afterwards so faithful to the simplicity of the gospel in ages of declension & darkness."

Given this summary, there is no need to press the point that *Cornelia*, though readable, is nevertheless hardly a major novel. Beecher's immersion in the historical setting was more than adequate; given his purpose, his representation of Cornelia's and Valerius' conversion was successful; and the characters that serve as comic relief were delightfully drawn. But these cannot balance the inadequacies of his epistolary devices to convey information, his appropriation of sentimental devices in the love story, the tedium of the long, textbook descriptions of the ancient society Beecher knew so well, or the expository quality of most of the dialogue. As fiction *Cornelia* fails. As an attempt to recreate by fable most of the central experiences of Beecher's life, and to embody in the fable his attitude toward them, however, *Cornelia* is a remarkable success. Cornelia's religious problems are Catharine Beecher's; Marcus Aurelius plays the role Lyman Beecher played in 1822, and Beecher's attitude toward him is appropriately ambiguous; Roman society is the equivalent of American society, 1830–

60; the Christians of the second century live by a theology that sounds much like that of the *Conflict* and *Concord*; their persecution by the Romans is the equivalent of Alton's persecution of Lovejoy. In *Cornelia*, Beecher was still writing about the relation between religious experience and social regeneration in America. He must have read with satisfaction Uhlhorn's comment that in the early centuries after Christ "all political questions were at bottom religious," and would have wished to add only that, to a large extent, the reverse was also true.[38]

After the *History* and *Cornelia*, Beecher's activity in retirement slowed down, but only a little. His letters to Charles Beecher reveal him in 1883 reviewing a new book on baptism and writing four "pieces" for associations and clubs; in 1884 evaluating Henry George's books; in 1885 writing his estimate of Henry Ward Beecher's orthodoxy, commenting on the treatment of evolution in European magazines, and following with care the reviews of a new book in the *Andover Review*; in 1886, not only preparing an article on the atonement to be read before a New York association, but wishing he had the time, energy, and money to write the three books he had "conceived" on the atonement, on communion with God, and on the "sanctifying power of divine analogies."[39] Much of his contemplation during these years was retrospective, as it had been at least since 1876. Invited to Boston to celebrate the fiftieth anniversary of his settlement over Park Street Church,

38. Gerhard Uhlhorn, *The Conflict of Christianity with Heathenism*, edited and translated with the author's sanction from the third German edition by Egbert C. Smyth and C. J. H. Ropes (first published in translation, 1879; New York: Charles Scribner's Sons, 1894), p. 438.

39. EB, as quoted in "Life," pp. 485–517.

he gave an address dealing with the religious history of New England (which men in 1826 "fully understood, as the present generation cannot").[40] He was never more retrospective than when, at Charles Beecher's urging, he considered buying the plates of *The Conflict* and *Concord* and publishing an edition of them with "notes up to date," only to abandon the project for lack of funds. We may be sure he died feeling that the arguments contained in those two books were unanswerable.[41] He never abandoned the revelations of 1827. As *Cornelia* shows, he never could forget Alton. And if in "one aspect" his life "seemed a failure," if he failed to "revolutionize theology," his attempt informed all his social and political thought and allowed him to be involved in the central conflicts and inner drama of his time as perhaps few other men were.[42]

40. EB, "Life," p. 401. CB reproduces the Address.

41. EB to CB, November 23, 1881, reproduced in "Life," p. 442. EB, *History*, p. 299.

42. CB, "Life," p. 526.

Acknowledgments

Because this book has taken several preliminary forms and because I have been working at it a long time, I find myself obliged to many people and institutions for gracious and helpful acts. I want to acknowlege as many of those acts as I can.

I am indebted to: D. C. Ritter, formerly librarian at Illinois College, for sending about 1,000 pages of Beecher manuscripts to the University of Minnesota, where I could transcribe them, and for his kindness in opening the doors of his library to me one Sunday; C. B. Russell, his successor at the Illinois College Library, for transcribing important passages from the Trustees Record Book; L. Vernon Caine, President of Illinois College, for permission to use freely and quote from the Beecher manuscripts; Harvey Arnold, now librarian of the Chicago Divinity School, for the better part of a day spent talking about Beecher and exploring the library of Chicago Theological Seminary; Cushman McGiffert, for information about Beecher's position at the seminary in its early years; John Gill and Merton L. Dillon, biographers of Elijah P. Lovejoy, for explanatory letters; Seymour V. Connor, Professor of History and Director of the Southwest Collection at Texas Technological College, for transcribing a crucial letter from Beecher to Lovejoy; Flora B. Ludington, formerly librarian at Mount Holyoke College, now deceased, for guiding me through her library's Beecher manuscripts and for lunch and conversation; Hermann R. Muelder, Dean of Knox College and author of *Fighters for Freedom*, for talking to me about Illinois abolitionism; John R. Adams, author of the Twayne series biography of Mrs. Stowe, for an explanatory letter; H. Crosby Englizian, for information about Beecher at Park Street Church; Truman Nelson, whose magnificent novels about the New England abolitionists Theodore Parker and John Brown are rich sources of ideas, for a tour of his area, for talk, for correspondence; John Beecher, Edward Beecher's great-grandson and himself a writer of great stature, for bibliographical leads, for exciting correspondence, for moving poetry; Cyril I. Nelson, E. P. Dutton editor, for his good work in publishing an edition of Beecher's *Narrative*; Mary Lee Tipton, assistant editor of the Vanderbilt University Press, for conscientious and perceptive editing.

I want also to name and thank: Elizabeth de W. Root, archivist of the Hartford Seminary Foundation; Katherine Day and Joseph S. Van Why, of the Stowe-Day Foundation in Hartford; John A. Harrer, head librarian of the Congregational Library, Boston; Nelson F. Adkins, Professor of English and custodian of the Index to Early American Periodicals at New York University; Margaret A. Flint, Assistant State Historian, Illinois State Historical Library; Harold B. Noyes, Edward Beecher's great-nephew; William L. Walcott, Clerk of the Parkville Congregational Church; Nancy Berlo, typist; and Barbara Mielecki, typist and assistant.

I have either visited the libraries or corresponded, sometimes at length, with the librarians at the following institutions: Andover-Newton Theological School, the Library of Congress, the Boston Public Library, Marietta College, Massachusetts Historical Society, the William L. Clements Library of the University of Michigan, the Litchfield Historical Society, the Connecticut State Library, Yale University Library, Knox College, McCormick Theological Seminary, the Historical and Philosophical Society of Ohio, the Houghton Library of Harvard University, the Schlesinger Library of Radcliffe College. To all those involved, anonymous here, as well as to those who wrote me saying their libraries had nothing to offer me, I am grateful. For extended help I am also grateful to the librarians at the University of Minnesota, where I began this book in the form of a seminar paper, then a dissertation, and to Lee Dutton and John A. Weatherford, librarians at Miami University.

My work has been subsidized, in part, by a fellowship granted by the Graduate School of the University of Minnesota and by Miami University in the form of a Summer Research Appointment, a Faculty Research Committee grant for typing and clerical assistance, and released time from teaching duties (arranged through the efforts of Spiro Peterson). Members of a graduate seminar in American Studies at the University of Minnesota read and criticized a first version of Chapter III. Members of the graduate faculty read and criticized the first complete version. David Hernandez read parts of later drafts. Merton L. Dillon and James Hastings Nichols read and criticized the sections on the *Narrative*. Roland DeLattre, Louis Schaeffer, and Ralph A. Stone read and criticized the whole of the next-to-last draft. All this help, financial and critical, was indispensable.

To Charles H. Foster, who has followed the development of the book from the beginning, I am indebted for kindness and encouragement now far beyond the call of duty. To my wife, Elizabeth, I owe the benefits of her constant consideration and support. To my parents, to whom the book is dedicated, I give, with it, both my gratitude for their efforts on my behalf for so long and my love.

RM

Bibliographic Essay

MANUSCRIPTS

Charles Beecher wrote that he was "moved to prepare" his 543-page "Life of Edward Beecher" because he only "of the children remaining" could "do justice to its subject" and because he only sympathized with the doctrines of pre-existence and a suffering God. (He observed in a deleted footnote that the latter doctrine was held also by HWB, HBS, Catharine, and William. But they were now dead.) CB was in some respects, of course, biased in favor of his subject. But if his facts were sometimes inaccurate, and if for personal reasons he omitted some events in EB's life that in retrospect seem crucial, he nevertheless provided insights and information impossible to find elsewhere. His "Life" is indispensable. Unfortunately, sometime between the writing of the manuscript and its delivery by Mr. John Beecher, EB's great-grandson, to the Illinois College Library in 1950, Chapter 26, "The Fugitive Slave Law," presumably dealing with *Uncle Tom's Cabin* and HBS, was lost. The remainder, however, is intact and available not only in Jacksonville but on microfilm at the Illinois State Historical Library, Springfield.

CB mentions and quotes, all too briefly, EB's diaries. To have had them available to me, as CB had them when he was writing the "Life" in the mid-1890s, would have been a great help. But they have disappeared. I have, however, been able to locate EB's manuscript novel, *Cornelia, A Tale of the Second Century Under the Reign of Marcus Aurelius,* written, as both internal and external evidence indicate, between 1885 and 1890, and now at the Illinois College Library. CB, I suspect, knew nothing of it.

Most of EB's letters, so far as I have been able to learn, are deposited in three libraries. Yale University owns thirty-three letters bearing directly upon EB's life, most of them written by EB, most of them mixed in the large Beecher family collection, but some scattered and indexed in the Kingsley, Woolsey, and Stokes collections. In the Beecher family collection there appear also eighteen letters from CB to Leonard Bacon on the subject of CB's heresy trial and his edition of LB's *Autobiography,* as well as a number of miscellaneous items (such as a "Skeleton Plan of a Sermon" preached by EB in Boston in 1847, sermon No. 233 from the text Romans 8:31). Mount Holyoke College Library owns a number of Beecher family documents, including eight letters from Catharine to EB, six from EB to LB, twelve from LB to EB, six outlines for sermons and lectures delivered by EB presumably in Galesburg in the early 1870s, and Frederick Beecher's notes (1858–1859) on EB's lectures at Chicago Theological Seminary. In the Schlesinger Library, Radcliffe College, there are eighteen letters from EB to Catharine, all dated 1822, as well as three letters from EB to LB (1822, 1836, 1847) and one letter from CB to EB (1846). The Beecher collection there was given to the library by Lyman Beecher Stowe and is extensive. For the letters I describe, see the Beecher-Stowe Collection, Folders #20 and #23.

Other relevant letters are scattered. The Library of Congress owns a letter from Isabella Beecher Hooker to EB, Hartford, January 16, 1873; and a letter from EB to Salmon P. Chase, Boston, December 21, 1854. The Massachusetts Historical Society owns letters from EB to Joseph Worcester, Boston, November 24, 1847, from EB to the Reverend Dr. Jenks, July 1827, and from CB to His Excellency John A. Andrews, Georgetown, January 31, 1861. The William L. Clements Library, University of Michigan, owns two letters from EB to Owen Lovejoy, one headed Jacksonville, November 14, 1837, the other, Illinois College, December 25, 1837. In the Wickett-Wiswall Collection of Lovejoy Papers, in the Southwest Collection, Texas Technological College, Lubbock (and also on microfilm at the Illinois State Historical Library, Springfield), there is a letter from EB to Elijah P. Lovejoy, Illinois College, December 20, 1835. The Boston Public Library owns letters from EB to E. A. Park, Boston, November 25, 1850, to [HWB?], Galesburg, March 16, 1863, to [?], Boston, March 14, 1853. The New York Public Library has a note from EB to [?], Boston, March 23, 1848, and a letter from HWB to [?], Brooklyn, October 24, 1882, observing that "with the exception of my brother Edward, I am alone, in religious companionship." Knox College owns an unsigned fragment from G. W. Gale to EB, Galesburg, July 13, 1857, EB's "Address on the State of Knox College," July 27, 1857 (which, in print, took up sixteen columns of news type), and a letter from EB to the college, Brooklyn, May 23, 1879. The Illinois State Historical Library owns a brief note from EB to "Dear Sir," Illinois College, September 10, 1839. And the Illinois College Library has various notes and letters by EB bearing upon college finances.

Though there are no EB documents either in the large and uncatalogued pile of Beecher materials at HWB's Plymouth Church in Brooklyn, or at the Stowe, Beecher, Hooker, Seymour, Day Foundation in Hartford, or at the Rutherford B. Hayes Library, I have found useful materials in the records of the Georgetown, Massachusetts, Congregational Church; the records of the First Congregational Church of Galesburg, Illinois; the records of the Parkville Congregational Church, Brooklyn; the Trustees Record Book, Illinois College; and the Record of the Illinois Association (which reproduces EB's letter accepting the presidency of Illinois College). The Congregational Library, Boston, owns a manuscript entitled "Address to the Church and People of Park Street Church Boston at the Ordination of Rev. Edward Beecher, Dec. 27, 1826," but the author does not name himself. He is probably the Reverend Mr. Fay, who is listed on a broadside at the Massachusetts Historical Society ("Order of Services at the Ordination of Edward Beecher") as giving the *Address to the Church and People*.

PUBLISHED WORKS

Edward Beecher's family was large, his salary small. He tried, as he wrote on October 4, 1855 (Yale), to "make up the deficiency by writing." It is virtually certain that I have not discovered some of those casual essays he wrote in order to feed his family and which belong on this list of published works. Moreover, I have not included articles in the *Congregationalist*, the *Spirit of the Pilgrims*, and the *Christian Union*, which in some cases can be only uncertainly attributed to him. I have been unable to locate articles he alludes to in letters (as, for example, a lecture on "The Last Times" in 1841) and a document Lyman Beecher Stowe lists in his brief bibliography (*The Right Use of the Passions and Emotions in the Work of Intellectual Culture and Development*: Address delivered at the Annual Meeting of the American Institute of Instruction). Everything else is arranged chronologically, by publication date. Whenever an item is rare, I have noted its location. Whenever items might be conveniently grouped, as in the case of the essays on baptism, I have arranged them after the major entry. Whenever plausible, I have included after the major entry a sampling of reviews, with the exception of reviews of *The Conflict*, which are adequately described in the footnotes.

An Address, Delivered at the Eighth Anniversary of the Auxiliary Education Society of the Young Men of Boston; Feb-

ruary 10, 1827 (Published by Request of the Society; Boston: T. R. Marvin, Printer, 1827). Available at the Congregational Library, Boston.

EB and Theron Baldwin, *An Appeal in Behalf of the Illinois College, Recently Founded at Jacksonville, Illinois* (New York: Printed by D. Fanshaw, 1831). Available at Yale University Library.

EB and Thomas H. Skinner, *Hints Designed to Aid Christians in Their Efforts to Convert Men to God* (Hartford: James W. Judd and Company, 1832). Available at the Connecticut State Library, Hartford.

Six Sermons on "The Nature, Importance, and Means of Eminent Holiness throughout the Church," *The American National Preacher: Or Original Sermons—Monthly*, X, Nos. 1 & 2 (June and July 1835), 193–224. See the long review, "On Symmetry of Christian Character," perhaps by the Reverend Mr. Andrews of Woodbury, in *The Quarterly Christian Spectator*, VII (December 1835), 546–564.

"To the Friends of Free Discussion," Alton *Telegraph* (October 18, 1837).

Narrative of Riots at Alton: in Connection with the Death of Rev. Elijah P. Lovejoy (Alton: George Holton, 1838; reprinted, New York: E. P. Dutton and Company, 1965).

EB to "Dear Sir" [Chairman of the Committee of Arrangements for the 1838 meeting of the American Antislavery Society], Illinois College, March 11, 1838. *The Pennsylvania Freeman*, IV, No. 11 (May 24, 1838).

Y. Z. [pseudo-initials for EB], "Reply to 'A. B.' on Slavery," a series of seven articles in the Boston *Recorder*, XXIX, Nos. 15–21 (April 11–May 23, 1844). See also the articles preceding EB's series: one by HWB appearing in XXIX, No. 4 (January 25, 1844); two by A. B. responding to HWB appearing in XXIX, Nos. 9–10 (February 29, March 7, 1844), 33, 37.

Proceedings of a Public Meeting in Behalf of the Society for

the *Promotion of Collegiate and Theological Education
at the West, Held in Park-Street Church, Boston, May 28,
1845. Including the Addresses of Rev. Drs. Hopkins, E.
Beecher, Bacon, and L. Beecher* (New York: Printed by
J. F. Trow and Company, 1845), pp. 4–7.

*Faith Essential to a Complete Education. An Address Delivered
at the Anniversary of the Charlestown Female Seminary,
July 31, 1845* (Published by Vote of the Trustees; Boston:
Haskell and Moore, Printers, 1845).

"Dr. Beecher on Organic Sin" appeared in twelve successive
weekly issues of the Boston *Recorder,* XXX (October 16,
1845) through XXXI (January 1, 1846). Each "letter" was
headlined and 2–10 numbered. Letter 9 began on December 11 and continued on December 18; letter 10 appeared
on January 1; in between, on December 25, appeared "Dr.
Beecher's Letter to the Rev. A. A. Phelps." With EB's first
letter (October 16) there appeared also a letter from Calvin
Stowe defending the Report of the Committee of the
American Board. On October 23, A. A. Phelps's preliminary letter responding to Stowe and EB appeared, promising a full rebuttal. In the same issue, the editors of the *Recorder* observed that other papers were beginning to reprint EB's letters, which was good, they thought; they
hoped Phelps's eventual reply would also be reprinted.
The subject, they said, is "most important" and "one that
is perplexing thousands of honest minds." "Perhaps no
two men in the country are better qualified" than EB and
Phelps to get to the heart of the matter. On November 6,
as EB's letter 4 was appearing, the editors noted that
Phelps's reply would, by agreement, be held off till EB
was finished, that it would be addressed to Stowe, that EB
expected his statement would continue only two more issues (it went much longer than that). Beginning with No.
4, then, EB's letters were addressed directly to Phelps. And
when EB finally finished, Phelps's reply, in the form of

letters to Stowe, began. The exchange, I believe, is crucial to understanding abolition and the church in the forties.

"Dr. Beecher's Address," *History of the Formation of the Ladies' Society for the Promotion of Education at the West; with Two Addresses Delivered at Its Organization by the Rev. Edward Beecher, D.D., and the Rev. E. N. Kirk* (Boston, 1846), pp. 7–13.

"Remarks on Stuart's Commentary on the Apocalypse," *The Biblical Repository and Classical Review*, 3rd Ser., III, No. 10 (April 1847), 272–304.

"Influence of the Literature of the Saracens," *The Biblical Repository and Classical Review*, 3rd Ser., IV, No. 13 (January 1848), 145–166.

"Pharaoh and His Host Drowned in the Red Sea," *The Sacred Tableaux: Or, Remarkable Incidents in the Old and New Testament*, edited by Thomas Wyatt (Boston: John M. Whittemore, 1848), pp. 105–110.

"Address" to the members of the New England and California Trading and Mining Association, delivered at the Tremont Temple, on Thursday evening, January 25, 1849, in *Constitution and By-Laws of the New England and California Trading and Mining Association, Together with the Names of the Officers and Members, the Order of Exercises at Tremont Temple, and Rev. Dr. Beecher's Address* (Boston, 1849), pp. 21–34. Available at the Houghton Library, Harvard.

"Life and Times of Leo the Great," *The Biblical Repository and Classical Review*, 3rd Ser., V, No. 20 (October 1849), 571–599.

"The Doctrine of the Trinity, Rational and Scriptural," *The Biblical Repository and Classical Review*, 3rd. Ser., V, No. 20 (October 1849), 706–739.

Baptism, with Reference to its Import and Modes (New York: John Wiley, 1849). A series of articles preceded and was incorporated into this book, all appearing in *The Biblical*

Repository from 1840–1848, beginning with 2nd Ser., III, No. 5 (January 1840). See also the small pamphlet, *President Beecher's Letters on the Subject of Baptism, Addressed to Rev. William Hague* (Boston, 1843), by EB; available at the Congregational Library, Boston. The controversy, which lasted ten years and which involved nearly all important Baptists and many Congregationalists and Presbyterians, produced too long a list of publications to reproduce here. One may, however, wish to consult EB's "Strictures on Wilson on the Mode of Baptism," *The Biblical Repository and Classical Review*, 3rd Ser., V, No. 17 (January 1849), 48–79; and "Beecher and Wilson on Baptism," *The Biblical Repertory and Princeton Review*, N. S., XXI (April 1849), 206–236, an anonymous review of EB's *Baptism* and related books.

The Question at Issue. A Sermon, Delivered [on October 30, 1849] *at Brooklyn, New York, before the Society for the Promotion of Collegiate and Theological Education at the West* (Boston: Press of T. R. Marvin, 1850).

"Man the Image of God," *The Bibliotheca Sacra and Theological Review*, VII, No. 27 (July 1850), 409–425.

"The Works of Samuel Hopkins," *The Bibliotheca Sacra* [No. 37] *and American Biblical Repository* [No. 89], X (January 1853), 63–82.

Address to the Citizens of Massachusetts. Read at the State Temp[erance] Convention, Held Sept. 12 & 13, 1853.

The Conflict of Ages: Or, the Great Debate on the Moral Relations of God and Man (1st ed.; Boston: Phillips, Sampson and Company, 1953; 7th ed., 1855; British ed., London: Sampson Low, 1856).

"Dispensations of Divine Providence Toward the Apostle Paul: an Expository Dissertation on 2 Cor. 12:7–10," *The Bibliotheca Sacra* [No. 47] *and American Biblical Repository* [No. 99], XII (July 1855), 499–527.

The Papal Conspiracy Exposed, and Protestantism Defended,

in the Light of Reason, History, and Scripture (Boston: Stearns and Company, 1855). The British edition is entitled *The Papal Conspiracy Exposed; Or, the Romish Corporation Dangerous to the Political Liberty and Social Interests of Man* (Edinburgh: James Nichol; London: James Nisbet and Company, 1856), with a "Preface to the British Edition" by the Reverend James Begg, D.D., and an Appendix in the form of a "Letter to the Hon. Joseph R. Chandler." The chapter headings have a more temperate tone in the British edition. Orestes Brownson reviewed the book, which had originally been given as a series of lectures, in *Brownson's Quarterly Review*, 3rd Ser., III (April 1855), 246–270. See also the anonymous review, "The Romish Hierarchy," *North American Review*, LXXXII (January 1856), 111–128.

"From the Rev. Edward Beecher, D.D.," Galesburg, Illinois, June 2, 1856. A letter to Bennett Tyler providing EB's "recollections" of Asahel Nettleton, printed at the end of Tyler's sketch of Nettleton in William B. Sprague, editor, *Annals of the American Pulpit; Or, Commemorative Notices of Distinguished American Clergymen of Various Denominations, from the Early Settlement of the Country to the Close of the Year Eighteen Hundred and Fifty-five* (New York: Robert Carter and Brothers, 1857), II, 552–554.

The Concord of Ages: Or the Individual and Organic Harmony of God and Man (New York: Derby and Jackson, 1860).

"Evening Discourse," *The Semi-Centennial Celebration of the Park Street Church and Society; Held on the Lord's Day, February 27, 1859. With the Festival on the Day Following* (Boston: Henry Hall, 1861), pp. 59–83. Available at the Connecticut Historical Society, Hartford.

"The Great Religious Controversy of England," a series of fifteen articles reviewing *Essays and Reviews* in *The Independent*, from XIV, No. 720 (September 18, 1862) through XV, No. 735 (January 1, 1863). Installment #7 (October 30) was misnumbered #6. There was no installment on December 18; instead, installment #14 appeared on December 25.

"Address," in EB and the Reverend George W. Field, *Address and Sermon Delivered in Salem Church, Boston, on* [the] *Occasion of the Death of Gilman S. Low, Who Died August 16, 1863* (Boston: Press of George C. Rand and Avery, 1863). Available at the Congregational Library, Boston.

EB and CB, *The Result Tested. A Review of the Proceedings of a Council at Georgetown, Mass., Aug. 15, 16, and 22, 1863* (Boston: Wright and Potter, Printers, 1863); available at the Congregational Library, Boston. For an anonymous Unitarian review of the Beechers's protest, see "Some New Attempts at Conformity," *The Christian Examiner*, LXXV (November 1863), 387–395. For an indication of the publicity the trial received, see the New York *Observer*, XLI, Nos. 31–33 (July 30, August 6, 13, 1863), 243, 250, 258.

EB to CB, Galesburg, October 24, 1864, in *Autobiography*, II, 580–587.

"The Scriptural Philosophy of Congregationalism and of Councils," *Bibliotheca Sacra*, XXII, No. 86 (April 1865), 284–315.

"Secret Societies. A Paper Adopted by the General Association of Illinois of the Congregational Churches, at Their Meeting in Ottawa, 1866," in David MacDill, Jonathan Blanchard, and EB, *Secret Societies: A Discussion of Their Character and Claims* (Cincinnati: Western Tract and Book Society, 1867), pp. 79–92.

Funeral Sermon of Matthew Chambers (January 29, 1869).

"Address of Investiture," in *Addresses Delivered at the Inauguration of Rev. John P. Gulliver, D.D., as President of Knox College, Galesburg, Illinois, June 25th, A.D. 1869* (Galesburg: Published by the Trustees, 1869), pp. 5–9.

History of Opinions on the Scriptural Doctrine of Retribution
(New York: D. Appleton and Company, 1878). Most of the
first thirty-two chapters appeared serially in the *Christian
Union*.

"Lyman Beecher and Infant Damnation," *North American
Review*, CL (April 1890), 529–531.

Index